Security and Data Protection with SAP Systems

Security and Data Protection with SAP Systems

Werner Hornberger and Jürgen Schneider

Translated by Jason M. Miskuly

 Addison-Wesley

an imprint of **Pearson Education**

London • Boston • Indianapolis • New York • Mexico City • Toronto • Sydney • Tokyo • Singapore • Hong Kong • Cape Town • New Delhi • Madrid • Paris • Amsterdam • Munich • Milan • Stockholm

PEARSON EDUCATION LIMITED

Head Office:
Edinburgh Gate
Harlow
Essex CM20 2JE
Tel: +44 (0)1279 623623
Fax: +44 (0)1279 431059

London Office:
128 Long Acre
London WC2E 9AN
Tel: +44 (0)20 7447 2000
Fax: +44 (0)20 7240 5771

Website: www.it-minds.com
        www.aw.com/cseng/

English edition first published in Great Britain in 2002

© Galileo Press GmbH 2001
First published in 2001 by Galileo Press,
Gartenstr. 24, 53229, Bonn, Germany
as *Sicherheit und Datenshutz mit SAP-Systemen*

The rights of Werner Hornberger and Jürgen Schneider to be identified as authors of this work have been
asserted by them in accordance with the Copyright, Designs and Patents Act 1988.

ISBN 0-201-73497-4

British Library Cataloguing in Publication Data
A CIP catalogue record for this book can be obtained from the British Library

Library of Congress Cataloging in Publication Data
Hornberger, Werner, 1946–
        Security and data protection with SAP systems / Werner Hornberger and Jürgen
    Schneider; translation by Jason M. Miskuly.
        p. cm.
    Includes bibliographical references and index.
        1. Computer security–Congresses. 2. Data protection–Congresses. 3. SAP R/3. I.
    Schneider, Jürgen M. (Jürgen Mathias), 1961–II. Title

    QA76.9.A25 2001
    005.8–dc21   2001053637

The programs in this book have been included for their instructional value. The publisher does not offer any
warranties or representations in respect of their fitness for a particular purpose, nor does the publisher
accept any liability for any loss or damage arising from their use.

10 9 8 7 6 5 4 3 2 1

Designed by Claire Brodmann Book Designs, Lichfield, Staffs
Translated by Jason M. Miskuly
Typeset by M Rules, London, UK
Printed and bound in Great Britain, by Biddles Ltd of Guildford and King's Lynn

The Publishers' policy is to use paper manufactured from sustainable forests.

Preface

SAP products provide the infrastructure that enables many companies to monitor and control their activities and to handle business processes. In addition to systems for core business functions, SAP has also recently developed numerous Industry Solutions and other products for data warehousing, modern reporting, optimization of the logistics chain, customer relationship management, enterprise portals, and internet marketplaces. Both enterprises and their employees count on the reliable functions of SAP systems for their daily work.

SAP produces distributed systems that place high demands on the completeness and effectiveness of security mechanisms, system administration, and system monitoring during daily operation. The IT landscape of companies today consists of a steadily growing number of systems composed of numerous hardware and software components with differing architectures.

This situation sees the creation of global, internal networks that are increasingly connected to the internet so that employees, business partners, customers, and vendors can use direct, electronic means to communicate with each other. Yet, a high degree of threat and an increasing need for security stand opposite the promising potential for optimization of business processes and the creation of new distribution channels.

Please note that the term data protection can mislead the unwary. It actually refers to the protection of privacy, the privacy of the person to whom the data relates. An alternative term, such as privacy, would be equally misleading, as it does not connote the active measures necessary to protect it.

Controversy has colored past discussions of security and data protection because no direct profit results from the effort needed to produce them. Recently, however, more and more companies have come to realize that they cannot implement e-business and services without security and data protection. Recent events on the internet have certainly contributed to this realization.

Contents

This book offers a complete overview of the security functions available in SAP products and the use of those functions within a company-wide security policy. Based upon these security functions, it also discusses the basics of data protection and their global implementation with SAP systems. Against the background of the growing importance of the internet and the integration of SAP systems into this open environment, we present what we hope is an exciting topic for our readers.

From the outset, the authors knew that the book would speak to a diverse audience composed of both specialists with an extensive knowledge of operating systems and databases and those with intimate familiarity with SAP applications. It also offers specialists in security and data protection without comprehensive knowledge of SAP products an opportunity to become familiar with the means to meet the demands placed upon them.

To deal with the varied audience, the book does not repeat all the details on inspection and security contained in SAP security guidelines or guidelines produced by SAP customers and partners. The guidelines were developed for specialists and demand a high level of knowledge. Instead, we have attempted to strike a healthy balance between introductory and detailed material and offer a presentation that is neither too simple nor too complicated. We know that we cannot meet the needs of every reader in every section.

This book is composed of two major sections: security and data protection. A third section treats selected special topics that we approach specifically. The attentive reader will notice that a different author, each with his own style, wrote each section. We have worked hard to link the two sections and how data protection depends upon the foundation provided by security. We know that some will use the book as a reference manual, so we have included some repetitions, cross-references, and a comprehensive index.

To separate out basic presentations, explanations, and recommendations from technical information, we generally treat the latter in a technical section at the end of individual chapters. These technical sections offer a simple glance into the technical implementation in an SAP system of the issues discussed; they do not replace any formal, technical documentation. In some places we offer only a summary of technological basics to provide interested readers with a deeper understanding.

A look ahead

The internet makes us believe that the future is already the past: a true philosophical statement. While we worked on this book, SAP developers continued to introduce innovations that we had to include in our material. However, we also learned that the basic principles and rules for security and data protection, even when written several months previously, held true in the long term.

Today, both the communications landscape and legislation are breaking new ground. Here, at the beginning of the internet age, we touch an unknowable future that awakens equal measures of hope and fear. Will the gulf between those moving onward and those staying behind become impossible to span? Politics tries to keep up with the demands of globalization and legislation can hardly keep pace with technological progress. Only greater self-responsibility by all those involved can address this situation. Uniform frameworks are a basic precondition for using new possibilities economically for the benefit of humankind. At the very least, EU guidelines for data protection strive for a uniform level of protection in the EU market and for gentle pressure on other countries.

We end this book with the knowledge that some of what we have written will become obsolete in a few years and that some predictions will turn out to be incorrect. It's no consolation that legislation for the internet, designed to regulate security and data protection, will be even more distant from the true state of affairs. We hope that we have been successful in highlighting the constants, and have built upon the basic global principles of security and laws on data protection.

Acknowledgments

We wish to thank all our colleagues who did not shrink from proofreading such a comprehensive book and who provided many suggestions for improvement.

Werner Hornberger
Jürgen Schneider

Contents

ix

3   SECURITY IN THE SAP SYSTEM LANDSCAPE   82

Part 3   Special Topics 269

9   THE SPECIAL ROLE OF THE ADMINISTRATOR 271

10   REMOTE SUPPORT 283

11 DATA WAREHOUSES AND DATA PROTECTION – A CONTRADICTION 298

Part 1

Security

## CHAPTER 1

Enterprise security

Recent events on the internet have made security a central topic of public interest. Events include stolen passwords, purloined credit card numbers, hacking into e-mail accounts, and full-scale denial of service attacks on e-commerce websites, to name only a few examples.

Of course, security is by no means a new topic. The spread of distributed information landscapes that include several servers and workplace computers has already made protection of enterprise information and processes a formidable task. Without over-emphasizing the topic or offering inappropriate criticism, this author has always been amazed at how many companies simply take network security within the enterprise as a given, and fail to mandate any specific security measures. An enterprise network (intranet) with several thousand internal and external users is actually a small internet itself, and can be exposed to attacks daily.

In any case, the time is ripe for this book on security and data protection with SAP systems. Just as security is itself not a topic specific to SAP, this introductory chapter offers general observations on the topic that apply to all IT applications rather than SAP-specific applications. Security also is not a new issue for SAP products; the earliest versions of SAP products contained extensive security functions. But the topic has become more significant recently, and customers have changed their attitudes. Customers now place more value on practical security functions that they can implement easily, and SAP has responded with changes in the scope and design of its security functions.

Later chapters will treat SAP security functions and tools in detail, in the context of the previous SAP system landscape and in the context of the new SAP approach to the internet. This chapter, however, serves as a general introduction to those considerations. It describes the basic principles and terms involved. In addition to a presentation of guidelines for security and data protection, this section treats another crucial topic: embedding the security of SAP systems in the security policies of the enterprise itself.

1.1   INTRODUCTION

SAP is a market leader among suppliers of business application software (with a market share of 30 percent in 2000) and one of the few European high-tech firms that can determine trends in the US SAP products offer a palette of enterprise solutions that enable its customers to increase their competitiveness and implement integrated business processes. SAP solutions are offered around the world and are available for all regions.

In addition to its previous business software products, the R/2 System and the R/3 System, SAP also offers Industry Solutions that tailor SAP products to the needs of individual industries. SAP New Dimension products supplement the product palette. Combined with the R/3 System itself, these products deliver the building blocks for a real-time enterprise, including sales, marketing, product development, procurement, production, distribution, customer service, strategic enterprise management, and financial management.

The SAP R/3 System, the Industry Solutions, and the New Dimension Products have become components of mySAP.com. As an internet solution-environment, mySAP.com, with its Workplace and Marketplace portals, enables SAP customers to provide their employees with tailor-made workplaces connected to the internet. SAP also offers non-customers virtual marketplaces that can handle cooperative business processes. A presence on the internet improves an enterprise's business and competitive advantages. mySAP.com creates cross-enterprise markets and simplifies maintenance of dynamic business relationships.

In this context, SAP application systems store and process all the important business data. They are crucial to an enterprise and its ability to handle business processes on an intranet and the internet. To avoid damage that might have massive effects on the enterprise, the security of data used by systems that process information and of those who use the systems must be guaranteed. To do so, the security functions created by SAP must be implemented within the context of the security policy established by the enterprise.

The issue of data protection is closely linked to that of security. Here, a company must not only define the means to ensure meeting its own goals, but also observe national and international laws and regulations. With the EU guidelines on data protection, Europeans strive for a uniform level of data privacy. The guidelines also provide gentle pressure on the most important international business partners outside the EU to create a corresponding security standard.

Economic and social progress in Europe is to create a closer union of peoples. Progress in IT is an absolute prerequisite for enterprise-wide communication that processes and exchanges data relating to persons. The processing and transmission of this data must observe and respect basic rights and the privacy of the individual. Germany, for example, has adopted a law on the self-determination of personal data as an inalienable, basic right: all persons have the right to determine for themselves when and where their personal data may be used. This approach agrees with the EU guidelines on data protection.

But an enterprise does not protect its personnel data and confidential customer data only because of legal requirements. It has its own interest in dealing carefully with this valuable company property.

1.1.1 Breaking out on to the internet

Entry into the internet market will accelerate cross-enterprise and cross-border data transfer without restraint. Even confidential and personal data must be transferred, and time constraints in many cases will temporarily push the important clarification of security and legal questions into the background.

The internet is booming, enterprises are acting, legislation is pending, and everyone responsible for security and data protection tries to remain at the cutting edge of technology. The responsible parties require established and up-to-date knowledge for the tasks that require solutions. Otherwise, when they implement new projects, they face the danger of first being mocked as inimical stumbling-blocks to the company and then being ignored as inhibitors of innovation when they make their decisions. Software manufacturers must provide a transparent and comprehensible presentation of the security mechanisms present in their systems.

At the beginning of the internet age, we can only imagine the future effects of the expected total communication for companies, private life, and public life. The internet forces states, companies, and the workforce to rethink.

An internet-year now lasts about three calendar months; it's already evident that governmental provisions and regulations cannot keep up with the speed of innovation. Many states will weigh whether they will 'grant' companies and citizens the freedom of the global data stream or use regulations, controls, and sanctions to retain at least part of their monopoly on information.

The telecommunications industry is hoping for an explosive eruption of data that will lead to a massive upgrade of existing networks and bandwidth and trigger a fall in connection fees.

We know that the markets will expand. Previously local companies will suddenly have an opportunity to offer their wares worldwide and become global players. Business processes will involve customers and vendors directly. Open markets with their transparency will come closer to the ideal of a market economy where supply and demand can meet briefly to exchange goods internationally at a fair price. Groups that already operate worldwide will attempt to strengthen their positions of power and to influence the market in their favor by mergers and acquisitions.

Availability (just-in-time production), market analysis with rapid reaction times (time-to-market), and reliability will all play a decisive role in this new market, but only with the support of modern information technology. The use and operation of IT within a company must be reliable and secure; IT must operate with the newest level of technology whenever possible. Rapid and problem-free upgrades to the latest versions and the corresponding knowledge transfer will become a new challenge for manufacturers and customers.

We are utterly certain that even companies that still treat their IT environment as a stepchild will be forced to change their approach. Simply observing the market will not suffice. Revenue lost to sales on the internet and the accompanying lost profits will force companies to deal with the situation precipitously. This pressure will often mean that security and data protection will receive insufficient attention, which can hardly benefit a company's reliability as a business partner and the long-term customer loyalty that should arise from it.

In particular, Germany has already experienced how a threatened loss of competitive position erodes the lofty idea of co-determination. Quick functionality and availability enjoy the highest priority; everything else is subordinated to them. In addition, companies that missed the internet train or were run over by it are now asking for government support to counter the structural crisis and threatened loss of jobs in the company, none of which is reputedly the company's fault.

Employees on the most advanced internet-front are always being confronted with new challenges: lifelong learning is becoming a matter of course. Continuous, dynamic adjustments and change ever more frequently replace long-term planning.

The mySAP.com e-business platform offers a wide spectrum of software, services, information, and infrastructure technology for the internet. Companies can use directories of virtual marketplaces to create business relationships and process business over the internet. mySAP.com offers industry-specific, cross-industry, and private services for professional, commercial, and private interests. A large selection of external products and services enhance the offering. Together with its customers and partners, SAP will establish internet markets for cross-company collaboration and electronic commerce.

Despite this forced move to dynamic growth and constant striving for innovative, new products, companies must strike a balance if they are to respect the requirements of their existing customer base. The long waiting times for an SAP release have managed to hold back the pressure to jump on the train of innovation. It's doubtful that the competitive situation will permit remaining with proven application scenarios in the future.

The strategy behind mySAP.com also aims at putting gentle pressure on users to observe measures designed to enhance security and data protection. On the one hand, more and more users are linked to the previously isolated personnel system with employee self-services (ESS). These users can display, create, delete, or lock their own personnel data. They have information on address, banking, vacation, insurance, communications, and other data about them stored in the system. They can retrieve the information at any time, and can correct or delete any incorrect data. Employees regard the security provisions for their own data with the greatest suspicion; they do not ignore security lapses or fail to observe the required care.

On the other hand, increased communication with the world outside the enterprise will test companies. Service and reliability will become a decisive criterion along with an economical price. The suspicion that security holes exist or that a company misuses personal data will trigger a loss of customers.

1.1.2 Security controversies

Do SAP products meet customer requirements for security and data protection?

Interestingly, such customer requirements often do not actually exist. Every company has different groups with different tasks and goals. Many items enjoy a higher priority than the security of data. The list includes user-oriented, high-tech functions, the quick availability of innovations with a minimal risk of operating interruptions, comprehensive business processes beyond the limits of the company itself, unlimited maintenance and upgrade opportunities, ad hoc evaluations, economical IT infrastructure, quality, reliability, and availability.

Within the company, those responsible for security must constantly convince others of the need for security. They must broker with decision makers to convince them that only balanced security measures can guarantee the necessary reliability, availability, audit security, ability to reproduce data, and adherence to legal requirements. Company management ultimately decides on the intensity and cost of the security measures, based in part upon the estimated risk. It is precisely this estimation that requires the participation of those responsible for security issues. On the one hand, they must forcefully indicate and direct the attention of management to potential dangers. On the other hand, they can't continually cry wolf and lose their credibility. If the threatened dangers never appear, security personnel are called to task for instigating cost-intensive measures unnecessarily. They then face the difficult task of explaining that without the existing security measures, security breaches are sure to have taken place.

Our customers have varied security requirements for these very reasons. Security experts and those familiar with data protection are brought to a project only at the start of production; the implementation project simply passed over or forgot them. Those responsible for the implementation ultimately have to work with the basics: speed, functionality, and cost-saving allocation of scarce resources, both in personnel and hardware.

Customer demands on SAP products are similar. During presales and in the implementation phase, the focus is directed toward the error-free functions that must be provided as soon as possible. Those connected to the SAP applications during this phase include management, project management, subject experts, and end-users. Security requirements can only put the brakes on a project here, especially since a real security breach cannot yet exist. Administration comes into the foreground during the production phase, which builds upon the experience gained in the test systems. It is now time to implement the security norms required by the company with the appropriate security measures. Contact with the manufacturer usually takes places via consultants. A group of requirements for individual product components is rare here.

Other cases, however, require working through a detailed catalog of questions before the company even decides on a specific system. The questions represent the requirements for security and data protection of the security personnel and often those of the employee representatives.

Do the ever-shorter innovation cycles for SAP products allow for too little attention to security issues?

No. Security has always been an integral component of SAP products. Some users find the options already available too comprehensive – in reporting or in implementing the SAP security guidelines, for example.

The installation must observe and convert the available supply of security precautions into reality. Delivery of a software product does not guarantee that the production systems operate securely and according to law, only the creation and maintenance of an accountable level of security does. The security standard must exist at the same level for all areas, given the differing needs of each area. After all, just one weakness is enough to compromise the security of the entire system.

The statutory technical and organizational requirements and the reliability of participants in the project are both preconditions for success. To become partners in matters of security and data protection, both administrators and users of SAP systems need adequate training and explanations of their responsibilities.

However, please note that no one-size-fits-all recipe for the security of an SAP system exists. The management of each company ultimately decides the level of security toward which the firm will strive. The security policy or company principles express that level. Decisive factors include the sensitivity of the data, the openness of the system, the subjective estimate of the risk involved, and the costs required to reach a specific level of security. A company chooses and implements specific options of an SAP system according to how it estimates the relative importance of those factors.

Security personnel have the task of giving management the correct basis for a decision. That basis must include both existing risks and the options for mitigating risk offered by the preventative measures. A cost–benefit analysis suffers from a major problem, however: it is as difficult to estimate future, potential costs as it is to estimate the damage that will be avoided. Existing security holes cannot always be recognized, and (currently) loyal employees and partners do not use them. If confidential data are copied and given to third parties without anyone noticing, the costs cannot be calculated.

To portray the security options available in SAP systems, this book will summarize all the information previously published in SAP documentation, notes, and guidelines. It will comment on the information from the viewpoint of security and data protection. As noted, although the authors cannot give any general recommendation, they can speak of their experience and discuss examples.

This book treats the topics of security and data privacy from the viewpoint of practical operations with SAP systems. This approach makes clear that both can be reached only in accordance with the existing security philosophy in a company and in consideration of the practical ability to execute the security measures and rules.

The authors have established the goal of presenting not only a description of the functions and applications available in SAP systems, but also how those functions work together and what they mean in the context of increasing security needs and international regulations on data protection. Accordingly, the book is oriented to system administrators, those responsible for IT security, protectors of data privacy, employee representatives, human resource professionals, inspection authorities, and boards of directors. Readers of this book should be able to become familiar with the security functions and tools offered in SAP products and to evaluate and implement them according to the security and data protection requirements of a company.

1.2   GUIDELINES FOR SECURITY AND DATA PROTECTION

Before we deal with the options available to provide SAP systems with security and data protection, we need to formulate some general guidelines on this topic. Here, at the beginning of this book the guidelines can serve as a better way to evaluate the meaning and purpose of security measures.

1.2.1 Minimalists and maximalists

The positions taken range from minimalists to maximalists. The German literature in the area since the 1983 census authorized by the Federal Constitutional Court increasingly differentiates proponents of minimalist and maximalist proponents of data protection. Some positions of each group are diametrically opposed to the other group (Fiedler, 1989, p. 131).

The minimalists espouse the following positions.

- Nothing has happened so far, why should anything happen in the future?
- The company has nothing to hide.
- The system we use is secure and will take care of security automatically.
- There's no such thing as absolute security anyway.
- The company trusts its users and administrators absolutely.

As a consequence, these companies take only minimal security measures. Further efforts are regarded as having a disproportionate negative effect on the growth of profits, and are therefore not cost-effective.

Maximalists regard security as the highest good in a company, and want the firm to take every conceivable security measure.

- The company guidelines specifically highlight security and data protection.
- Those responsible for security and data protection must approve all relevant projects in writing.
- A comprehensive set of rules determines behavior when dealing with the system in great detail. There are security guidelines for operating the computer center, for building security, for use of PCs, and for the recording, disposal, archiving, and deletion of data.
- All users undergo regular training on the meaning and practice of security and data protection.
- To enable clear re-creation of any misuse at any time, exact logs record all system and user activity.
- Regular checks are performed to ensure that security provisions are being observed.
- Internal and external resources regularly check the system; the company seeks certification.
- A security instance exists in which decision makers can exchange information and report directly to the board of directors.
- Transmission of any personal data to third parties requires the written permission of the person involved.

In actual practice, pure maximalists may not exist, although their goals are seen as an ideal worth striving for. Minimalists are found more often, usually because of missing information on security criteria or existing laws.

1.2.2 Guidelines

Before we examine the details of each approach, we must explain some guidelines on security and data protection.

1 It's certain that nothing is certain.

This remark by Karl Valentin, a famous German comedian, holds true for IT. There is no absolute security in the area of IT.

Those who want to misuse a system will find a way to do so. Those who absolutely want to break in will find their way in. Those who want to hack passwords or codes know that it's merely a matter of time and cost until they are successful. Consider psychological and physical pressures such as blackmail, bribery, or sabotage: an unauthorized third party can use each of these methods to gain access to a system.

Those responsible for security can only consider the risks and estimate the damage, and then set the barriers to access as high as possible. Damage estimates must include material and immaterial damage. For example, the effects of a security breach on a company's public relations and image cannot be ignored.

Security personnel are bound to bring the risks and means of avoiding risk to the attention of management. But there are situations in which management will ignore a known risk because the costs of the suggested security measures are too high to allow complete implementation.

2 Management is responsible.

The authority, the company, or group management decides its own level of security. The risk assessment is based upon the experience of the company. A company with a small number of employees that works with secure data has different security needs than a multinational airline group. The latter would regard the security of manufacturing or air traffic as a vital and valuable asset. In this case employees must deal with security from the time they enter the property until they arrive at their workstations. A small company can reach optimum security with physical isolation of its systems and a restrictive access policy.

3 Functionality must not compromise security.

As noted, the threat of lost profits forces companies to react too quickly to implement new functions. The new functions are pushed through at whatever price; security and data protection take a back seat in the discussions and then must be added to systems after the start of production – an onerous task. Early and thorough consideration of security concerns can avoid this problem.

4 The employee is the greatest risk to security.

In an age of information overload, it becomes a special challenge to provide employees with optimal information, without, however, setting the bars for information processing too high. The trust granted an employee should lead to more creativity, not to misuse.

Everyone hates putting together comprehensive sets of rules. Practice has shown that such compilations are seldom read or soon forgotten. In Germany, for example, contracts require employees to observe confidentiality. Even if some employees still don't know about their obligation, they would at least know that there's something about it in their personnel file. They would have to ask themselves just what the non-disclosure statement was all about and similar questions.

The obligations can easily become nothing more than alibis. The obligation to protect the privacy of data as a legal safeguard becomes wastepaper if the company itself fails to develop and implement security standards. Security is part of the most important goals of a company. Management should propagate and sponsor security across the enterprise in a security policy that reflects its importance. A uniformly high level of security and data protection must be created, particularly in companies that operate globally. Since each country has its own, often differing, legal regulations, a company would do well to use the EU guidelines as a common basis for its overall approach to the issue.

Companies can go even further, and have employees collaborate on improving security. Although a company can allow (internal) hacking to uncover security holes only with special permission, it can encourage employees to report security problems immediately. The firm should accept constructive suggestions and, if possible, reward an employee financially. Many companies already have a system in place for employee suggestions.

In no case may employees become used to lapses in security and fail to report them, so that an easy source of information continues to flow.

5   Respect employees' sense of responsibility.

An employee's conscience and sense of responsibility control the intensity of rules and controls at each location.

Many areas absolutely require laws, regulations, guidelines, and other rules as a precondition for a high level of security. But the regulations must keep up with constant innovation and those affected by them must understand and keep them.

Nonetheless, a good manager knows that employees who are usually responsible for the performance of their own tasks need some freedom. Just how much depends upon the results, but these employees do not need a detailed list of rules that describes how to deal with their computers, other devices, and internal work environment in great detail.

Company management and decision makers must use their own experience and requirements to determine if they should invest more in their employees' sense of responsibility or in regulations and the effort required to produce, monitor, and enforce them. If security manuals are produced, they must not only be up to date, but also given to, understood by, and monitored for each employee.

6   Coordinate the security staff.

The security staff must be able to work collegially with all employees, especially with specialists. All-knowing generalists are becoming extinct: specialists are in demand. Equally, the security staff can handle only portions of their area of responsibility thoroughly. Several shoulders should carry responsibility for the required tasks, a basic principle of distributed responsibility. The goals here include mutual support, the exchange of information, and the distribution of risks.

We recommend that you set responsibilities and processes without any ambiguity. But you cannot only place responsibilities on the security staff; they also need broad rights to design their tasks optimally. Trusting collaboration can set free an amazing amount of creative power. Once the rights and obligations on personnel, administration, and security staff have been determined and openly documented, the only task remaining is the coordination of employees working together in mutual trust.

In most cases, the security staff follows the same interests when responding to a security question. It's worth it for a company to establish a group to deal with security issues, a sort of security council. Members of the group can use this forum to report on their experiences and to report on grievous security problems – directly to management. Reporting can occur through minutes of meetings or in regular reporting. Members might include the following:

- person responsible for administration
- selected employee representatives
- data protection officer
- IT manager
- security manager
- HR representative
- auditing.

7 Develop measures to prevent misuse by third parties.

A company or group of companies usually has its own interests at heart when it considers the results of sensitive company and personnel data leaving the company. Management expects IT directors to guarantee compartmentalization against those outside the company. In the view of the group, legally autonomous firms within the group are not external, third parties. But according to the German data protection law, all those outside of the storage location are considered third parties.

Efficient information management must be in effect throughout the group; limitations in this area can result in competitive disadvantages. According to suggestions made by an EU commission, contracts can offer safeguards that provide a legal basis for the internal exchange of data, even personnel data. A company might well ask if it should protect itself in general through the use of contractual agreements.

A general distinction is drawn between purely internal, group-wide, and public access to data. The greatest danger, however, lies in circulating data to external parties. Data can circulate when accessed externally or internally – intentionally or unintentionally by users of the internal systems. These users make up a broad spectrum:

- company employees
- group employees
- partners
- customers (with permission)
- maintenance technicians
- trainees.

8   Overcome the discrepancy between potential dangers and occurrences.

As long as no security-relevant breaches occur, only those in the know are aware of the risks that exist. To an external observer, and often to management itself, systems with little or no security measures are regarded as secure.

The request to implement security measures is often a balancing act for those responsible. How can a company analyze the realistic risks if no security breaches have been registered? Damages not yet incurred cannot be calculated, parallels from the market are seen as individual cases and therefore not accepted, and many cases go unreported because the victims wish to protect their reputation. The person in charge of security often becomes a notorious pessimist, and no one is willing to authorize funds for measures that seem unnecessary or exaggerated and that do not translate directly into commercial success. The parallel with ecology is unmistakable.

As early as 1986, the 10th data protection congress (DAFTA) in Cologne formulated the following comment:

> It's quite true that no other potentially dangerous area of our time displays the extremely large discrepancy between predicted dangers and actual damage as does data security. Compare our area with the accidents that occur in traffic, on the job, and at home. Yet this by no means implies that our security measures are sufficient in every case (Weise, 1997, pp. 228–29).

9   Ensure proportionality of security measures.

The effort involved in implementing the technical and organizational security measures at a company must stand in reasonable proportion to the desired level of protection. The security staff must always ensure that an incremental increase in security justifies the efforts needed for special security measures.

The security staff often confront a problem. They must make their demands on management palatable because management thinks in terms of costs and cannot calculate the cost of imaginary damages.

> Data protection costs money, and does not contribute directly and in the short term to company profits (Weise, 1997, pp. 228).

This empirical finding must not mislead a company into avoiding the measures required to protect data. No one requires absolute protection of all the data that requires protection. The measures taken depend upon the category of the data involved and the security needs of the company (for sensitive company data) or the security needs of the individual involved (for personnel and private data). The protection needed for data involved in public communications differs from that required by sensitive medical information.

10 Improperly implemented transparent security regulations can be misused.

The details in publications of security-relevant information can be used to uncover points of attack. Such information includes data protection, inspection, and security guidelines in addition to detailed descriptions of the organization, registers of IT systems, file registers, floor plans, data flow plans, and extensive descriptions and disclosures of security programs.

For example, if SAP security guidelines are published at a company before they are actually implemented, readers can do more than evaluate the level of security and how well management is fulfilling its responsibility to provide security. Targeted use of the guidelines, however, can also uncover weaknesses in the standard settings of the system as delivered. This can lead to deceptive security when the data is discovered and copied early in the project. Later resetting of the security measures and inspections do not always uncover a misdeed. The damage here usually goes unnoticed.

The publication of security-relevant information must also occur as part of the overall security concept and only after the required security measures have actually been implemented.

11 Use quality assurance as an additional security measure.

The only constancy is change. Companies regularly look for opportunities to improve. Improvements in SAP implementations occur through constant enhancements, customizing, and changed business processes.

Pressure to remain competitive and current can mean that the security measures taken for software previously in use have not undergone enough testing for the version currently in use. This problem applies equally to application software, the operating system, the database, and the network. All these systems undergo constant change, caused by the implementation of new functions, correction of errors, further developments, modifications, and customizing settings.

If an analysis for the board of directors runs in production, many overzealous employees feel forced to work around security precautions and set up a development authorization for the production system as a standard. This abbreviated process avoids the official transport path from development, to quality assurance, and then to production. Good quality assurance avoids such problems.

12 Understand the motivation of consultants.

Decision makers are offered many suggestions, rulebooks, forms, tools, seminars, and meetings in the area of security and data protection. The sheer mass of information often leaves experts in despair. Since the relevant laws are open to a broad range of interpretation, decision makers need concrete, practical advice. However, the well-intentioned suggestions of external consultants do not always help in actual practice: they are counterproductive in many cases.

We recommend that decision makers examine the motivation of external experts very carefully. As is true of a mystery, the motivation provides the reasons for the actions. Bad consultants can divert a company from essential matters and direct limited resources in the wrong direction.

We wish to reveal the motivation of the authors of this book. Because we work with security and data protection for SAP systems in everyday practice, we often hear the opinion that SAP products are not secure or do not protect data. Many uninvolved persons even go so far as to claim that SAP systems offer no security at all. But if you press those who raise the issue as to whether or not they are familiar with the authorization and authentication concepts, you are greeted with unsure answers or the observation that such issues are far too complicated to deal with.

Admittedly, such remarks got under our skin and provided the primary motivation for putting together a book on security and data protection with SAP systems. The authors are part of contemporary trends: we both gained our expertise at SAP AG. The years of experience we have with the development and maintenance of standard software along with our constant contact with customers, partners, and SAP administrators on the topics of security and data protection have encouraged us to present this topic from our viewpoint.

1.3 SECURITY MANAGEMENT

Our guidelines on security and data protection feature some aspects of security management. We understand security management as the total organizational, personnel, infrastructure, and technical measures to achieve and maintain a uniform security level within a company. Security and data protection in SAP systems can be guaranteed only when they form part of a security level that applies throughout a company. Accordingly, we present an overview of the essential components of functioning security management. This overview is based upon the presentation in a document issued by the German federal bureau for IT security[1].

---

1 This document is only available in German. (Bundesamt für Sicherheit in der Informationstechnik. *IT-Grundschutz Handbuch*. Bundesanzeiger-Verlag: Bonn, 1997.

1.3.1 Security process

Security and data protection do not reflect a status that is achieved once and for all. Rather, both issues must be understood as part of a continuous process within a company. The process includes security analyses and the creation, implementation, and monitoring of security concepts. An illustration from the report issued by the German federal bureau for IT detailed in footnote 1 clarifies the security process (*see* Figure 1.1).

Company management must initiate and sponsor the security process (see the second guideline in section 1.2.2). Without support from above, a company cannot reach its protection goals. The recent German law on control and transparency in business and comparable laws in other countries provide management with a legal requirement to do so.

The first task in the definition of a security process is the creation of a security policy that lists the company's protection goals in a general form. The policy must also name those responsible for reaching and maintaining the goals. The list of responsibilities usually reaches from top management to individual employees (*see* the fifth guideline in section 1.2.2).

A team made up of experts and decision makers from individual areas of the company creates the security policy and attends to the security process (*see* the sixth guideline in section 1.2.2). This security management team initiates the registration and documentation of all IT systems and application in the company. It also evaluates the results of the security analyses that it may have undertaken.

The first goal here is the creation of a security concept that considers the needs for protection in individual systems and applications. The second goal is the creation of

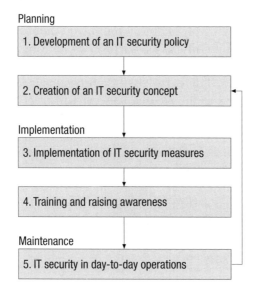

FIGURE 1.1   Security process (Copyright © SAP AG)

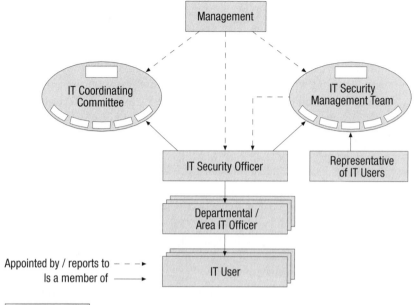

FIGURE 1.2   Security organization

a catalog that lists the security measures to be undertaken. Consultants and manufacturer's guidelines can help here (the SAP R/3 Security Guidelines [SAP-SG][2] for example).

The next step implements the security measures that have been agreed upon. To this end, security management defines priorities, appoints persons to be responsible for the areas of the company involved, and monitors the implementation of the measures. These procedures must arise as a consequence of information and sensitization in the company. All employees should become familiar with the security policy and have access to it at all times (*see* the eleventh guideline in section 1.2.2). Regular review of and updates to the security concept whenever the IT landscape changes will help ensure that no one rests upon the laurels of a job done well once and for all.

Figure 1.2 (see footnote 1 for source) illustrates the place of the security management team. The team is constituted by upper management and consists of experts and user representatives from various areas of the company. In our view, a company that uses SAP systems should also include at least one representative from the SAP application level in the team. Through its lead, the security management team reports to the security officer, the IT coordinating committee, and the board of directors.

---

2   Codes in square brackets like this example indicate that full details are available in the reference section.

| **1.4** | **SECURITY SERVICES IN IT SYSTEMS** |

To protect systems, data, and users, IT systems contain security functions at various levels. Depending upon what needs protection, the security functions aim at different protection goals. The same approach applies to the security functions in SAP systems, the functions treated in this book. The following serves as a general introduction to the essential terms for protection goals.

1.4.1 General protection goals

General protection goals in IT systems include the following.

■ Identity and authenticity

Protecting identity means that no one can impersonate the system or one of its users or trigger actions in the system under a false identity. Users, system components, and their communications partners should always undergo authentication. The identity of the author of data accepted by and stored in the system must always be available.

■ Integrity and confidentiality

No one without the proper authorization should be able to view or manipulate the data processed in and stored by systems. This principle applies to the data within a system and to data transmitted over a network.

■ Testability and repeatability

You must be able to repeat any of the current procedures in the system and for a specific period in the past.

■ Binding character and provability

Business transactions require the presence of binding data that also supports the provability of the business transaction. This approach ensures that no one can dispute a given transaction.

■ Availability

The system must be available for information processing and for dialogs with its users at any time.

To achieve these general goals, you must set up and use appropriate security functions for information processing. This book treats the security functions of SAP systems for these general goals in detail.

1.4.2 Security services

The logical structure of IT systems can combine security functions into services that stand available at several locations within the system architecture to reach the protection

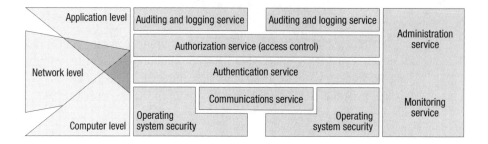

FIGURE 1.3   Security services in system architecture (Copyright © SAP AG)

goals (*see* Figure 1.3). The services distinguish between the computer, network, and application levels (see the suggestions on safeguarding an intranet in Rawolle 1999).

From the viewpoint of a distributed application, the following basic security services exist.

▨ Operating system security

The protection of resources (files, processes, devices) and operating system users occurs at the operating system level of each computer. These items control which users have access to the computer and what resources and applications they can use.

▨ Communications service (network security)

The communications service links the individual computers in a company. Today's operating systems usually include and integrate local portions of the communications systems. During the transmission of data between the application processes, the communications service guarantees the integrity of the data. With encryption, the communications service can also guarantee confidentiality between the individual computers on the network. Safeguarding integrity and confidentiality during data transfer can occur at the transport level between application processes or even within the application level.

▨ Authentication service

The authentication service inspects the identity of system components and users when they access the system and when they establish communications links. Computer addresses serve as the primary tool at the network level. Firewall systems or remote access servers can also add stronger authentication mechanisms at the network level. The operating system level usually involves a logon process with passwords or another tool (smart cards or biometrics). Distributed operating system environments also support cross-system user administration and network logon. Simple passwords are used at the application level. Authentication can be taken away from the operating system or network level. For example, the SSL (Secure

Sockets Layer) protocol on the internet uses digital certificates with cryptographic procedures to authenticate communications partners at the level of communications between two system or application processes.

- Authorization service (access control)

  Based upon the identity of system components and users, the authorization service controls access to resources and applications. At the operating system and network level, this service involves processing capacities, files, and network services. Application-specific access controls occur within applications.

- Auditing and logging service

  Log files at the operating system and network level handle auditing of system processes. Depending upon the desired level of detail, logging can record file accesses, requests for connections, network addresses, the type and length of access, and so on. The application log at the application level records events relevant to the application. In business application systems, the creation of documents plays a special role in supporting audits of the system. The use of digital signatures at the application level provides a high level of audit for e-commerce: the system cannot create the signatures on its own and they can have significance beyond the system itself.

- Administration and monitoring service

  The administration and monitoring service plays a significant role at all levels. This service organizes and controls the entire IT landscape. The tasks here are distributed to various tools and administrators at various levels. In the best case, the tools are concentrated in one location and made available over a common system-management console.

Figure 1.3 illustrates the need for different security services in somewhat different forms at all levels. The functionality can be supplemented at each level or it can overlap. The security services should contain the complete security concept of a distributed application but should not contain too much redundancy.

   This presentation of general protection goals and security services serves as an introduction to the structure of security functions in SAP systems.

## CHAPTER 2

Security in the SAP system

The data processed in an SAP system and the business transactions supported by that system are vitally important to a company and thus deserve a great deal of protection. This chapter treats the various security functions offered by the SAP system. The discussion will indicate that the central protection mechanisms are implemented in the SAP system itself and are therefore independent of the associated operating systems, databases, networks, and hardware platforms.

Two separate reasons illustrate that the implementation of a specific and complete protection concept in an SAP system is a necessary and important component of this standard software.

1   The completeness of business application functions and their high level of integration in an SAP system testify to the scope and complexity of computer-assisted business control. All these tasks need appropriate security functions that are not directly supplied by the operating system or database. The business objects and transactions that need protection are not identical to the resources protected at the operating system level. The means available to the database alone do not provide protection to these objects and procedures, which require a protection concept integrated into the application.

2   The structure of the distributed system architecture in SAP systems means the distribution of overall functions to various computers and several loosely coupled

application processes. The breadth of the hardware, operating system, and database products supported by SAP systems and the mixed use of such products hardly permits complete mapping of the protection concept by the mechanisms contained in the underlying infrastructure.

SAP systems therefore use a design that incorporates the protective functions of the operating system and database for the system itself. However, the system internally implements its own user management, a reporting system tailored to business needs, auditing, and logging at the application level. Supplemental cryptographic products that use direct interfaces to the SAP system, such as digital signatures, provide additional protection.

The following sections treat the security functions in SAP systems. The application of these functions enables implementation of a complete security concept. As noted in Chapter 1, the security concept must be completed by organizational measures and agree with company-wide regulations. Chapter 3, on the security of the SAP system landscape, treats the dependencies for the remaining environment: the operating system, the database, and the network infrastructure.

2.1 USER MANAGEMENT

Knowing who uses a system, and why, is an essential basis for providing security for the system. The course catalog for the training department or the catalog of a book company is quite different from the personnel or management information system of a company or the control of a nuclear power plant.

The system and its protective functions need information on users: such information must be available at system runtime. The information includes a user's identity (authentication) and the user's role in the company (authorization). A record of all actions and events triggered by the user must also be available (auditing and logging).

Depending upon the level of protection in the system, various mechanisms can provide authentication of users. In the same way, the reporting system can operate at a greater or lesser level of detail because a business environment includes comprehensive requirements. Logging of user and system activities enables repeatable transactions and the ability to log transactions. The following sections treat these topics.

2.1.1 User master records

SAP systems store information on users in user master records. Several tables in the database hold the user master records. Dialog transactions or function modules maintain the records and ensure the authenticity of the data. The creation and maintenance of user master records also require authorizations that are, in turn, checked by maintenance transactions (*see* the technical section).

Figure 2.1 illustrates the most important contents of SAP user master records. User master records exist for each client, itself a logical SAP system according to the SAP client concept. A user ID identifies a user master record, which must be unique to each client. The logon data in the user master record indicates the time at which the record was created and until when it remains valid. The *user type* attribute indicates which types of access this user is allowed. The current user types include dialog, CPIC, and batch. A user master record with a *dialog* attribute allows the user to work in the system via dialog logon, via SAP remote function call (RFC), and in batch mode. A user master record with a *CPIC* attribute permits RFC logon and batch operations. A user master record with a *batch* attribute permits operations only in batch mode. Since Release 4.6C of the R/3 System, the user types have been slightly renamed and an additional type for a purely technical user was introduced – namely "service user".

Users can be assigned to a user group, which affects a user's authorizations. The standard SAP system uses passwords to authenticate users. The user master record stores the hash value of a password. To monitor misuse, the system stores the time of the last logon and displays it at the next logon dialog. The account number is used to assign the costs of system usage to cost centers. The user master record also includes a status, because users can also be locked.

If external security products are used for user authentication and connected to the SNC and SSF interfaces offered by SAP products, the user master record also contains this required information. Later sections will treat these interfaces.

The user master record stores the authorizations that a user of the SAP system has by assigning users to activity groups. Section 2.3 treats the functions of the SAP authorization concept.

Individual settings and the address information provided by the user enhance the logon-authorization information of the user master record.

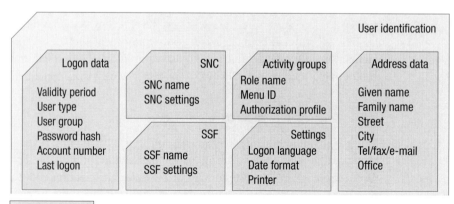

FIGURE 2.1   User master record (selections) (Copyright © SAP AG)

2.1.2 Maintaining user master records

You can create user master records with a dialog maintenance transaction or with an ABAP function module. Release 4.5 of the R/3 System also contains a BAPI interface for internal or external user maintenance. You can use the same techniques to display and change user master records.

The same holds true for deleting user master records. However, you should not delete users as soon as they leave the company. The system employs user IDs to log business transactions, so they should remain in the system long enough to enable an audit, should one prove necessary.

2.1.2.1 Distribution of roles in user and authorization maintenance

The creation of users and the granting of authorizations are critical security actions in an SAP system. Since all actions occur in the system under a user ID and log entries always reference a user ID, security measures must guarantee that unauthorized users cannot be created. Because creation of a user master record includes assigning the user to activity groups and maintaining the user's authorizations, no unauthorized person may make the assignment. Of course, misbehavior on the part of one authorized person is therefore enough to open the system to an attack by a dishonestly created user with powerful authorizations.

To counter this danger with good management, we suggest establishing and operating a separation of functions for maintaining users and authorizations. This approach distinguishes between two or three roles in the administration of users and authorizations. The authorization system also forces this division of roles (*see* Figure 2.2).

- The user administrator holds responsibility for user maintenance. The person holding this position creates new user master records and assigns a new user to one or more activity groups that correspond to the user's roles in the company. After the assignment, however, the user does not receive all the required authorizations immediately. The user receives the authorizations only after the user master record has been matched with the role definition. The user administrator has the authorizations needed to maintain user master records, but cannot maintain activity groups or perform a match.

- The role administrator maintains activity groups and establishes the authorizations that result from the groups. The role administrator cannot create user master records or match roles to the user master records.

- The activation administrator performs the user match, which can occur from within user maintenance or role maintenance. After the match, users have the authorizations that arise from their roles. If the separation of functions calls for two people, the user administrator or the role administrator can perform the activation, but if the separation calls for three people, the third can do so.

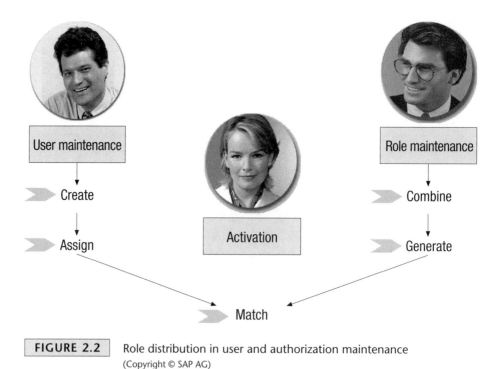

| FIGURE 2.2 | Role distribution in user and authorization maintenance |
(Copyright © SAP AG)

The distribution of tasks within these roles for user and authorization maintenance offers additional protection against attackers who possesses or have stolen administrator rights. Think of completely dissatisfied company employees who begin an attack from the inside, from the company's internal network.

2.1.2.2 Individual and technical users

User master records exist not only for real persons, but also for technical users. For example, the standard SAP system always includes the predefined technical users DDIC and SAPCPIC. Technical users are also created for all ALE (application link enabling) scenarios and for internet application components (IACs) that are processed over the SAP Internet Transaction Server.

Authentication of technical users occurs just as it does for individual users. Accordingly, you must take special care to protect the passwords of technical users, because they represent worthy targets for attackers. Misuse is easier for technical users, since no one can actually inspect each logon of a technical user, as can occur for actual users. Technical users along with their passwords exist immediately after installation of an SAP system. SAP customers must change the passwords as indicated in the SAP security guidelines [SAP SG].

Automatic operation of SAP systems almost always requires technical users. When creating technical users, however, you must ensure that they receive the correct user type. User type CPIC is sufficient for most technical users because such technical users are employed in automatic procedures that run without any user dialog, such as ALE. Accordingly, an attacker cannot employ this type of technical user in a dialog activity. This approach prevents any simple changes to SAP programs through the ABAP Workbench.

In addition, technical users should always have a minimum of authorizations, only exactly as many as they need to perform their automatic functions.

2.1.2.3 User maintenance with directory services

SAP customers increasingly use directory services to administer system and user informa-tion in the IT infrastructure of a company. This procedure is based upon strategies to lessen the effort required to administer systems and users by storing and maintaining such data in only one place, the directory service. With this approach, a company's IT systems no longer access user information from their own databases, but access it directly in the directory service. Modern directory services offer internal and external replication mech-anisms optimized for data that changes only rarely and to which the application itself does not need to attend.

As of Release 4.5, the SAP R/3 System offers an interface to directory services that uses the LDAP (lightweight directory access protocol – see Wahl, Howes and Kille 1997) as stan-dardized by the IETF. The SAP system contains ABAP function modules for this interface to create, display, write, and delete directory entries. The SAP security development group is currently working on the use of this interface to export and import user information to and from a directory service. This will be provided with SAP Web Application server Release 6.10.

2.1.3 Locking users

An SAP system administrator can lock a user. This action can become necessary when an employee leaves the company or occur automatically if the user makes a certain number of incorrect logon attempts.

The automatic locking of users after a specific number of failed logon attempts avoids dictionary attacks, in which an attacker systematically tries to log on with a predefined dic-tionary of passwords. Programs that automate this task exist. They attempt to log on by going through all the combinations and permutations of terms contained in the diction-ary. The programs are also known as crack programs, familiar attack tools. Their authors show a great deal of imagination and emulate familiar mnemonic devices (such as wild-cards or special characters).

Locking user master records after a few failed logon attempts is an effective response to such attacks. However, an attacker can prevent an employee from doing almost any work if the employee remains locked as a user. At the beginning of the day, the standard system automatically unlocks user master records that were locked the previous day because of failed logon attempts. At that point, the user can log on with the correct password. You can use profile parameters to configure automatic locking.

Users who find themselves locked even though they have not made any unsuccessful logon attempts should contact the system administrator immediately to identify the cause of the lock. It might well indicate an attack. Security audit logs (*see* section 2.5) can help fix the time of such attacks and follow them back to their source to track down the attacker. External system programs, such as fax servers, for example, frequently trigger user locks if the programs no longer possess valid user information.

Technical

Creating user master records

The SAP system contains a dialog transaction to create user master records. Follow the menu path: *Tools • Administration • User Maintenance* (su02). You enter the name of the user master record and the desired action through the initial screen (*see* Figure 2.3). In this manner, you can also create user master records as copies of existing records. If you do so, pay particular attention to the assigned activity groups and authorization profiles; change them if necessary.

Maintaining user master records

Maintenance of user master records also occurs through the dialog transaction for user management. After you enter the transaction, several tabs provide you with an opportunity to display and change user information (*see* Figure 2.4 for an example of changing address data).

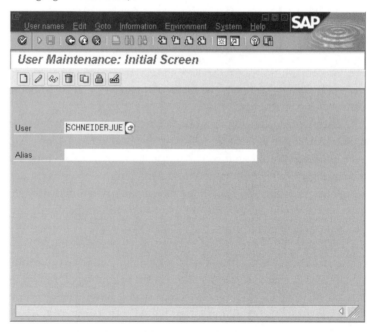

FIGURE 2.3   Dialog transaction for user maintenance (1) (Copyright © SAP AG)

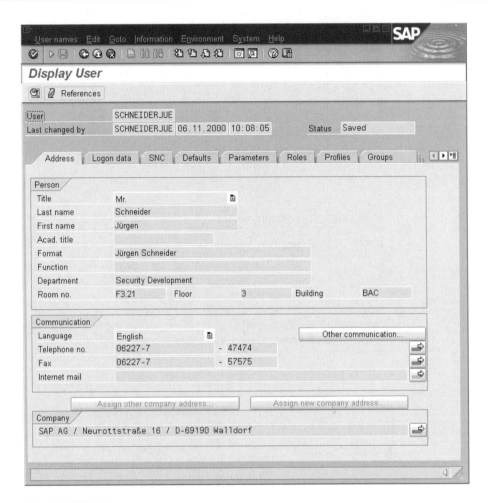

BAPIs for user maintenance

Release 4.5 of the SAP R/3 System offers a group of BAPIs for automatic management of user master records. Table 2.1 lists a small selection of the available functional scope. You can also use this interface to perform SAP user maintenance with an external tool. Some manufacturers offer tools for system administration that support the management of SAP users via these BAPIs.

SAP standard users

SAP products have some technical users that are already present in the standard systems after installation (*see* Table 2.2). To avoid any misuse, you must change the passwords for

TABLE 2.1   BAPIs for user maintenance

BAPI	Description
BAPI_USER_CREATE	Creating user master records
BAPI_USER_GET_DETAIL	Displaying (reading) information in user master records
BAPI_USER_CHANGE	Changing user master records
BAPI_USER_LOCK	Locking user master records
BAPI_USER_UNLOCK	Unlocking user master records
BAPI_USER_DELETE	Deleting user master records

TABLE 2.2   Standard users

USER	Description	Clients
SAP*	Super user for the R/3 System	000, 001, 066 (as of Release 3.0D) all new clients
DDIC	Super user for the ABAP Dictionary and software logistics	000, 001
SAPCPIC	CPIC user for the R/3 System	000, 001
EARLYWATCH	Dialog user for the EarlyWatch-Service in client 066	066

TABLE 2.3   Authorizations for user maintenance

Authorization object	Fields	Description
S_USER_GRP	User group (CLASS) Activity (ACTVT)	Checks during all transactions involved in user maintenance. The user group can be used to limit authorization to specific groups of users. The activity field can differentiate between create, change, display, lock/unlock, delete, and some additional actions. This field also includes the assignment of users to activity groups, which is used to assign authorizations to users with the concept of activity groups.
S_USER_PRO	Authorization profile (PROFILE) Activity (ACTVT)	Checks during the assignment of authorization profiles to users. The field for authorization profile can limit the profiles that may be assigned to users. The activity field is used here as it is for user maintenance.
S_USER_AGR Role (ACT_GROUP) Activity (ACTVT)	Roles	Checks during the assignment of roles to users. The field for role can limit the roles that may be worked on. The activity field is used here as it is in user maintenance.

such users after installation. For example, user SAP* exists in the runtime environment of the SAP system and has all authorizations there unless you explicitly create a user master record for it. To avoid misuse of this powerful, standard user, you must create a user master record for SAP* for all clients and assign each SAP* its own password. The user master record for SAP* should be then locked for logons.

Authorizations for SAP user management

Table 2.3 lists an overview of the technical authorization objects that are used by the separation of functions principle during user and authorization maintenance.

<table>
<tr><td>2.2</td><td>USER AUTHENTICATION</td></tr>
</table>

User authentication ensures that only specific users have access to the system at specific times. Because access authorization and the logging of transactions are linked to user IDs, it's crucial that it be as difficult as possible to sneak into the system as a foreign user.

System administrators have a special responsibility here. Sneaking into a system with administration rights has an enormous risk potential for an SAP system.

2.2.1 Rules for password protection

As the standard mechanism for user authentication, the SAP system uses a password procedure. Practical experience has shown that users often treat PINs (personal identification numbers) and passwords lackadaisically. They either choose passwords that are easy for others to guess or post them at their workplaces. A misunderstanding of collegiality causes many users to reveal or exchange their passwords, and the same users are then surprised when data is manipulated under their names.

Weaknesses in the system can also defeat the protection of passwords: maintaining unencrypted codes in easily accessed tables, using reserve decoding, or ignoring password rules.

The near future will see company networks offer self-service scenarios for a large portion of the workforce. Employees will be able to enter data directly into the personnel system, data such as changes of address, banking information, and insurance policies along with notifications of absence and records of hours worked. It's clearly in the best interest of all users that they can access and change only their own data.

The following lists the recommendations of data protection agencies and the federal German agency for IT security (SBI) on passwords and indicates how to implement them in SAP systems.

The specifications can be implemented as follows.

▨ Each person receives a unique user ID.

A user can be created only once in a client, although the same user can be created in different clients. The latter is often the case for system administrators. In this case, however, the authorizations and passwords can differ.

▪ A user ID is valid only as long as required.

You can adjust the validity period for each user with the *from* and *to date* setting. At the very least, assignment of user IDs for maintenance or emergencies should have a temporal limitation.

▪ The file for passwords and user IDs demands special protection.

Passwords are stored as hash values, and cannot be converted back to actual values. Transmission from the frontend occurs with compression. If you use secure network communications (SNC), the password must no longer be transmitted over the network (*see* section 2.7 on the authentication of external users).

▪ Automatic limits to logon attempts and locking the user.

You can set the number of invalid logon attempts before the session ends or the system locks the user at any value between 1 and 99.

▪ Logging of failed logon and administrative information.

The system log records user locks that occur once the value set of invalid logon attempts is exceeded. You can also record both successful and unsuccessful logons in the security audit log, by user name and terminal (*see* section 2.5 on auditing and logging).

▪ Display of last logon for monitoring purposes by authorized users.

The system status contains the date and time of the last logon.

▪ Automatic logoff after a long period of inactivity.

You can set the maximum period of inactivity in seconds.

▪ Supplemental security measures when dialing in to a public network (such as automatic return calls).

You can require these features.

▪ Minimum length of six characters.

Settings permitted between three and eight characters.

▪ No given names or trivial passwords.

Table USR40 can contain a list of all forbidden passwords; placeholders make the task easier. In addition, the first three characters of the password cannot be identical to the user ID.

▪ Passwords must be changed at specific intervals.

You can set this value in days.

- Avoid the use of old passwords.

  Users may not reuse their last five passwords.

- Default passwords must be replaced by individual passwords.

  At delivery, the system uses initial passwords for standard users. The SAP security guidelines expressly note that these passwords must be changed. Monitoring programs detect the failure to do so (*see* section 2.5 on auditing and logging).

- Users must be able to change passwords at any time.

  Passwords can be changed once a day. The change requires correct entry of the old password.

- No display of a password during entry.

  The SAP system operates in this manner.

The following recommendations have not been implemented.

- Temporal limitations, such as working hours.

  Establishing this function would demand excessive administrative and system effort. Working hours are becoming increasingly flexible. Exceptions to normal working hours would have to be implemented by user management. Given the separation of functions, several employees would be needed around the clock to perform them. At the end of office hours, the system would have to remove the user: merely blocking a new logon attempt would not satisfy the recommendation. However, removing an active user poses problems. Who wants to prevent willing employees from working?

  As described above, you can limit access to the system by date. This feature also enables you to block a user who may be absent for an extended period, such as a vacation.

- Passwords should contain a number or a special character.

  This function is available, but not required. Users who change their locations and have special characters in their passwords may find it impossible to log on when using a different keyboard.

The following recommendations must be set in the rules for password use.

- Passwords may not be stored in programmable function keys or in objects on the PC desktop.

- Passwords may be known only to a user, and must remain confidential.

- Written passwords should be stored as carefully as a bankcard.

- If a password has been discovered, the password must be changed or the user blocked until the situation is clarified.

- The entry of passwords must not be observed by anyone.

2.2.2 Monitoring adherence to password rules

In addition to creating rules for password use and informing all users of the rules, you should also monitor adherence to the rules at regular intervals. Such monitoring covers more than direct access by SAP users; it also includes a study of access to the operating system, the database, and the network.

The market currently offers crack programs that mechanically examine the quality of passwords even when reverse encryption is unavailable. The programs require only the encrypted password and the encryption algorithm to try the most common words in a dictionary on a very fast computer. Almost half of all passwords are cracked in a short time.

When communicating password regulations, you should place value on the transparency of the security measures: ensure that both administration and users are clear about the meaning of password protection.

We recommend that the security staff should not determine the actual passwords during monitoring. Instead, they should simply determine the users who have easily decrypted passwords. These users should be asked to select a secure password according to the rules already in place. However, if the staff first determine passwords and then the users, a suspicion can easily be raised that the staff themselves can operate dishonestly. This concern is particularly important when you consider that users can select one password and then use it in multiple systems. We cannot exclude the option of using PIN codes or other numbers from the private area as the basis for designing passwords.

Technical

Standard logon dialog

Figure 2.5 shows the standard logon dialog to a SAP system with the SAP graphical user interface (GUI) for Windows. SAP users know the dialog well: they execute it at least once a day. Users must enter a user ID and a user-specific password, which the system occludes from view. Entry of a client and a logon language is optional. If users enter nothing here, the system uses the default values it has already stored for the user (system parameters or fixed values for the user).

The use of external security products to authenticate users with secure network communications (SNC) makes the standard logon dialog and a user-specific password unnecessary. Section 2.7 on external user authentication outlines this option, which has been available in the standard SAP R/3 System since Release 3.1.

Table 2.4 lists the profile parameters that you can use to set password rules on SAP application servers.

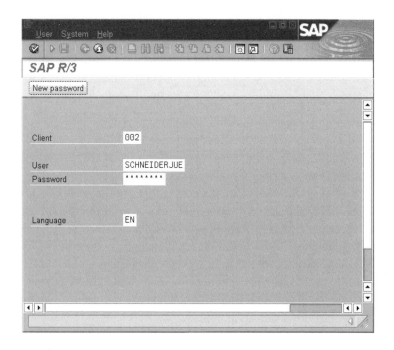

FIGURE 2.5 Standard logon (Copyright © SAP AG)

TABLE 2.4 Profile parameters to set password rules

Parameter	Description	Standard	Valid values
Login/password_expiration_time	Forces a change in password	0	0–999
Login/min_password_lng	Minimum length	3	3–8
Login/fails_to_session_end	Failed attempts until the session ends	3	1–99
Login/fails_to_user_lock	Failed attempts until the user is locked	12	1–99
Login/failed_user_auto_unlock	Release lock at midnight	1	0–1
Rdisp/gui_auto_logout	Logout after inactivity	0	> 0

2.3 AUTHORIZATION CONCEPT

After successful authentication, a user has access to the SAP system. At that point, however, not all the applications and data in the system become available to users. That availability depends far more upon the role that users play in the company and upon the authorizations they possess in the system.

The authorization concept has existed in the SAP system since the very first versions of the product. From the beginning, SAP realized that different tasks and responsibilities exist in a company, and that standard software to handle business processes must be able to map these roles and responsibilities. In this regard, business transactions make high-level demands that differ from similar roles in operating systems. For example, an employee in the finance department may not have the authority to trigger payments. Employees who may trigger payments may often do so only up to a specific amount, from specific banks, and from specific accounts. And they often need the approval of other users to do so.

2.3.1 Authorization objects, authorizations, and roles

SAP applications define authorization objects that protect business objects or transactions. The SAP system recognizes several hundred authorization objects that are distributed throughout SAP Basis and all applications. An authorization object includes the definition of several fields of differing meaning, each of which can accept different values. Figure 2.6 provides a sample.

To access a business object or execute an SAP transaction, an SAP user must have the appropriate authorizations. The authorizations represent instances of generic authorization objects and are characterized by the roles and responsibilities of the employee.

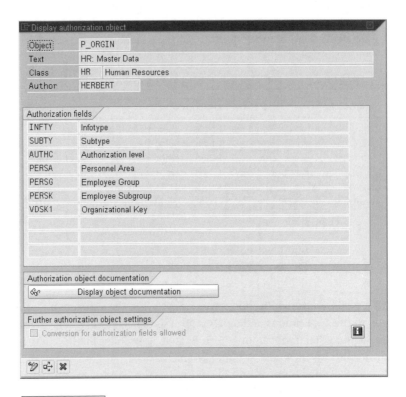

FIGURE 2.6   Sample authorization object (Copyright © SAP AG)

The activity group entered in the user master record (*see* section 2.1.1 on user master records) defines the assignment of a user to a specific role.

2.3.2 Authorization check

Whenever a program runs in the SAP system, it does so under the identification of the user who logged on to the system. A user is also indicated when planning batch jobs: a job runs under a specific user. In both cases, the user's authorizations are checked at various levels.

2.3.2.1 Authorization check in SAP applications

The significant program portions of an application contain a check to determine if the user possesses the appropriate authorizations. The SAP programming language, ABAP, has its own construct for this function (AUTHORITY-CHECK, *see* Figure 2.7 overleaf). This function checks if the user has a specific authorization and if it is properly defined, that is if the fields contain the appropriate values. Both concrete and generic values can be entered into authorizations.

Figure 2.8 (overleaf) provides an overview of how authorizations function in SAP applications. The system authenticates the users at logon. The system loads the authorizations assigned to users' roles and assigns them to users at logon. The applications used check for the presence of the authorizations at runtime and decide if a given transaction is executed or terminated.

2.3.2.2 Authorization check in the SAP runtime environment

Basic authorization checks occur in the SAP runtime environment. Checks are performed during the following actions:

- start of SAP transactions (authorization object S_TCODE)
- start of reports (authorization object S_PROGRAM)
- call of RFC function modules (authorization object S_RFC)
- table maintenance with generic tools (S_TABU_DIS).

These authorization checks occur before a program is started or data is read from a table; SAP applications cannot suppress the checks. To perform a check with authorization object S_PROGRAM, reports must be assigned to authorization groups. In the same manner, the authorization object S_RFC affects groups of function modules and S_TABU_DIS affects groups of tables.

AUTHORITY CHECK

Basic form

```
AUTHORITY-CHECK OBJEKT object ID name1 Field f1
ID name2 Field f2
...
ID name10 Field f10
```

Effect

Explanation of the identifier

- object

    Field that contains the name of the object that is to undergo the authority check

- name1 ...name10

    Fields that contain the names of the authorization fields defined in the object

- f1 ...f10

    Fields that contain the values that are to undergo the authority check

FIGURE 2.7 ABAP language element: AUTHORITY-CHECK (Copyright © SAP AG)

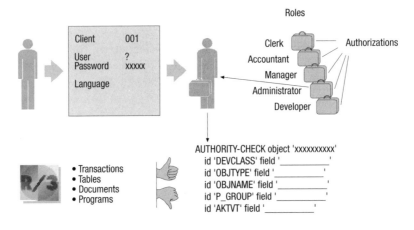

FIGURE 2.8 Authorization concept (Copyright © SAP AG)

2.3.3 Authorization maintenance

At the technical level, the SAP system stores user authorizations in authorization profiles. Administrators formerly needed detailed knowledge of the authorization objects in Basis and applications. They also needed knowledge of the relationships between the business objects and transactions that the authorization objects were designed to protect. However, the number of authorization objects in SAP Basis and SAP applications grew steadily between each R/3 release, and the authorization objects themselves became subject to changes. These developments made the need for support with tools very clear and led to the development of the SAP profile generator, which has been part of the standard SAP offering for several years.

2.3.3.1 SAP profile generator

The profile generator aims at automating authorization objects and profiles for the authorization administrator at the technical level, and to enable the creation of an authorization concept at the level of executable SAP transactions. To abstract from technical authorization profiles, SAP introduced activity groups which contain information on users' activities. With the internet direction of SAP provided by mySAP.com (*see* Chapter 4 on mySAP.com and security on the internet), SAP consistently developed this strategy further into a role concept. A role represents a summary of all the activities permitted in the system. At an abstract level, it replaces the activity group.

The role administrator uses the profile generator to create the activity menu of a user from among all the functions available in the system. From a menu of all functions, the role administrator selects one or more application areas or even single transactions from these application areas and combines them into a new group of activities: a role. In turn, individual roles can be combined into collective roles.

With the profile generator, the authorization administrator works at the level of the business transactions offered by the SAP system. The administrator selects specific transactions and creates a new, role-specific menu. The tool itself finds the authorization checks that occur in the runtime environment when the transactions start. In addition, data on the authorization checks performed in individual applications is collected automatically during the development of an SAP release.

Accordingly, for an SAP release, tables store information on the authorizations needed to perform specific transactions. Using that data, the profile generator can automatically suggest the required authorizations to the role administrator, who can then process the suggestions further. In particular, the role administrator can refine the values suggested by the tool for various organizational areas and responsibilities within a company's structure, such as plants, company codes, and so on, for a specific company.

Finally, the technical authorization profile for a role is generated. It can be assigned to users within role maintenance and matched with the user master records. As stated in section 2.1.2 on the maintenance of user master records, the matching requires various system administrator authorizations to allow for the distribution of tasks required for security.

The profile generator makes authorization maintenance much simpler, but still implements and administers an authorization or role concept efficiently within a company. We always advise our clients to use this tool and to bring their authorization management into line with it.

2.3.4 Creating the authorization concept

SAP customers can use the means available in the SAP system to create an authorization concept that corresponds to the individual requirements of their companies. In general, the creation of an authorization concept requires specialized knowledge of individual areas within a company and a familiarity with SAP tools. The affected departments must participate in the creation of the authorization concept. In the final analysis, only user departments can determine which activities are allowed in the SAP system within the context of a specific role.

Our experiences with the creation of authorization concepts vary. Small or mid-size companies often have two or three employees who work in accounting. With such a small group of people, it makes little sense to distinguish between plants, company codes, or responsibilities for specific customers. An authorization concept that essentially functions at the level of SAP transactions is sufficient here, and the profile generator can produce it in a short time.

For larger companies, authorization at the transaction level is too broad. Here, the use of transactions must be differentiated according to responsibilities. For example, authorizations should be assigned only for specific plants, customers, or groups of persons. The creation of an authorization concept tailored to the needs of this type of company represents a major task for which the profile generator can offer comprehensive support.

Criticism was often raised in the past on the structure of authorizations, which was regarded as too complex. Examined closely, however, the authorization scenarios for business transactions are very multifaceted and can proceed differently in different companies. Dealing with these requirements properly demands a flexible concept that can map complex authorization contexts at a fine level of detail. The same concept must be able to create much simpler authorization concepts at a broader level. The tools available in an SAP system, along with the profile generator, offer both possibilities.

Technical

Manual profile and authorization maintenance

The SAP system includes a dialog transaction for manual profile and authorization maintenance. Use the menu path: *Tools • Administration • User Maintenance • Manual Maintenance • Edit Profiles Manually* (su02). However, we do not recommend use of this dialog transaction because the profile generator has replaced it. You enter the name of the authorization profile and the desired action in the initial screen. The transaction can create and change both individual profiles (*see* the same in Figure 2.9) or insert individual profiles into a collective profile. Individual profiles receive individual authorizations that specify authorization objects.

The SAP system includes a dialog transaction for manual definition and administration of individual authorizations. Use the menu path: *Tools • Administration • User Maintenance • Manual Maintenance • Edit Authorizations Manually* (su03). The transaction offers functions to create, display, and change authorizations. However, we do not recommend use of this dialog transaction because the profile generator has replaced it. To edit a specific authorization, you first select the object category and then an object class from that list.

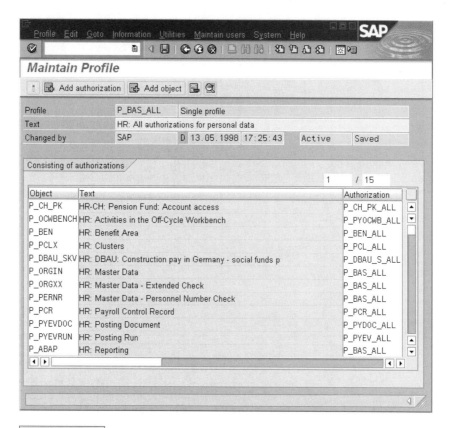

FIGURE 2.9   Manual maintenance of authorization profiles (Copyright © SAP AG)

You then create or change an authorization for the authorization object and specify the field values (*see* the sample in Figure 2.10 that applies to the authorization object in Figure 2.6).

SAP profile generator

Call the profile generator via the menu path: *Tools • Administration • User Maintenance • Roles* (pfcg). The initial screen displays the individual steps to define a role for a user in a series of index tabs. After a textual description of the role, you create the user menu for the role by interactively selecting transactions that apply to the role from the overall menu (*see* Figure 2.11).

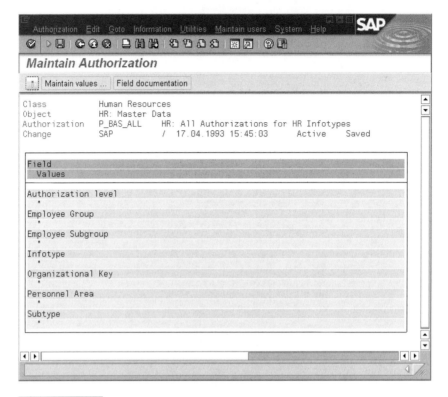

FIGURE 2.10 Manual maintenance of authorizations (Copyright © SAP AG)

After the transactions are combined into a role, the profile generator knows which authorizations are needed for the role. In a second interactive step, you examine the fields and values for the authorizations more closely and refine them according to the role and the organizational units of the company (*see* Figure 2.12). Wherever possible, the profile generator first suggests the maximum value area, which the role administrator can then adjust. The organizational units and responsibilities must be entered specifically for a customer. The dialog screen displays a red light for each menu entry that does not contain values for all fields.

All the lights should be green at the end of this step. Once you have designed the user menu in light of organizational structures and responsibilities, you can generate the technical authorization profile. You can then assign roles to users with the user tab (*see* Figure 2.13).

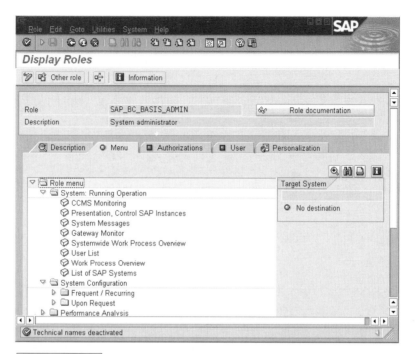

FIGURE 2.11 Creating a role with the profile generator (Copyright © SAP AG)

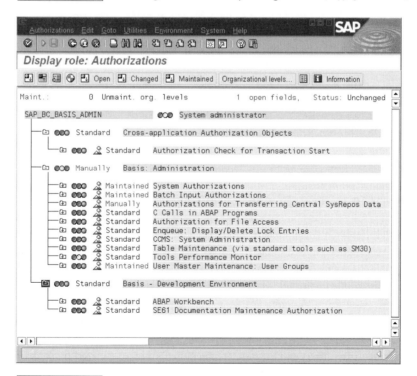

FIGURE 2.12 Refining a role with profile generator (Copyright © SAP AG)

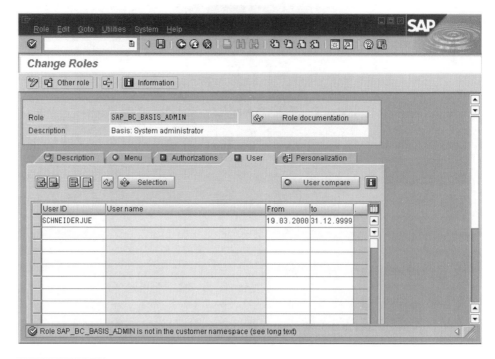

FIGURE 2.13 Assigning roles to users (Copyright © SAP AG)

Displaying authorization at runtime

To monitor authorizations, you can use a dialog transaction to display the authorizations that a logged-on user possesses. Use the menu path: *Tools • Administration • Monitor • User Buffer* (su56). The system lists the authorizations loaded into the system buffer for the logged-on user (*see* the sample in Figure 2.14).

2.4 DATA INTEGRITY AND CONFIDENTIALITY

The data processed and stored in an SAP system is worth protecting, whether it involves sales figures, balance sheets, employees, customers, or system settings.

The protection of data integrity means that data is not modified on purpose or in error. Accidental changes to data can also arise from program errors; user error is not the only explanation. Deliberate falsification of data, however, is a criminal act. The damage done to data integrity and authenticity in both cases represents a significant threat to a company.

The same is true for data confidentiality. Companies must always ensure that only authorized users can view data. The ability of unauthorized persons to view confidential data poses a major threat to a company.

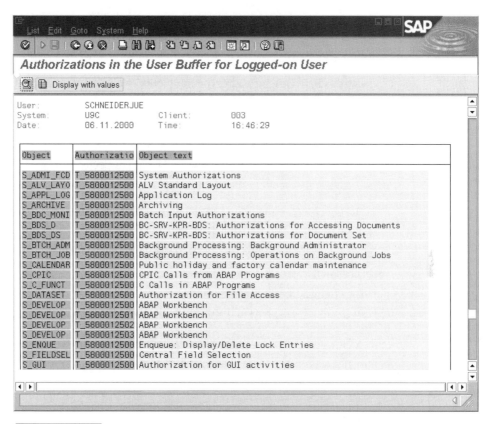

FIGURE 2.14   Displaying the authorizations of a logged-on user (Copyright © SAP AG)

This chapter has already treated some of the mechanisms contained in the SAP system for the protection of data integrity and confidentiality:

- user management (*see* section 2.1)
- user authentication (*see* section 2.2)
- authorization concept (*see* section 2.3).

These features ensure that an SAP system knows its users. It authenticates them when they enter the system, and it monitors their actions with authorization checks. The authorization concept can also ensure that users can see and change only the data for which they possess the appropriate authorization.

2.4.1 Transaction and posting concept

The SAP transaction and posting concept provides additional protection for data integrity. An SAP transaction is subdivided into one or more sections called logical units of work (LUW). An LUW represents a transaction at the database level and is therefore secure because of normal database technology. In particular, this means that the classic characteristics of database transactions are also guaranteed over the SAP database interface.

■ Atomicity

The database either executes the transaction completely or rejects it completely: all or nothing.

■ Consistency

The transaction maintains the consistency of data: no data is changed incompletely or ever falsified. Dependencies between data are respected.

■ Isolation

The effects of a transaction can be executed independently of other transactions, even those that may run in parallel. No dependencies between transactions running in parallel exist, or such transactions are synchronized by a locking mechanism.

■ Permanence

The changes effected by the transactions are permanent and will not be lost. The logging and recovery mechanisms in the database contribute to this feature.

The architecture and implementation of the SAP database interface and runtime environment ensures that these characteristics operate. *See* [SAP-Enqueue] for a more detailed description of each system component.

2.4.2 Encryption methods

The security functions used in the standard SAP system guarantee data integrity and confidentiality at the level of the SAP system. The SAP mechanisms do not, however, work during access to the database with normal database tools or with the applications of other manufacturers. We advise our clients that the use of other software can lead to consistency problems in the SAP database. An attacker who wants to gain unauthorized access to the data in an SAP system will hardly follow this advice.

Accordingly, structural measures and measures at the network level make sense. The measures should prevent an attacker from gaining access to the SAP application and database servers. For more detail, see Chapter 3 on security in the SAP system landscape.

The use of an encryption method can provide additional security for the integrity and confidentiality of data in an SAP system. Both checksum methods and encryption can help here. The standard SAP system contains an interface to external security products, secure store and forward [BC-SSF], that are themselves not part of the standard system. Section 2.8 on digital signatures and encryption treats the options offered by the BC-SSF interface for the use of cryptographic products in detail.

| 2.5 | **RECORDING, LOGGING, AND AUDITING** |

The recording and logging of events relevant to security in the system form an important part of a complete security concept. When such events occur or when they deviate from defaults, the system administrator can be informed immediately and then check the situation. If a security concern is discovered only later, the log information permits a more detailed analysis of the incident and its effects. As a rule, administrators check logs daily or weekly for irregularities to recognize unauthorized manipulation early. Log information also provides the basis for system audits that allow for the inspection of security throughout the system and for secure administration of the system.

The SAP system features several complementary functions for these purposes. In addition to the SAP applications, the central administrative applications (such as user and authorization maintenance) write documents that the database stores. There is also logging of table changes made in Customizing that notes the old and new values of a table entry. As delivered, table logging is already switched on for central tables. Customers can extend this logging to other tables. The system log records messages on general error conditions in the system.

As of Release 4.0 of the R/3 System, two additional applications record security-relevant events and check the security status:

▓ Security Audit Log

▓ Audit Information System.

The following sections describe these components in more detail.

2.5.1 Security Audit Log

The Security Audit Log helps the system administrator observe and record security-relevant system events. It is activated with profile parameters in the application server and it records information in log files written to the file system of the application server – in areas accessible only to the system administrator.

The system administrator uses filters to set the scope of the events recorded by the Security Audit Log and the information on these events. The system administrator first defines the filters in a dialog transaction and then activates them either globally throughout the system or locally on one application server (*see* the technical section). At each location in the runtime system or application the filter settings are checked when an event occurs during system operations and, if required, recorded (*see* Figure 2.15).

Security-relevant events cannot only be recorded in audit files: they can also be displayed directly in the Computer Center Management System (CCMS). The CCMS is part of the standard SAP system and helps with general system administration. For

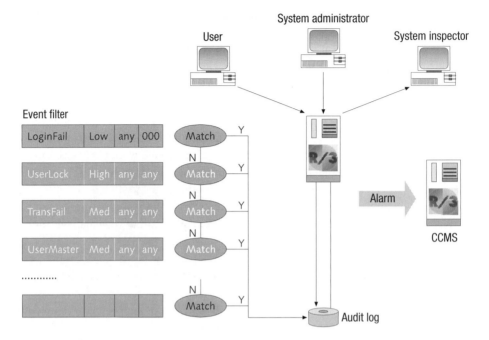

FIGURE 2.15   Principle of the Security Audit Log (Copyright © SAP AG)

monitoring system security, CCMS Monitoring has a special security monitor that can be displayed with the situations set in the Security Audit Log (*see* the technical section).

The Security Audit Log currently supports observation of the following classes of events in an SAP system:

- starting and stopping of application servers
- successful and unsuccessful dialog messages
- successful and unsuccessful logons via Remote Function Call (RFC)
- successful and unsuccessful transaction calls
- successful and unsuccessful report calls
- successful and unsuccessful calls of function modules via RFC
- changes to user master records
- upload and download methods
- signature methods via the SSF interface
- changes to setting in the Security Audit Log.

To analyze the recording locally or throughout the system, the Security Audit Log offers the system administrator a dialog transaction. The analysis can sort according to the time of the recording, the type of event, and importance. An additional dialog transaction is available to administer audit files (*see* the technical section).

The Security Audit Log provides central logging and monitoring functions in the SAP system; you can configure the log to meet the security requirements of your system.

2.5.2 Audit Information System

Permanent recording and monitoring of system security includes regular audits of the security status and system settings. These should occur according to a fixed audit plan that schedules one or more audits every year.

The system buffer in a SAP system has a comprehensive information system available for this task, the Audit Information System (AIS). A dialog transaction offers a selection of reports that give the auditor an overview of the basic settings in the system along with an ability to see more detailed information on individual aspects of system security.

The newer versions of the Audit Information System provide a menu that corresponds to the structure of the SAP security guidelines [SAP SG].

- User authentication.
  - Password rules.
  - Protective measures for standard users.
  - Protective measures against unauthorized logons.

- Authorization concept.
  - Authorization maintenance and profile generator.
  - Information system for authorizations.
  - Organization of authorization management.
  - Settings for authorization checks.

- Network infrastructure.
  - Network structure and SNC settings.

- Protecting the operating system.

- Protecting access to the database.

- Protecting the production system.
  - System landscape and transport paths.
  - Settings for system convertibility.

■ Remote communications.
  – Settings for SAP Remote Function Call (RFC).
  – RFC destinations with logon information.
  – External commands via RFC client programs.

■ Secure store and forward mechanisms and digital signatures.

■ Logging and auditing.
  – Audit Information System.
  – Security Audit Log.
  – System logs.
  – Daily statistics.
  – Logging specific activities.

■ Special topics.
  – Internet settings.
  – Application Link Enabling (ALE).
  – Protecting the SAP service connection.

The technical section includes some samples of the choice of reports offered by the Audit Information System.

The Audit Information System is used within a company for more than inspections and audits. Consulting firms and auditors will also find it a welcome aid. SAP continually works closely with companies and its partners to improve the functional scope and structure of the Audit Information System.

The Security Audit Log and the Audit Information System offer important functions for monitoring and checking the security of SAP systems. Unfortunately, the activities associated with these functions are all too often underestimated during daily operations, even though the functions can protect against attacks. Security holes uncovered during a system check can be filled before they can be used for an attack on the system. Security holes often exist for months before discovery. A responsible system administrator cannot simply operate on the principle that the discoverer has no dishonest intentions.

Technical

Security Audit Log – configuration

You can configure the event filter for the Security Audit Log with a dialog transaction. Use the menu path: *Tools • Administration • Monitor • Security Audit Log • Configuration* (sm19).

Although the sample (*see* Figure 2.16) shows that two filters can be set, you can also set more. Each filter has settings for the clients, users, events, and at what rank of an

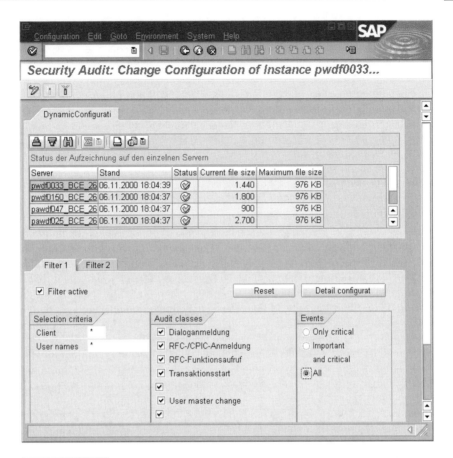

FIGURE 2.16 Security Audit Log – configuration (Copyright © SAP AG)

event logging should occur. A checkbox indicates if the filter should be active. Depending upon your needs, you can use this filter to define that all clients and users are monitored, but that only critical events are recorded. Additional filters are then defined to record additional events in a specific client and for specific users. The additional filters can first remain inactive, and be activated if needed in the event of misuse.

Security Audit Log – evaluation

A dialog transaction is available to analyze the entries in the Security Audit Log. Use the menu path: *Tools • Administration • Monitor • Security Audit Log • Analysis* (sm20). Here you can specify the events and period you wish to analyze, and whether you want to evaluate a specific application server or the entire system (*see* the same in Figure 2.17). After indicating the desired selection, the system administrator receives a display of the results (*see* the sample in Figure 2.18).

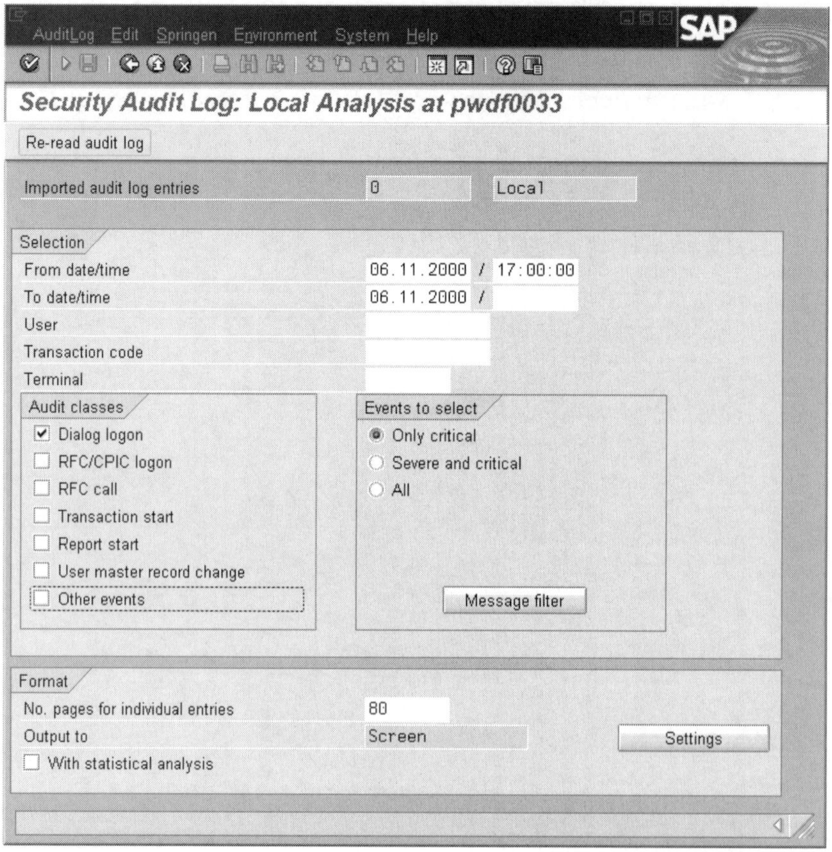

FIGURE 2.17   Security Audit Log – selections for evaluation (Copyright © SAP AG)

Security Audit Log – managing the audit files

You can manage the audit files of the Security Audit Log with a dialog transaction. Use the menu path: *Tools • Administration • Monitor • Reorganization* (sm18). The system administrator must, however, regularly back up and archive the material. The dialog transaction in the SAP system itself only permits the deletion of audit files depending upon a specific age, specified in days.

Security Audit Log – security monitor in the CCMS

The Computer Center Management System (CCMS) of the SAP system offers a specific security monitor. Use the menu path: *Tools • CCMS • Control/Monitoring • Alert Monitor* (rz20). Select *SAP CCMS Monitor Templates* for the security monitor, which provides immediate notification of events recorded in the Security Audit Log and generates alarms (*see* the sample in Figure 2.19).

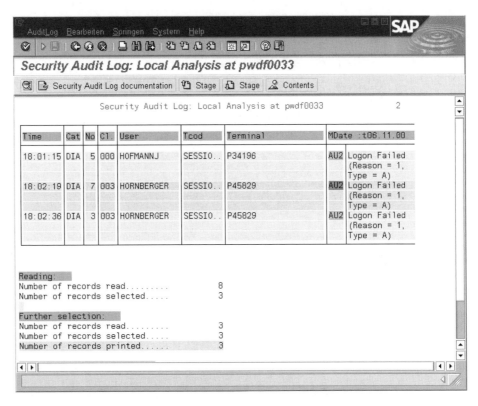

FIGURE 2.18   Security Audit Log – display of the results of an evaluation
(Copyright © SAP AG)

Security Audit Log – profile settings

Table 2.5 lists the profile parameter settings required for the Security Audit Log on SAP application servers.

You can start the Audit Information System (AIS) with a dialog transaction reached via the menu path: *Information Systems • Audit Info System* (secr). An overview lists the available reports. The system audit portion supports various views. Current versions of the AIS provide a menu structure that corresponds to the SAP security guidelines (*see* Figure 2.20). AIS users can also configure their own views. From within the AIS, you can display all the system settings that are relevant to security, and thereby quickly determine the security status of the system. You can also identify and correct any potential security problems. The following treats a few examples.

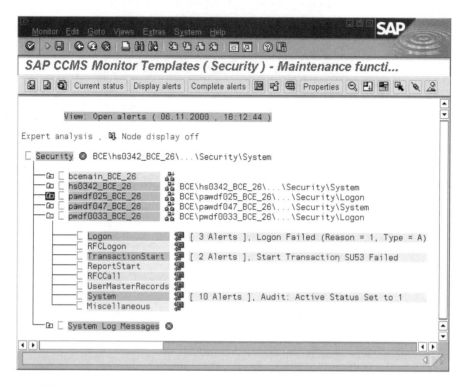

TABLE 2.5   **Profile parameters for settings in the Security Audit Log**

Profile parameter	Description	Standard or suggested value
rsau/enable	Activates the audit log on an application server	Suggested value: 1 (audit log not activated)
rsau/local/file	Indicates the directory of the audit log on the application server	Standard value: /usr/sap/<SID>/<InstNr>/log/ audit_<SAP instance number>
rsau/max_diskspace_local	Indicates the maximum length of the audit log	Suggested value: 1,000,000 bytes
rsau/selection_slots	Indicates the number of memory slots available for the selection options when recording security-relevant events	Suggested value: 2

List   Edit   Goto   Utilities   System   Help   SAP

Audit Information System: Display

Audit info view AUDIT_ALL   STANDARD

```
┌─ ⌷                  Introduction
├─ ⌷                  - - - - - - - - - - - - - - - - - - - - - -
├─ ⌷                  System Audit

    ├─ ⌷                  ▣ System Configuration
    ├─ ⌷                  ▣ Transport Group
    ├─ ⌷                  ▣ Repository / Tables
    ├─ ⌷                  Development / Customizing
    ├─ ⌷                  ▣ Background Processing
    ├─ ⌷                  System Logs and Status Displays
    ├─ ⌷                  ▣ User Administration
    └─ ⌷                  Checklist According to R/3 Security Guidelines

        ├─ ⌷                  2-1:  User Authentication
        ├─ ⌷                  2-2:  R/3 Authorization Concept
        ├─ ⌷                  2-3:  Network Infrastructure
        ├─ ⌷                  2-4:  Operating System Protection
        ├─ ⌷                  2-5:  Database Access Protection
        ├─ ⌷                  2-6:  Protecting Your Productive System (Change&Transport)
        ├─ ⌷                  2-7:  Remote Communications (RFC & CPI-C)
        ├─ ⌷                  2-8:  Secure Store&Forward Mechanisms and Digital Signatur
        ├─ ⌷                  2-9:  Logging and Auditing
        └─ ⌷                  2-10: Special Topics

    ├─ ⌷                  Checklist According to Data Protection Guidelines
    └─ ⌷                  Human Resources Audit / Data Protection Audit

└─ ⌷                  Business Audit
```

FIGURE 2.20   Audit Information System – report selection (Copyright © SAP AG)

Audit Information System – sample: standard user

Via the menu path *Checklist According to R/3 Security Guidelines, 2–1: User Authentication*, you can find the report 'Protecting Standard Users Have you changed the default passwords?' This report lists the standard users in the SAP system and the status of their passwords. The sample given in Figure 2.21 indicates that new passwords for the standard users SAP* and DDIC have been assigned in client 000.

The report also indicates that user SAP* has been created. Creation of this user is a crucial security recommendation. Without it, the programmed user SAP* can be used in the runtime environment with a standard password. The password has not been changed for standard user SAPCPIC, so that the familiar starting password is still valid. No SAP* user has been created in client 005.

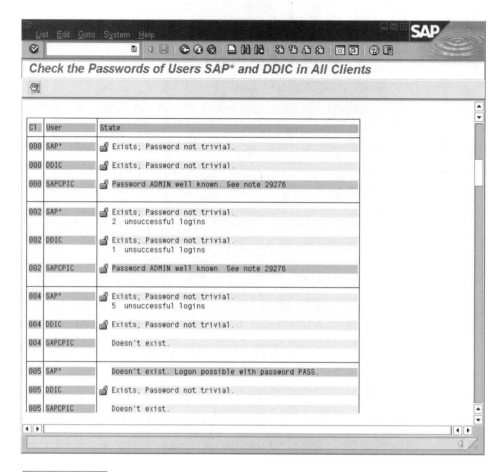

FIGURE 2.21 Audit Information System – standard user (Copyright © SAP AG)

Audit Information System – sample: user with special authorizations

You can enter authorization object S_TCODE with a value of "se38" and the authorization object S_DEVELOP with activity '02' (change) in the report "User By Authorization Values." The resulting report lists the users in the system who have development rights and can therefore change program objects (*see* the sample in Figure 2.22).

The SAP security guidelines recommend that this list remain empty in a production system, and that any exceptions to the rule be made only for a very short time. The Audit Information System can check the status of this recommendation.

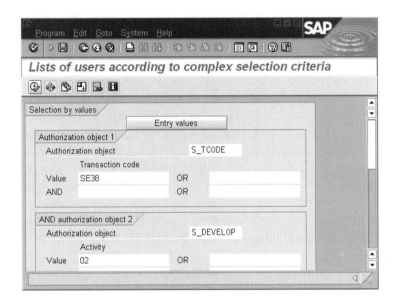

2.6   EXTERNAL SECURITY PRODUCTS AND CRYPTOGRAPHY

The use of cryptographic methods and algorithms offers an extremely beneficial tool for the implementation of security functions. Cryptography can provide a significantly higher level of security for the confidentiality of data and the authentication of system components and persons. State security agencies throughout the world have made good use of this characteristic for quite some time. The internet has increased the importance of mathematical and cryptographic work for modern IT in recent decades. The technical section offers a short overview of the methods used today.

2.6.1 Cryptography and legal regulations

Cryptographic processes can be used for different purposes.

- The encryption of data provides confidentiality. Only recipients with access to the required key can decrypt the data.

- Knowledge of a secret key can be used for authentication, to determine the identity of a system component or a person.

- Digital signatures calculate a mathematical seal for specific data. The seal protects the integrity, authorship, and authenticity of the data.

■ Cryptographic hash methods can give data a unique fingerprint that protects the integrity of this data (one-way function).

Modern cryptography can help companies and private individuals protect their data reliably and prevent unauthorized persons from accessing it. Of course, nothing prevents the use of encryption techniques to conceal illegal deeds and subversive activities targeted against national and international security interests. And as has ever been the case, the military also uses encryption techniques.

Accordingly, the laws of some countries limit the use of encryption (currently Russia and China, for example). Many countries, even those in the industrial West, legally restrict the export of cryptographic products. Such products include software that can encrypt data. Digital signatures and hash methods can be exported freely, however. Germany has its own laws on the subject, and the European Union has issued regulations on dual-use goods, which can be used for civilian and military purposes [EU Crypto].

The US has long had very restrictive laws that generally prohibit the export of strong encryption products. The length of the keys permitted for export has risen steadily in the past few years, but only after the computing power needed for decryption also increased. (*See* the technical section for a discussion of key length.) The computer time required for decryption remained practically unchanged. With the means available to national security agencies, the time needed to systematically decrypt data with a short key length currently takes a few hours, and sometimes even just a few minutes.

In the Wassenaar Arrangement of 1998, most industrial countries in the West have taken up the American position and committed themselves to controlling the export of encryption techniques beyond a given key length. To adhere to the arrangement, the signatories must retain current, domestic legal requirements or adopt new laws in a reasonable time. Such export control can come very close to an outright prohibition. In many cases, an export license is needed for every customer in every country. Customers must sign statements regarding the end use of the products in their companies. The approval process can last weeks, and must be repeated for every software update.

January 2000 saw a loosening of export regulations in the US, so that the export of strong encryption technology is now permitted in most commercial software products. (*See* the technical section for a discussion of strong encryption.) The new regulations (*see* [USA Crypto]) already mean that strong encryption is available in Microsoft internet Explorer and Netscape Navigator outside the US. The rest of the world is waiting to see if other industrial countries in the West will adopt the same attitude.

The question of who should have the most protection, private individuals, companies, or the government, is not new and is often discussed publicly. Changes sometimes come as a surprise: in the US and France for example, where almost total bans on encryption were in force until 1999. Limiting the protection of data with cryptography by legal means seems illogical. After all, those who operate outside the law will certainly take little notice of legal requirements. This approach stymies the legitimate interests of companies and private individuals to protect data, and technology is still misused for criminal purposes.

2.6.2 The SAP position

SAP is well aware of the differences in national and international approaches, the propensity toward unexpected change, and the significant effects that regulations have on the production and delivery of software. Accordingly, SAP has decided not to support encryption in its standard systems, and avoid any possibility of violating German export law or country-specific import laws anywhere in the world. This position, however, does not mean that the standard SAP system offers no security. Mandatory protection with logon passwords, the authorization system, and the recording of transactions and changes are all possible without encryption.

To meet even higher security needs for SAP installations (such as human resources or production control), SAP offers open interfaces to external security products and partner solutions. The interfaces enable problem-free integration of these products into the SAP system. In this manner, cryptographic products can be used with SAP software at any time, still respect the legal situation, and remain at the leading edge of technology. In this case, SAP customers decide on the optimal security products for their purposes and environments.

Nonetheless, SAP still hopes that future legal developments regarding cryptography will enable it to simplify the delivery of appropriate products along with SAP software.

2.6.3 SAP interfaces for external security products

In addition to options offered by the SAP Business Framework [SAP BFA], SAP Remote Function Call (RFC) [SAP RFC], and SAP User Exits [SAP LIB] to integrate security products, two other standard interfaces exist. These interfaces are integrated directly into the SAP runtime environment and are present in all other required SAP product components. Each interface and the supplemental services of each external security product have different aims, but provide a very high level of security when taken together.

Secure Network Communications (SNC) enables you to implement user authentication and to protect data transmitted over network connections in an SAP system with the cryptographic tools of an external security product. Options here include the use of smart cards and encryption of network communications. The protection afforded by user and system identity by SNC refers to the length and context of communication relationships between the various components of an SAP system (frontend, application server, RFC, SAPlpd, SAProuter, SAP Internet Transaction Server, and so on). Packing and unpacking data by the external security product occurs at the Basis levels; applications in the ABAP runtime environment make data available to applications in its usual format, so that encryption and decryption remain transparent to the application. The security product can use completely different methods and protocols.

The interface for secure store and forward (SSF) was developed as an enhancement to SNC and to protect data and documents that require protection independently of an existing communications connection and for an unlimited period. This category includes data and documents stored in the database or file system, data that for whatever reason was exported from an SAP system and stored in any medium, and data transported insecurely (such as by normal e-mail). The mechanisms for digital signatures available with SSF are also used to create digital seals for business transactions that can then be stored in the SAP system as evidence of the transaction. The SSF interface uses only security products that employ public key technology (*see* the technical section). SSF functions can be called via ABAP function modules directly from the applications.

Both interfaces have been designed as C programming interfaces and are integrated directly into the Basis level. Both SNC and SSF feature SAP certification as part of the SAP Complementary Software Partner (CSP) Program, to guarantee the interoperability of the partner products with SAP software [SAP CSP].

Section 2.7 on user authentication treats the SNC interface in more detail. Section 2.8 discusses the SSF interface.

Technical

This section offers a short overview of cryptographic methods and their use. The presentation does not refer to SAP and helps readers in two ways. It helps them understand the functions available in SAP security interfaces treated in this book better. It also helps them evaluate the use of external security products with SAP systems. Readers already familiar with this area can skip this section.

Cryptography

Cryptography deals with the theory and practice of transforming information into another form so that it can no longer be viewed directly, and with its re-conversion into a visible form. Cryptography helps information remain secret and its redundancy helps ensure the integrity of information. Both are classic applications for militaries and secret services, but have also proven useful in everyday dealing with confidential information during this age of electronic communications.

Cryptography uses mathematical algorithms and the corresponding keys to transform data. The algorithms are known publicly; the international community of cryptographers continually studies and inspects their strength. The internet even has worldwide contests that challenge competitors to decode encrypted messages. The strength of encryption with this familiar technique lies exclusively in the length of the key used, which must be sufficiently long. Attempting to guarantee security by keeping the method used a secret is not a good approach. Secret methods are often decoded after a short time. Mathematical proofs for the value of a method are difficult, and most methods don't even have proofs.

Cryptography distinguishes between symmetrical and asymmetrical encryption methods and hash methods. The following provides a short overview of popular, current methods. Interested readers can learn more by consulting specialized literature, such as Schneier (1995) and Menezes (1996).

Symmetrical methods

In symmetrical methods, both sender and receiver have the same, secret key. To encrypt a message, the encryption function E with key k is applied to the plain-text message m to deliver the encrypted message c (cipher text):

$$c = E_k(m)$$

To decrypt a message, the decryption function D with the same key, k, is applied to the encrypted message c (cipher text) to deliver the plain-text message m:

$$m = D_k(c)$$

In many common symmetrical methods, functions E and D are identical. The US Bureau of Standards developed the DES (data encryption standard) method in 1977, which uses a key 56 bits long. Today, this key length is no longer considered secure, since the computing power of normal PCs can now break a key of this length in a relatively short time (a few hours or minutes). Newer methods, such as IDEA or RC4, use keys with 128 bits; Triple DES uses 112 bits or even 168 bits (*see* the overview in Table 2.6). Trying all the possible combinations would take several thousand years. Other ways to decrypt such messages without knowledge of the key have been discovered, but they also require a very long time.

Symmetrical methods can be implemented very efficiently in hardware or in software. These methods, however, have a problem with key exchange. For two parties to exchange confidential information, they need a common key that they must exchange over a secure channel. In actual practice, however, the multiplicity of insecure communications connections and initially unknown communications partners makes this exchange a significant problem. The asymmetrical methods treated in the next section offer important advantages here.

TABLE 2.6	Cryptography – symmetrical methods	
Method	**Key length**	**Patent**
DES	56	IBM
Triple-DES	112, 168	–
RC2	128 or more	Rivest
RC4	128 or more	–
IDEA	128	Ascom

Asymmetrical methods

Asymmetrical methods use a pair of keys that consist of a secret key and a public key. To distinguish it from the secret key used in symmetrical methods, the secret key here is also called a private key. Both keys have a strict mathematical relationship, so that data encrypted with the public key of one person can be decrypted only with the corresponding private key. The reverse is also true. Data signed with the private key can be checked only with the corresponding public key. Knowledge of the public key does not help discover or calculate the private key.

To encrypt a message, encryption function E with public key kpub is applied to the plain-text message m to deliver the encrypted message c (cipher text):

$$c = E_{kpub}(m)$$

To decrypt a message, decryption function D with the private key (kpriv) that corresponds to the public key is applied to encrypted message c (cipher text) to deliver the plain-text message m:

$$m = D_{kpriv}(c)$$

Asymmetrical methods are rather new. Although Diffie and Hellman published the basic idea in 1976 (Diffie et al. 1976), Rivest, Shamir, and Adelman developed the needed mathematical method only in 1978 (Rivest et al. 1978), a method that bears their initials: the RSA method. The RSA method is based on the (so-far unproven) complexity of factoring large prime numbers. It is the most common asymmetrical method in use today. Current research is looking at methods based upon elliptical curves.

In addition to encrypting information, asymmetrical methods are most important as signature methods. For a digital signature, the private key is used to calculate a digital seal for the data. The seal can check the integrity of the data, since the additional information it contains (fingerprint) can be used to recognize any change in the data. The public key can also be used to check the authenticity of the data, that is the identity of the signer. Checking the digital signature requires use of the public key associated with the private key.

To sign a message, the signing function S with the private key kpriv is applied to the text message m that is to be signed to deliver the digital signature ds_m:

$$ds_m = S_{kpriv}(m)$$

To check a digital signature, the verification function V with the public key (kpub) associated with the private key is applied to the digital signature ds_m and compared to the original data. The result determines if the digital signature is valid or not:

$$V_{kpub}(ds_m, m) = \{TRUE, FALSE\}$$

RSA is the most common signature method used today, along with the DSA method developed by the US Bureau of Standards [DSA]. In that method it is typical to sign only a cryptographic fingerprint of the message, the hash value (h), rather than the entire message m. Table 2.7 lists the two most commonly used asymmetrical methods.

TABLE 2.7	Cryptography – asymmetrical methods	
Method	Key length	Patent
RSA	1024 or more	Rivest, Shamir, Adelman
DSA	1024 or more	–

Hash method

Hash method H maps message m on to a characteristic hash value, h, for the message. The hash value (h) is also known as a cryptographic fingerprint.

$$H (m) = h$$

Depending upon the specific hash method, the hash value is 128 or 160 bits long: it does not depend upon the size of the original message. It is calculated in several iterations that include the outgoing message and the intermediate results.

A cryptographic hash method must fulfill several requirements. Mapping a given message to the hash value should always produce the same result and be calculated efficiently. But because the number of possible messages is much larger than the number of possible hash values, some messages can produce the same hash value. The quality and suitability of a cryptographic hash method primarily depend upon the practical impossibility of calculating two meaningful messages leading to exactly the same given hash value. If it's relatively easy to produce such collisions, the hash method has been broken and is therefore insecure.

The American mathematician Ronald Rivest has developed a series of hash methods with 128-bit hash values (MD2, MD4, and MD5). Of these, MD5 is the most commonly used hash method today. But new and improved hash methods also exist, among them SHA and RIPEMD, which also generate 160-bit hash values (*see* Table 2.8).

TABLE 2.8	Cryptography – hash methods
Method	**Length of hash value**
MD5	128
SHA	128, 160
RIPEMD	128, 160

2.7	

EXTERNAL USER AUTHENTICATION AND PROTECTING NETWORK COMMUNICATIONS

The network connections that enable communications between system components in a distributed system provide opportunities for attack. This observation also applies to SAP systems.

Intercepting data over communications lines is quite simple, depending upon the type of connection. The technology overwhelmingly used in local networks for a common transmission medium in theory permits every computer connected to the system to listen to data. Several, freely available tools, or LAN Sniffers, can record and display intercepted data without the sending or receiving station noticing. With point-to-point connections, such as a dial-up number or ISDN line, interception is more difficult, but can still occur in telephone switching offices or at a PBX. It's very easy to intercept communications over the internet connections at routers if the routing cannot be monitored exactly. Only the use of encryption can help here.

Interception is not the only means for unauthorized access to data transmitted over network connections. If an attacker can use the identity of a system component or partner system, a process known as IP spoofing, the system under attack can actually transmit the desired data directly to the attacker. To protect communications on a distributed system, therefore, secure authentication of the communications partners occurs when a communications link is established. It also creates an important precondition for any later encryption.

Every company has to decide for itself how much exposure it has to these kinds of attacks. With hundreds or even thousands of employees, each of whom may have difficulties with the company, it's astounding that so many companies regard their internal networks as secure, without even taking any additional steps to protect them. Other companies take appropriate protective steps for their productive SAP systems and create internal, protective zones for the network. Chapter 3, on security in the SAP system landscape, treats this approach in more detail. These zones usually include particularly sensitive systems, such as human resources and production control. Extra security measures also apply to employees who dial in from home and for connections with partner companies.

Along with firewall systems and network protective zones, end-to-end authentication of communications partners and strong encryption offer the best protection possible for communications links. Cryptography plays the starring role here. To enable this high level of protection in the context of different legal requirements around the world (*see* section 2.6), SAP offers a software layer in its products and an open interface for Secure Network Communications (SNC). You can connect external security products to an SAP system via the SNC interface; the external product then handles the authentication of SAP users and the encryption of communications data.

To interact with the external security product, the SAP software uses an interface developed by the IETF (Internet Engineering Task Force) and written in C: Generic Security Services (GSS) API Version 2 (Linn, 1997). This generic interface permits the use of different architectures and algorithms in the security products, without having to pay special attention to any of these issues. The products allowed include both centralized architectures, such as Kerberos solutions, and decentralized architectures, such as products based upon public keys. The SAP system can be integrated into existing security infrastructures with SNC.

The SNC option is activated on SAP application servers, SAP frontends, Remote Function Call (RFC), SAProuter, and SAPlpd (for local printing) via profile parameters, configuration files, environment variables, and so on (*see* the technical section). The calls from the SAP components arise at the SAP Basis layer, which dynamically loads the calls into the external security product library, so that they therefore originate from the application layer of the overall system architecture. The authentication protocols and encryption functions used by the external security product therefore operate end-to-end between the communicating application processes. This approach, along with the use of strong encryption algorithms and protocols, means that a successful attack is very difficult.

The following treats user authentication and the protection of data integrity and confidentiality with SNC in more detail.

2.7.1 User authentication with SNC

When SNC is used, users are authenticated in the security environment of the external security product. In this situation, you can continue to permit user authentication and passwords in the SAP system as an alternative, or dispense with them entirely.

Figure 2.23 illustrates the flow of a logon in the SAP system with SNC. Initial authentication occurs with a single sign-on to the security product (1). The external security product determines the authentication procedure, which can include strong mechanisms and additional hardware, such as smart cards.

If an SAP system is accessed after logging on to the security product (2, over SAPlogon, for example), authentication of the communications partners occurs in the security products. The authentication protocol is processed via the connection established between the SAP components. Each application process uses GSS API Version 2 to communicate with the external security product (3). The external security product uses the single sign-on procedure to access the user's credentials, without the user having to interact with the system again.

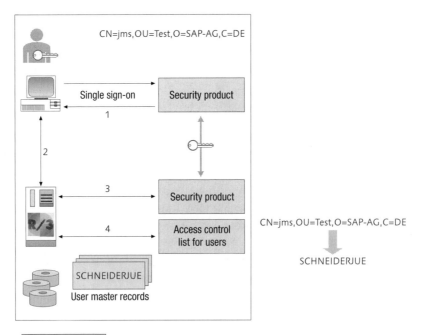

FIGURE 2.23 User authentication with SNC (Copyright © SAP AG)

At the end of the authentication, the SAP system learns the identity of the logged-on user, as it exists in the external security environment. The example in Figure 2.23 shows an X.500 name (with the structure of CN=, OU=, O=, C=), but it could just as easily be a Kerberos name or a Microsoft Windows NT Domain ID. To learn the corresponding SAP user ID, the SAP system features a mapping table that belongs to the user master record. The system administrator must maintain this table (4). Actual logon to the SAP system occurs with the user ID stored in this table. If the table contains several entries, the user must select one when logging on.

2.7.2 Protecting integrity and confidentiality with SNC

Once both communication partners have been authenticated, the extra features of the security product can protect the communications link that now exists. It can also protect data integrity against deliberate forgers during transmission. To do so, the product uses cryptographic checksum procedures. It appends cryptographic checksums to the data packets being transmitted to ensure the integrity of the data being received.

To protect data confidentiality along with its integrity, a security product can also add supplemental encryption to the data. The actual procedures and strength depend upon the capabilities of each security product itself. Various manufacturers offer strong encryption with the common methods (*see* the technical portion of section 2.6).

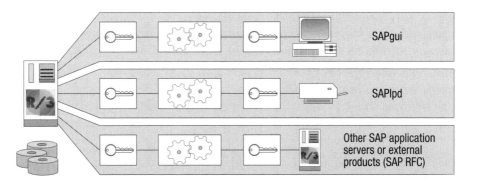

TABLE 2.9 Communications paths secured with SNC

From	To	Via	As of release
SAP GUI	SAP application server	DIAG	3.1H
External program	SAP application server	RFC	4.0A
External program	SAP application server	CPIC	4.0A
SAP application server	SAP application server	RFC	4.0A
SAP application server	SAP application server	CPIC	4.0A
SAP application server	External program	RFC	4.0A
SAP application server	External program	CPIC	4.0A
SAP application server		SAPlpd	3.1H
SAProuter		SAProuter	4.0A (SAProuter 3.0)
ITS Wgate	ITS Agate	Wgate/Agate	4.5
ITS Agate	SAP application server	DIAG, RFC	4.5

Figure 2.24 illustrates encryption and the protection of data integrity during communications between SAP system components with SNC. Table 2.9 provides an overview of the communications paths secured with SNC.

Technical

SNC interface to security products (GSS API Version 2)

The interface that SNC uses for interaction with an external security product, the Generic Security Services API Version 2, was standardized by IETF with the participation of SAP developers. The actual standard maps the interface in various programming languages; C is used in SAP products.

To guarantee the interoperability of external security products with SAP system components and the programming interface GSS API Version 2, the SAP Complementary Software Partner (CSP) Program includes GSS API Version 2 (BC-SNC interface in SAP CSP Program [BC-SNC]). The CSP program certifies security products and subjects them to several tests. These checks and the granting of an SAP certificate are particularly important for SNC. Otherwise, it would be impossible to establish a communications link between the system components, and the SAP system could not function.

Numerous security products from various manufacturers have been certified for the BC-SNC interface. *See* [BC-SNC] for a current list.

SNC user settings

The dialog transaction for user maintenance (*Tools • Administration • User Maintenance* (su01)) also maintains the SNC entries for users. The settings are found on the SNC index card that is visible only on application servers that are running an active SNC. Figure 2.25 shows an example.

The SNC name is a description of the identity that an SAP user has in an external security environment. From the viewpoint of the SAP system, this external identity is mapped with an entry for each SAP user in user maintenance. This entry can also indicate if the user can still log on with a normal password. The effectiveness of this setting depends upon the SNC setting of the application server, stored in the profile file. You maintain the SNC settings for SAPlogon on the frontend computer while maintaining the characteristics of the SAPlogon entries. *See* Figure 2.26 for an example.

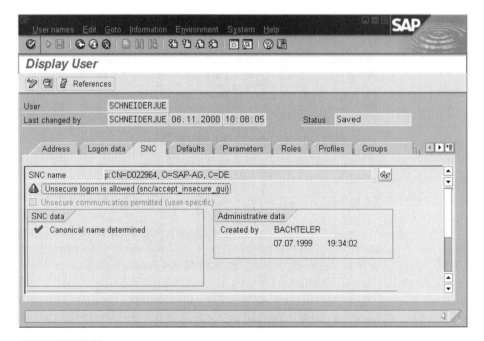

FIGURE 2.25   SNC settings in user maintenance (Copyright © SAP AG)

The SNC settings for the application server have several profile parameters. The profile parameters activate the SNC option and assign the external identity of the application server. You can also make settings that affect which security level should be used and accepted for the links with SNC and whether or not insecure links without SNC should still be permitted. Table 2.10 provides an overview of the SNC profile parameters for the application server.

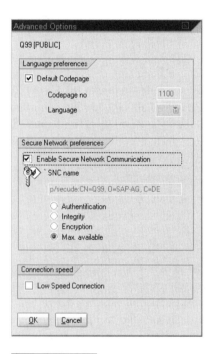

| FIGURE 2.26 | SNC settings for SAPlogon (Copyright © SAP AG) |

| TABLE 2.10 | SNC settings on the application server |

Profile paremeter	Meaning
Profile parameter	Meaning
Snc/enable	SNC active or inactive
Snc/gssapi_lib	File path to the program library of the security product
Snc/data_protection/min	Minimum data protection level (authentication, integrity, and confidentiality)
Snc/data_protection/max	Maximum data protection level (authentication, integrity, and confidentiality)
Snc/data_protection/use	Security level used for outbound connections
Snc/accept_insecure_gui	Allow or disallow insecure dialog connections
Snc/accept_insecure_rfc	Allow or disallow insecure RFC connections
Snc/identity/as	External identity of the application server

For more technical information, see the SNC user handbook, available to SAP customers and partners at [SAP-SNC].

2.8 DIGITAL SIGNATURES AND ENCRYPTION

Cryptographic solutions are important for more than network communications. Extra security is needed whenever sensitive data and documents are stored in an SAP or connected system. They are particularly crucial when such data leaves an SAP system for storage in another, insecure medium. Accordingly, SAP R/3 Release 4.0 (and higher) features an additional interface to external security products: secure store and forward (SSF).

We have already noted the security requirements for the SSF interface several times. Here, too, the task is to ensure that data remains unchanged (integrity), that the creator of the data can be identified uniquely (authenticity), and that the data cannot be viewed by unauthorized parties (confidentiality). To provide this protection at all times, that is, outside the context of an existing communications link as is the case with SNC, the SSF interface in an SAP system offers two basic mechanisms:

- digital signature
- digital envelope.

A digital signature protects the integrity and authenticity of a document. A cryptographic signing method is used to generate a digital signature, which represents a digital seal identifying both the document and the person (or system) who signed the document (*see* the technical portion of section 2.6). A change to a signed document invalidates the digital signature and can be seen readily. The signer can also be determined uniquely: only the signer's public key results in a positive evaluation of the validity of the digital signature (*see* the technical portion of this section).

Digital signatures offer no protection against unauthorized reading. To achieve that type of protection, the data must be packed into a digital envelope. Here, the data is encrypted. Much like a letter which requires an addressee, the encryption here is always aimed at one or more recipients. The encryption uses the public key of the recipient. Only the intended recipient of the document can then decrypt the document with the correct private key.

Digital signatures and digital envelopes are applied directly to the data and documents that require protection. The cryptographic keys used depend upon the signers and recipients involved and are not determined in advance. This approach demands use of an existing public key infrastructure (*see* the technical section). The infrastructure is set up independently of the SAP system and is made available to the SAP system over the SSF interface.

External security products for the SSF interface are also certified in the Complementary Software Partner (CSP) Program for use with SAP software (*see* [BC-SSF]).

This approach guarantees the interoperability of the partner product with the SAP Basis layer and SAP applications.

2.8.1 The SAP system with SSF

As of SAP R/3 Release 4.5, each SAP system possesses an asymmetrical pair of keys that can be used for a digital signature.

This mechanism was first used to control access to archive systems connected to R/3. The authorization process in the SAP system regulates which users are allowed access to which documents in the archive system, and how (create, display, change, or delete). After the authorization check in the SAP system, a digitally signed ticket is generated. The ticket is transferred as part of the URL referencing the document via a web browser which is then started on the user's frontend computer to access the document. The archive system receives the request for the document together with the signed ticket and uses the public key of the SAP system to determine if the SAP system has authorized access by verifying the digital signature of the ticket. If so, it then transmits the document to the user. *See* Figure 2.27 for an illustration of this process.

This archive scenario offers a model for the use of digital signatures to implement internal protective measures within a system. The digital signature generated by the SAP system can just as easily be used for processes that occur between the systems of different companies: business-to-business scenarios. For example, a business partner can process requests and orders automatically if the SAP system of the sender has given them a digital signature. The sender's digital signature provides a high degree of protection for the integrity and authenticity of the request. The recipient's system can also store it for auditing needs. The digital signature of the sending system represents the deal for the request,

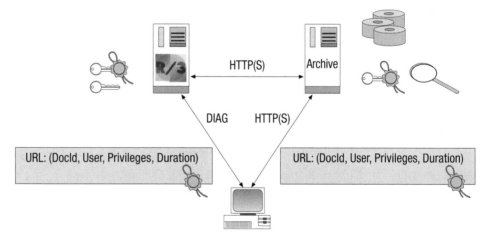

| FIGURE 2.27 | Use of a digital signature from an SAP system connected to an archive system (Copyright © SAP AG) |

ensuring that the receiving system cannot generate or forge it since the receiving system does not have the private key of the sending system.

To obtain the desired audit value, however, the digital signature must be generated within a very strict framework. Adherence to the framework ultimately decides the value of the digital signature in the event of dispute. How the private key of a given system is stored is one crucial factor. The system cannot let its private key be read or copied. The highest security therefore demands the use of additional hardware in the generating system. Here the private key is stored in a cryptographic plug-in card that also performs the cryptographic signing operations. The private key never leaves the hardware setup.

The standard SAP system generates an encrypted file to store the public and private keys. The file can also have password protection, but otherwise enjoys the features of the operating system to protect it from unauthorized access. The use of SAP-certified partner products also offers hardware solutions.

The use of a credible public key to authenticate a digital signature produced by an SAP system is yet another precondition for the security of the signature. If an attacker can produce a set of keys that give a system a false identity, and the receiving system trusts the identity, the entire process is compromised. The credibility of how public keys are assigned is a crucial part of the public key infrastructure. The infrastructure ensures that two partners can exchange the public key securely (for example on a diskette given by one person to another). But both parties must then store the key securely to protect against any possible exchange.

One general solution to the problem of the public key infrastructure is the creation of a third party trusted by all parties. The third party signs the public keys and thus guarantees their authenticity. A signed public key (with some additional information) is known as a digital certificate. The digital signature of a trust center ensures the validity of the certificate: it can even be transmitted across insecure communications channels. The technical section treats the functions of a trust center within the public key infrastructure in more detail.

Besides cryptographic characteristics, other contextual issues affect the security of a digital signature produced by an SAP system. None the less, this mechanism is much more secure than previous techniques that generated unsigned documents. It can also serve as the basis for trust between two business partners.

If system signatures are used as described in this section, you must also trust a system as a representative of a company. Many countries do not yet have a legal basis for such recognition, and only natural persons can execute legally binding transactions. Bilateral contracts between business partners on questions of validity and liability can create clarity in this area. Other countries already have laws on the use of digital signatures (*see* section 2.8.4 on SSF and signature laws). The use of digital signatures under generally legally binding conditions increasingly makes bilateral contracts unnecessary in these countries.

The standard SAP system features a program library in Basis that provides functions for digital signatures; it has formed part of the system since R/3 Release 4.5. The functions of the library are limited to the creation and verification of digital signatures; it does not contain encryption functions for digital envelopes. Since the functions are called in the SAP system over the SSF interface, you can easily replace this program library with a partner product certified for the SSF interface. Doing so would enable you to use the SSF functions for encryption as well.

2.8.2   SAP users and SSF

The signature of the SAP system is insufficient for many applications to sign and encrypt documents. To ensure that certain persons participate in business transactions, the SAP system can require a digital signature from these users and store it along with the business transaction. This feature is important for the release of work processes or payments. To ensure that only the intended recipient can read a confidential document or message, digital envelopes offer an effective approach. A typical example here to protect e-mail would include digital signatures and digital envelopes.

Users of Release 4.0 (and higher) of the SAP R/3 System can use the SSF interface to generate and check digital signatures. The same features enable the encryption and decryption of documents at the level of users and user groups. A security product offered by an SAP partner and certified for SSF enables the use of these features. The standards and technologies used in a public key infrastructure also permit communications between SAP users and persons who do not use SAP software.

Within the public key infrastructure, users need an individual set of keys that is generated and managed outside of the SAP system. The user-specific private key must be protected, usually on a smart card that belongs to the user. The smart-card technology ensures that a user's private key does not leave the card. The cryptographic processor on a smart card processes cryptographic operations directly on the card. In addition to smart cards, other software solutions can store private keys. For example, they can be stored in an encrypted file. In such cases, access to a user's private key enjoys password protection with a password known only to the user.

The use of user-specific digital signatures and envelopes in an SAP system requires a solution to the following technical problem. The applications (such as a workflow application) run on an application server while the user's private key – needed to decrypt a confidential document – is available only locally, in a local file on the user's PC or in a smart card reader. That means that the document to be signed or decrypted must be transmitted to the user's PC. The SAP system uses remote function call (RFC) for this purpose. SAP delivers the appropriate RFC server program for the SSF interface with every frontend installation for R/3 Release 4.0 and higher.

Figure 2.28 illustrates the flow of user-specific SSF functions in the SAP system. To generate a digital signature, an application in Basis calls the signing function. Then an RFC call to the frontend occurs, the SSF server program is started on the frontend computer, and the data to be signed are transmitted (1). To generate the signature, the SSF server program loads the program library of the security product over the SSF interface (2). The result, the digital signature of the data, is transmitted to the application as the

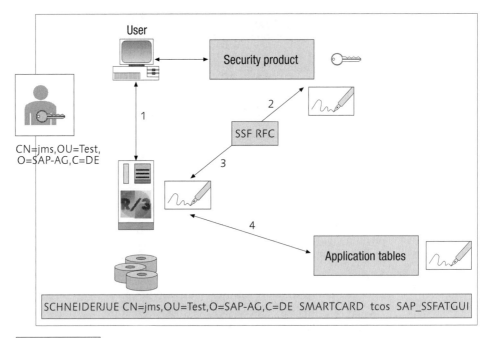

FIGURE 2.28 Using SSF on an SAP frontend (Copyright © SAP AG)

result of the RFC call (3) and then checked and stored by the application (4). The flow for decryption is similar, since it also requires the user's private key. Checking a signed file or decrypting documents can occur on either the application server or the frontend computer, since this task requires only the public key.

Either the SAP system or the security product can display data during these procedures with SSF. With a digital signature, for example, it is particularly important that the user can see a display of the document being signed, and that the user is informed of the signing process. Once the data is displayed, the system must ensure that only this document, and no other, is being signed. For the highest security requirements, a security product can use both the display functions of SSF and additional hardware, such as smart card readers with a display and a keypad for entering passwords. The same requirements can apply to decrypted data that should be visible only with the display function of the security product.

2.8.3 Applications of the digital signature

The SAP components for Production Control and Product Management were the first applications to integrate the use of digital signatures.

The US Food and Drug Administration, for example, has strict guidelines on the production of pharmaceuticals. A responsible person must release recipes for drugs and the subsequent production process; the release must uniquely authenticate that

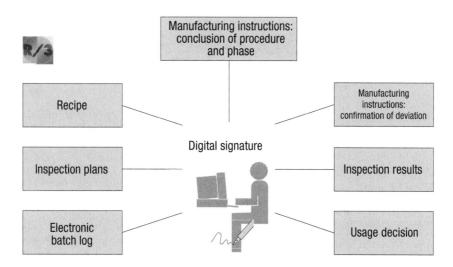

FIGURE 2.29 | Using a digital signature in SAP PP, PDM, and QM (Copyright © SAP AG)

person. This authentication requires means that enable identification by at least two components: possession of a smart card and knowledge of a PIN or password to access the information on the card, for example. Such a solution has been realized via the SSF interface for SAP Production Planning in Process Industries.

In this example, the digital signature serves to release a work process. To prove that the correctly authorized person has performed the release, the database stores the digital signature for the step in the work process. The same approach is possible for production data. The digital signature of an authorized person can also be used to ensure that the data has not changed. Figure 2.29 illustrates the work-steps secured with digital signatures in SAP PP, PDM, and QM.

2.8.4 SSF and signature laws

The SSF interface in the SAP system offers strong encryption and digital signatures to protect business transactions and documents. The digital signature uses a private key that can be uniquely assigned to one person (or one system). The digital seal calculated for a digital signature provides legally binding proof of a business transaction should it be contested, as long as misuse of the private key can be excluded.

Several countries have enacted laws to regulate digital signatures. Germany, for example, prepared and implemented such a law early on. The law requires a cryptographic method and lists comprehensive conditions for a trust center to operate in conformity with the law. In addition, the hardware and software involved in the signing procedure must pass a security certification conducted by a nationally or internationally recognized, official inspection agency. Laws were also passed on the European level [EU-DigSig] and in the U.S. to regulate the use of digital signatures.

To have standing as evidence in court, a digital signature must be generated under conditions that exclude the possibility of misusing the private key. Storage of a private key on a smart card almost completely excludes the possibility of misuse, at least without the cooperation of the owner. Modern smart cards have a locking mechanism that becomes operative if the PIN is repeatedly entered incorrectly or if someone physically tries to read the key information without having entered the correct PIN.

Security certification of signature components confirms that the signing process cannot be compromised. The data to be signed is displayed completely and accurately, and then the appropriate private key signs this data, and this data alone. The result, the digital signature, is counterfeit-proof as along as the basic mathematical preconditions continue to exist.

If a credible certification authority or trust center assigns the keys, it is certain that center has given a key-pair to the correct person, and that it has properly checked the person's identity. In this process, the trust center does not know the makeup of the private key.

Does adherence to these conditions suffice for the use of digital signatures in the context of a court case?

No precedents exist yet. Even the German signature law, one of the earliest, does not equate digital and manual signatures. In the event of a contest, the digital signature is subject to the free evidentiary decision of the court. Accordingly, the use of digital signatures will give e-commerce the experience it can gain only through practice. Still, the mechanism has the potential of making e-business worthy of trust for the business partners involved. In many instances today, a digital signature already increases the security of processes in the SAP system.

A great deal of literature on the topic of digital signatures exists: *see* Bizer (1999), for example.

Technical

Digital signature

A digital signature is calculated with a cryptographic method and gives data a digital seal. The calculation of the value of the signature requires the data and a cryptographic key (*see* the technical portion of section 2.6 on external security products). The digital signature thus guarantees the integrity and authenticity of the signed data. To identify the signer uniquely and as uncontestable evidence, an asymmetrical method is preferred, since this approach can ensure that the private key used to generate the signature is in the exclusive possession of the signer. The corresponding public key can be used to inspect the authenticity of the digital signature.

Figure 2.30 illustrates the technical flow of a digital signature. First, a hash value is calculated for the data to be signed. A cryptographic hash method is used here. The hash value represents a unique cryptographic fingerprint for the data to be signed. The hash value usually has a fixed length (128–160 bits are most common) that is significantly

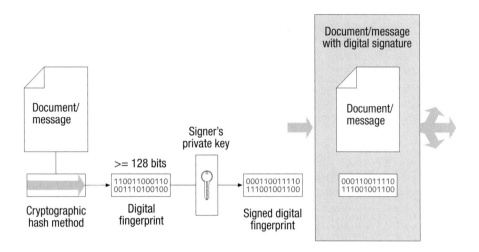

Document/message with digital signature

Document/message

Signer's private key

>= 128 bits

Document/message

Cryptographic hash method

Digital fingerprint

Signed digital fingerprint

| FIGURE 2.30 | Digital signature (Copyright © SAP AG)

shorter than the data being signed. A second step uses the private key to transform the hash value into the actual signature value. The digital signature can be stored or transmitted along with or apart from the data. The relationship between them, however, must always remain clear. The data remains readable before and after. To inspect a digital signature, the hash value is recalculated for the data with the same method. The public key of the signer is applied to the signature value, and the result is then compared with the recalculated hash value.

Digital envelope

Encryption is used to generate a digital envelope (*see* the technical portion of section 2.6 on external security products). A hybrid method is normally used here. Each document or message to be secured is encrypted with a new, randomly generated, and symmetrical key. The public key of the recipient then encrypts the randomly generated, symmetrical message key. Only the recipient has the private key needed to determine the message key and thus arrive at the actual message. Figure 2.31 illustrates this procedure.

Public key infrastructure and trust centers

If systems or persons are assigned asymmetrical pairs of keys that they use during a specific period for digital signatures and digital envelopes, the entire lifecycle of the keys requires proper support. Users themselves should have very little to do with the keys, which should feature intuitive use.

Generating an asymmetrical pair of keys is quite easy – the tools to do so have been

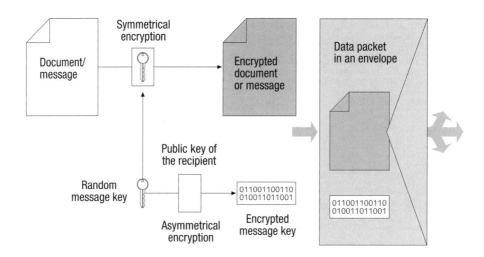

FIGURE 2.31   Digital envelope (Copyright © SAP AG)

available for quite some time. If a public key is required to check a digital signature or to encrypt a message, the person generating the data or performing the check must be sure that the public key actually belongs to the person who signed the message or generated the data. This requirement does not trigger a need to distribute public keys over secure channels. If a trustworthy third party confirms the assignment of a public key to a system or person, the key itself can be given along with the confirmation.

A trust center performs this function. A trust center operates a certification authority (CA) that confirms the assignment of a public key to its owner with a digital signature. The CA uses its own private key for the signature. The public key of the CA is sufficient to check the authenticity of other public keys that the CA has signed. In this approach, only the public key of the CA must be exchanged over a secure channel. For example, the exchange can occur if the public key of a CA is compiled in and delivered with the software. This is most often the case for some well-known trust centers included in web browsers and servers. Otherwise, the public key of a CA can be made accessible to the software via another secure channel.

A public key signed by a CA, along with information on the owner, the issuer, the method used, and the validity of the public key is known as a digital certificate. A digital certificate represents a digital ID for a system or person. For some years, X.509 has served as the worldwide standard for the creation of digital certificates [ITU]. Figure 2.32 displays the contents of a digital certificate according to the X.509 standard.

Digital certificates are usually valid for one to two years. After that, security reasons require renewal of the pair of keys or the generation of a new certificate. Certificates can also become invalid during the normal validity period, if, for example, the private key is compromised or an employee leaves the company. Accordingly, a CA can also revoke

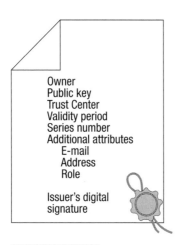

Owner
Public key
Trust Center
Validity period
Series number
Additional attributes
    E-mail
    Address
    Role

Issuer's digital
signature

FIGURE 2.32   Digital certificate according to X.509 (Copyright © SAP AG)

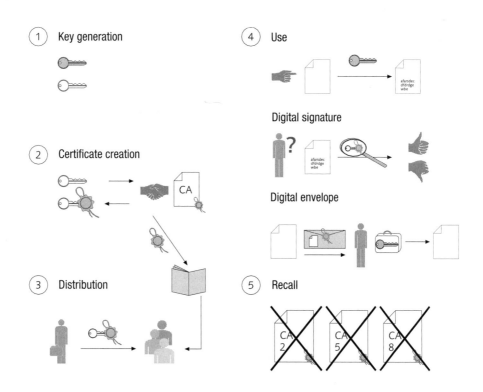

① Key generation

② Certificate creation

③ Distribution

④ Use

Digital signature

Digital envelope

⑤ Recall

FIGURE 2.33   Public key infrastructure (Copyright © SAP AG)

a certificate before its validity period runs outs. The CA periodically publishes certificate revocation lists (CRLs) that must be considered when using a public key. Once the validity period runs out, the pair of keys must be renewed and the user then receives a new certificate.

The public key infrastructure handles the creation, management, availability, revocation, and renewal of asymmetrical key pairs (*see* Figure 2.33). After generation of a key pair (1), a trust center certifies the public key (2). The owner stores the private key securely, but the public key can be distributed freely (3). The private key is used to generate digital signatures, and the public key is used to check digital signatures. The public key of the recipient is used for encryption of a digital envelope, and the private key of the recipient is used to decrypt a digital envelope (4). A digital certificate expires at the end of its validity period or as soon as the issuer revokes it (5).

SSF settings in user management

The SAP system features a dialog transaction to maintain the user information needed by SSF. Follow the menu path: *System • User profile • Own data • Other communication • SSF* (su3, *see* Figure 2.34). As soon as an SSF call occurs, this information informs the SAP system of the identity of a user as represented by a digital certificate and how the private key is accessed. The user must enter a PIN to give access to the private key, since the system does not store that information.

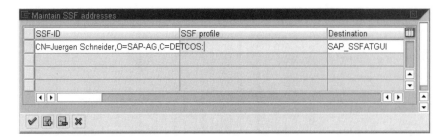

FIGURE 2.34   SSF user settings (Copyright © SAP AG)

SSF settings on the SAP application server

As noted in this chapter, every SAP system since Release 4.5 features a pair of asymmetrical keys and a program library for digital signatures in Basis. You can also use the SSF interface to connect an external security product to the application server. Profile parameters exist for the settings on the application server, as summarized in Table 2.11. For further information, see the documentation on SSF [SAP-LIB].

TABLE 2.11 SSF settings on the application server

Profile parameter	Meaning
ssf/name	Name of the SSF security product
ssf/ssf_md_alg	Hash algorithm of the SAP system for digital signatures
ssf/ssf_symencr_alg	Symmetrical encryption algorithm of the SAP system
ssf/ssfapi_lib	Path to the library for the digital signature and encryption

## CHAPTER 3

Security in the SAP system landscape

Secure operation of SAP systems requires more than the security functions presented in Chapter 2. The application software runs in a system environment that must be run and managed just as securely. The system environment includes the operating systems and supplemental programs on each computer as well as the database and the network that links the distributed components of an SAP system with each other. Accordingly, this chapter examines the system environment, the essential communications interfaces in an SAP system for importing and exporting data, and data traffic inside and outside the SAP systems.

Comprehensive treatment of the SAP system environment easily overwhelms the scope of this book. Nonetheless, we must treat it here: security gaps in the system environment can enable an attacker to degrade or circumvent SAP security functions. Those responsible for system security must always remember that a gap in one location can affect the security of the entire system.

Accordingly, this chapter examines only the essential aspects of security in the system environment. This approach benefits from the reality that the secure administration of operating systems or databases is not a special, SAP-oriented topic, but a basic precondition for the security of the entire IT infrastructure of a company. Likewise, the company network does not serve SAP systems alone, but supports communications throughout the enterprise and therefore requires appropriate protection.

We treat individual parts of the system environment in general, and mention specific operating systems or database products only as examples. The SAP security guidelines [SAP SG] contain extensive information on security for the operating systems and databases supported by SAP products. This book makes no claim to replace the SAP guidelines or the manuals and guidelines of individual manufacturers. We treat communications only in regard to the standard SAP interfaces.

Chapter 4 treats the security aspects involved in the use of internet technology with mySAP.com.

3.1   NETWORKS

Secure administration of the computers and applications at a company is no easy task. Limiting physical access to the systems offers one of the best methods of protecting the data stored by the systems. The days are long past when a mainframe computer remained isolated in an access-restricted computer center and had external links only via terminals. Today, company networks pose the greatest challenge to security personnel; networks demand very careful planning.

3.1.1 Setting up secure networks for a standard SAP installation

Planning and structuring the network setup contributes significantly to minimizing security risks. The employee responsible for the network must have an overview of the electronic communications channels in the company at all times. Accordingly, the network must be divided into different security zones, and only authorized persons may cross between the zones. The number of zones should not be too low: a distinction between internal and external zones is insufficient. A large company might well have over 100 different systems and thousands of users in its internal network. The security requirements of the systems and their users differ greatly between the computer center, user departments, management, conference rooms, and training rooms. Setup and expansion of the network must consider these differences.

The number of crossover points between network security zones should be as low as possible. Firewall systems usually protect the company network from external access (*see* the technical portion of this section), but they should also protect crossover points within the network. Various types of firewall systems keep the number of crossover points between network security zones low, so that the types of communications permitted over the points remain limited.

The typical network setup for a standard SAP installation uses a three-tier architecture, as illustrated in Figure 3.1. The application server and the database server operate within a distinct server LAN (local area network). Server LANs ideally exist for every SAP system, but should at least exist for each SAP system at the same security level (Figure 3.1 illustrates only one server LAN as an example). Within the server LAN, the database server allows remote access only from the application servers in the server LAN. The

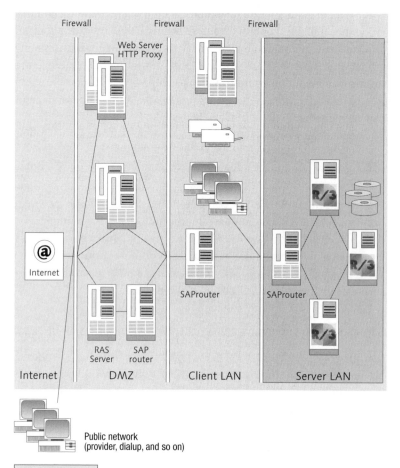

FIGURE 3.1 Network security zones in a standard SAP installation (Copyright © SAP AG)

application servers can invoke function calls between themselves and also use common services and directories as defined. Special workplaces for administration exist with the server LAN.

The expanded company network (client LAN) contains workstations for users. A firewall system protects access from the client LAN to the server LAN. The firewall system allows access to the application server only over SAP communications protocols (DIAG and RFC).

You can also use the SAProuter software as an option for improved protection. When using SAProuter, only a communications port to the SAProuter is opened at the internal firewall system in front of the server LAN. The SAProuter then creates all connections to the application server and functions as a bridge between the frontend stations in the client LAN and the application server (*see* section 3.1.2).

If SAP protocols are used to access an SAP system over a public network or the internet, access occurs over an additional, external firewall system. In this system, the first firewall monitors external accesses. This firewall, for example, can filter specific sender addresses and protocols. You can set the filters to permit access only by partner companies or from public, dial-in connections (*see* Chapter 4). However, bear in mind that counterfeiting computer addresses and names at the network level is not particularly difficult (IP spoofing and DNS spoofing). We recommend that you take additional protective measures, which we treat below.

A remote access server (RAS) is set up behind the first firewall. Here you can require authentication of users who dial in from outside the company network. A connection to the SAProuter is established after successful authentication. The SAProuter then creates the bridge to the internal network over a second firewall.

3.1.2 SAProuter

SAProuter software is available free of charge to SAP customers and represents an application proxy that determines connections between SAP system components. Figure 3.2

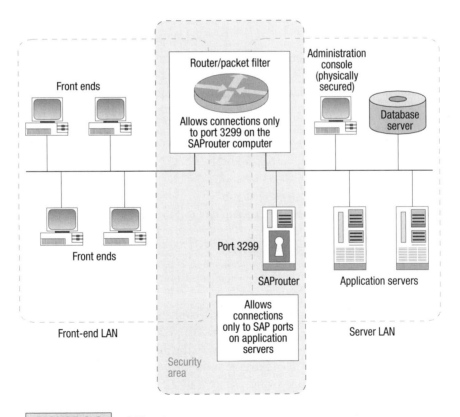

FIGURE 3.2 SAProuter (Copyright © SAP AG)

illustrates how an internal network area can be protected with a packet/port filter combined with a SAProuter. The packet/port filter permits requests for connections into secured network areas from selected network areas, but sends the requests only to the SAProuter behind those areas.

The configuration data of the SAProuter can determine the addresses that can access specific backend systems in the server LAN. The incoming request for a connection first ends at the SAProuter. The SAProuter creates a connection to an application server of the backend system and associates the connections with each other. During the following communications phase, the SAProuter transports the individual data-packets of the associated connections over the bridge it has created.

The following illustrates a sample configuration table for the SAProuter. It permits connections from a specific sub-network; the connections lead to application servers via the SAP dialog protocol.

In addition, connections to the message server are allowed for SAP logon groups to distribute and balance the load. Administrative access is limited to one specific workstation. You can assign passwords for establishing connections and enter them in the configuration file. *See* the corresponding SAP documentation [SAP Router] for more information on the SAProuter.

Sample:

```
# sample saprouttab
# permit connections from 155.152.22 subnet
# to the application servers (appsrv2...appsrv4)
# allow only dispatcher connections
P 155.152.22.* appsrv2 sapdp21
P 155.152.22.* appsrv3 sapdp21
P 155.152.22.* appsrv4 sapdp21
# only admin PC (IP address 155.152.23.3) can access appsrv1
P 155.152.23.3 appsrv1 sapdp21
# allow all access to message server (on appsrv1) for load-balancing
for appsrv1
P 155.152.*.* appsrv1 sapmsTST
```

3.1.3 Using SNC

Protective network zones, firewalls, and the SAProuter block undesirable access but permit desirable access: without the distinction, the SAP system would be unusable. But the SNC option (*see* section 2.7) offers the highest level of network security. SNC covers authentication from end to end: from the transmitting process to the receiving process. The communicant's system sets up only a communications link that both application processes can then use to exchange data. Each system encrypts the data itself. The approach destroys the effectiveness of attacks using IP spoofing and DNS spoofing.

SAProuter software also supports SNC. For example, to enable secure connections between SAP components at two company locations with little effort, you can create a tunnel protected by SNC between two SAProuters (*see* Figure 3.3). This type of configuration can also be used between companies. It is used for remote maintenance and in remote support by SAP.

Technical

Firewall systems

A firewall system monitors potential accesses in the network area that it protects. To accomplish this task, it uses a variety of mechanisms at different levels of the communications system (*see* Figure 3.4).

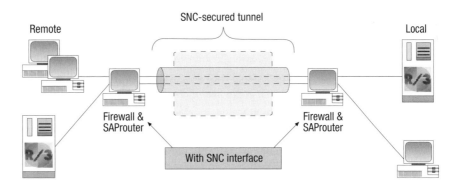

FIGURE 3.3   SAProuter–SAProuter communications with SNC (Copyright © SAP AG)

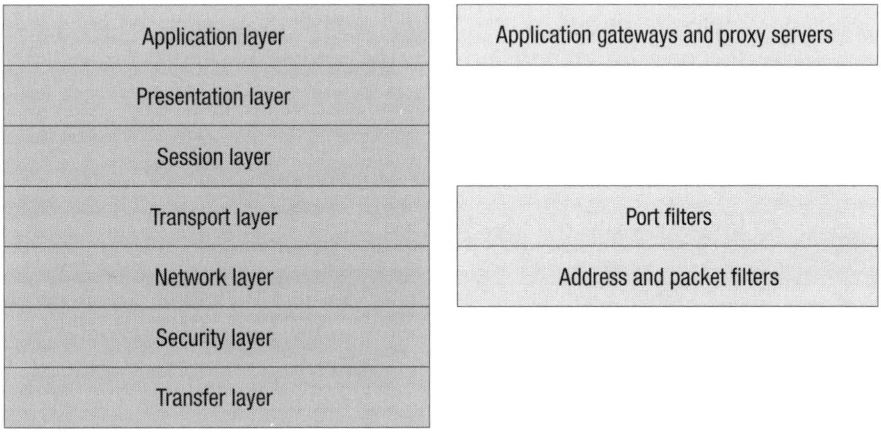

Application layer	Application gateways and proxy servers
Presentation layer	
Session layer	
Transport layer	Port filters
Network layer	Address and packet filters
Security layer	
Transfer layer	

FIGURE 3.4   Mechanisms of firewall systems (Copyright © SAP AG)

Packets and port filters are used at the network and transport levels. At these levels, firewalls monitor the network addresses of senders and reject undesirable packets. In addition, accesses are permitted only for communications services that implement specific protocols. As a result, you can accept specific services (such as SAP accesses, SMTP mail, FTP file transfer, or web accesses over HTTP), and block others (such as remote terminals with telnet, rlogin, or common data directories via NFS (network file system)).

An attacker would thus have access only to specific services. You can protect these services with additional application gateways that can offer additional controls, such as user authentication. The application gateways establish communications only with specific computers in the protected area.

You can create a firewall system in various ways. The simplest firewall consists only of an address filter or an additional application gateway on the same computer. To separate a protected network area from an unprotected one, a computer can have two network cards, each with its own address: a bastion host.

External firewall systems are usually larger installations that involve a first and second firewall (*see* Figure 3.1) and a series of interposed application gateways (screened sub-net). The area between the first and second firewalls is known as the demilitarized zone (DMZ), a no-man's-land between the internal and external network areas. Each network area has its own network address: at this level, each area knows nothing of the others. External accesses first go to a computer in the DMZ. Only after an inspection are they sent into the internal network. In the same way, all internal requests for communications links first go to the DMZ, and are then sent from there to the outside over a proxy server.

Why are firewall systems necessary at all?

The primary benefits of firewall systems arise because of weaknesses in operating systems and applications. If all operating systems and applications were free of security gaps, if they offered the requisite mechanisms for authentication and authorization of users, and if they were administered without errors, firewalls would be unnecessary. However, as noted, counterfeiting addresses at the network level is rather easy. But the protection offered by firewalls is deceptive: there are always open addresses and services that open doors in the firewall. The services and applications that are visited through these doors must have their own security functions and rely first and foremost upon their own security.

3.2 OPERATING SYSTEM

SAP system architecture normally distinguishes three levels for the distribution of system components: the presentation level, the application level, and the database level. The use of SAP internet connections involves additional, logical levels (*see* Chapter 4). Every level uses SAP software that can run on a variety of operating system platforms. This section treats the most important security requirements at the level of the operating system.

3.2.1 Security of the SAP workstations

SAP users normally work at a PC workstation; they use the SAP graphical user interface (SAPgui) or a commercial web browser (with mySAP.com: *see* Chapter 4) as an interface to the SAP system. Special SAP products, such as the SAP Business Information Warehouse, use a specific interface based upon Microsoft operating systems.

3.2.1.1 SAPgui

The SAPgui software establishes a dialog connection to application servers so that the user can work with SAP applications interactively. The GUI transmits user and application data, and displays the data graphically for the user. In the course of a normal dialog session, the data is neither processed nor stored locally. Only screens are transmitted. No data remains on the PC after the session has ended.

Potential damage to the information from the SAP system can develop from manipulation of the SAPgui program files. You must therefore ensure that all downloads of the SAPgui originate from a trustworthy location on the company network, a location supplied with files from the original SAP installation CD. Neither unauthorized persons nor applications may change the SAPgui program files. This requirement presupposes strict administration of PCs.

You must be cautious when using SAP shortcut technology with the SAPgui. SAP shortcuts simplify starting the SAPgui for a specific SAP system and open the desired SAP transaction directly. Every SAP user can set up this very practical function for day-to-day tasks. The SAPgui features a setup menu with a function for creating an SAP shortcut on the user's desktop. The shortcut offers the option of storing the SAP logon information, including the user's password. But users should go this route only when physical access to the PC is sufficiently secure.

3.2.1.2 Upload, download, and Office integration

In addition to dialog communications, the SAP system also offers users an upload function to transfer data to the SAP system. Users can also download data from the SAP system to hard disks in a user's PC or to a network drive. Section 3.4 also treats the upload and download functions. These functions are also used with Office integration to load data from SAP systems into Office applications, such as Microsoft Word, Excel, or PowerPoint, and process it there.

Once company data has been stored on a user's PC, the SAP system can no longer protect it. The security of the data depends upon the security mechanisms of the PC operating system. You must set up file access rights so that other users cannot access the data or have only limited access to it.

3.2.1.3 PC workstation

These comments clarify the importance of the physical security of a user's PC workstation. The requirements here include protecting the SAPgui software, logon information, and files that might contain data from the SAP system.

When using an SAP system, typical security recommendations apply to a PC workstation:

- boot protection based upon a password or the hardware itself
- forced network logon
- protection of shared directories
- screen protection switched on
- installation and regular upgrades of virus-protection software
- no installation of private or unknown software
- clearly regulated PC administration; only known users permitted to work on a PC.

We have particular concerns about the use of a PC workstation by several users. This situation often involves an SAP system used in a hospital or a warehouse. We must emphasize that the SAP products and the operating systems they support are not geared (today) for this type of shared use: see our comments in Chapter 9 on the role of the administrator. This restriction also applies to simultaneous logon of several users under Windows NT. Although users have often requested this function, the SAP software that runs on the PC operating system cannot guarantee the security of an SAP session, the logon information, or files stored on a PC shared by several users. The PC is a personal tool. This reality is evident in the design of a PC, and it results in the lack of any protective mechanisms at the level of the PC operating system. Effective separation of user data between individuals at the application level is therefore hardly possible.

Microsoft Windows Terminal Servers [MS-WTS] and the appropriate client software on a PC workstation offer an interesting and surer alternative for the shared use of a PC by several users. The terminal-server computer runs a separate session for each logged-on user and offers a simple connect/disconnect feature that does not require termination of the entire session.

3.2.2 Security of the SAP application servers

Given the characteristics of the operating system, SAP application servers must enjoy secure administration. Administration must pay particular attention to the existence and rights of operating system users, network services, and the file system. The short list of areas that require protection treated here clearly indicates that administration of the operating system demands special knowledge. That knowledge does not necessarily equate to the skills offered by an SAP system administrator. We therefore recommend a division of roles as treated below.

3.2.2.1 Operating system user

At the level of the operating system, SAP system processes run under an operating system user (<sid>adm for UNIX and SAPService<sid> for Windows NT, for example). Many operating systems also use another user for administration (<sid>adm for Windows NT, for example). Many analyst reports criticize this feature as a disadvantage because it means that protective mechanisms cannot be used at the level of different users. As we noted in section 2.3 on the authorization concept, we do not regard the protective mechanisms of the operating system as appropriate for mapping business processes – and they were not designed for this purpose. Access control for SAP users occurs in the SAP system with the support of the authorization concept. The authorization concept and the use of logical operating system commands can control access to the operating system (*see* the technical section).

Actually, it's an advantage that no operating system user must exist on the server for all SAP users. This approach makes user administration at the operating system level rather easy. To operate or administer the SAP system, there is one user at the operating system level. The administrator of the SAP system does not need to function as the server administrator at the operating system level. In fact, a division of labor is preferred here between the SAP system administrator and the server administrator. For example, the SAP system administrator on a UNIX system does not need to have the rights of a root user or to know that user's password. Similarly, the server administrator does not need access to the SAP system as an SAP user.

Nonetheless, the system resources available to the SAP system (file system, access right, main memory, and so on) are determined by the server administrator. The two administrators must therefore remain in contact. Even when server administrators have no direct access to SAP data, they can still access data that affects the security of the SAP system (such as profile parameters in SAP profile files). The comments made in Chapter 9 on the administrator's powerful position also apply to the server administrator.

If the application server is also the database server, there is also an operating system user for the database. Other than these two or three users, no other users should exist at the operating system level.

3.2.2.2 Network services

To protect the SAP application server, we recommend the network setup discussed in section 3.1 and a protected server LAN. The network services on the server are particularly worthy of protection because an attacker could use them to gain access to SAP system information.

Only limited use of the network file system is recommended within the server LAN to avoid unauthorized access to the server's file system. The network information service (NIS) can actually represent a security risk for operating system users and their passwords unless a shadow password file is used. You should also avoid creating trust relationships when using BSD UNIX services for remote terminals (rlogin and remsh/rsh) between servers with entries in the .rhosts or hosts.equiv files.

All these services identify computers only by their IP addresses, which other computers can counterfeit (IP spoofing). Most servers do not need other services such as file transfer (FTP) or sendmail (SMTP) at all; you can simply deactivate them. Other options that use the SAP remote function calls are available for operation of the SAP landscape – particularly Correction and Transport System and application link enabling (ALE).

When using Windows NT, the creation of separate NT domains for the client and server LANs offers additional security. But this approach can also limit the use of network services such as file servers or print servers. If the security functions available to Windows NT are used as a security product for SAP secure network communications (SNC, *see* section 2.7), you must also set up a trust relationship between the server domains and the client domains. The new SAP installation routines make security settings on the server (such as those for directory access) during installation, so that no separate NT domains are required. SAP development has therefore withdrawn its previous recommendation on the separation of NT domains.

3.2.2.3 File system

The directory structure at the operating system level clearly documents the files created and used by the SAP system. The SAP security guidelines (*see* SAP SG) list the recommended settings for access rights granted to operating system users. The rights were granted during installation.

Technical

Logical operating system commands

To determine what commands are available at the operating system level in the SAP system and how to call them in the various operating systems, you define logical operating system commands. Use the menu path *Tools • CCMS • Configuration • External Commands* to arrive at a dialog transaction (sm69, *see* Figure 3.5). You can use the transaction to create, display, change, delete, and copy external commands. Some characters within the defined commands for each operating system are forbidden. This feature helps prevent misuse by concatenating commands, for example.

The maintenance and execution of external commands is protected by the SAP authorization concept (authorization objects S_RZL_ADM and S_LOG_COM).

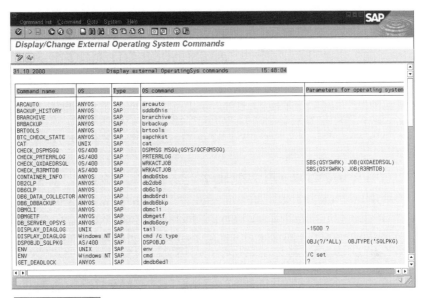

FIGURE 3.5   Definition of logical operating system commands (Copyright © SAP AG)

3.3 DATABASE

A database on a central database server stores the data and programs of an SAP system that require protection. SAP customers can choose a database from among the products of various manufacturers. The system uses a relational database that manages data in tables. Depending on the release level and the additional components in use, newer SAP systems use some 10,000 to 15,000 tables.

3.3.1 Database access and database user

The network structure recommended in section 3.1 (*see* Figure 3.1) is particularly important for the protection of the database. The database server runs in a protected server LAN. Access to the database can occur only from application servers in the server LAN. Depending upon the database product, you can also set network addresses on the database server for the database clients with access authorization, the SAP application servers in this case, and thus prohibit access by other computers. However, unless you use additional authentication mechanisms, other computers can obtain access by using false network addresses (IP spoofing). The comments made in section 3.2 also apply to the administration of the database server at the operating system level.

From the viewpoint of the database, the SAP system runs under a database user (SAPR3) with complete access to all SAP tables. Whenever a connection is established from the application server to the database, the system authenticates the database user. The standard version of all database products includes a simple password mechanism for this purpose. It is crucially important to change the standard password of database user SAPR3 (*see* the technical portion of this section).

To access the database with non-SAP applications, you should definitely use a different database user. Comprehensive authorization checks are performed on the application server for SAP applications, checks that might not exist in other applications. If the other applications need direct access from the client LAN to the database server, you must partially override the network separation in effect. In addition, when non-SAP applications change data in the database, a significant threat to the consistency of the database exists.

3.3.2 Database authorizations

Database user SAPR3 does not possess complete administrative rights for the database. Depending upon the database product in use, the rights are distributed to additional database users. The authorization concept in the SAP system (*see* section 2.3 on the authorization concept) regulates access for the SAP users.

Some have criticized SAP because the authorization concept does not use the mechanisms offered by each database for access control at the table and field level. But the use of the access control functions offered by a database become valid options only when the business processes can map the functions, not just for data access at the table and field level. In a process-oriented view, access authorization does not depend only upon the semantics of a table field, but upon the context of the transaction.

For example, the system can display a summary or average value to a user without letting the user know the individual values it read from the database. A user might easily access a table from within a specific transaction, without, however, having general access authorization. A highly integrated system such as SAP R/3 involves several cross-relationships between applications. For example, posting a material in Warehouse Management increases the sales stock, even though the warehouse manager neither possesses nor requires access rights to the database tables in Sales and Distribution.

The SAP system checks such scenarios on the application server before access to the database occurs. A general check at the database level is too short and does not supply the required flexibility. In practice, that approach would prove too much for the database and hinder operations. A two-level concept with individual authorization checks in the application and at each access to the database would create an unreasonable amount of maintenance.

3.3.3 Database administration

We recommend a further division of roles for database administration. The database administrator need not be the same person as the SAP system administrator. The various database products on the market all require special knowledge. Most databases support creation of various roles to administrative tasks. For example, an operator might be allowed to start and stop the database, and to manage operating tools, without being allowed to view the contents of the database. Another important part of data security is a concept for storing and archiving data. Standard SAP products offer useful tools here: *see* [SAP-DBA] for additional information.

No company can do without a database administrator with comprehensive rights who can set up database users and their rights. The database administrator has a very powerful position that we treat further in Chapter 9. Only a few, very trustworthy employees in a company may perform these tasks.

In this context, SAP customers often express a desire to use encryption to protect the contents of the database. Developers at SAP are watching and checking the technology that is already available, but so far no solution has appeared that truly increases security and does not lower performance of the SAP system to unacceptable levels.

Technical

Changing the database password and the Oracle OPS$ mechanism

Because the default password for database user SAPR3 is commonly known, you should change it when installing a productive SAP system. The SAP security guidelines [SAP SG] describe how to change the password for the various database products supported by SAP.

The standard SAP system includes tools to change the password for an Oracle database: chdbpass or sapdba. If you use Oracle, the OPS$ mechanism is set up when you change the password. This mechanism authenticates the database user via the operating system user under whom the database client application runs. The database no longer requests a password, but simply takes over the identity of the operating system user.

The Oracle OPS$ mechanism offers an advantage because you don't need a password any longer and no password must be transmitted. But caution is also required. The Oracle parameter REMOTE_OS_AUTHENT = TRUE is set because a connection to the database must be possible from the SAP application servers. Since authentication of the operating system user occurs on the client computer, attackers can enter the operating system user <sid>adm and then log on to the database as this user. A correct network setup (*see* section 3.1 on the network) offers the remedy here: the client LAN cannot address the Oracle services. You can also use the protocol.ora file to limit the network addresses that are allowed to establish a connection to the database.

The operating system user <sid>adm is assigned to the operating system group oper for database administration. The command *connect / as SYSOPER* from SAP tools gives the requestor only limited database administration rights, but no read or write rights for SAP tables.

| 3.4 | **UPLOAD/DOWNLOAD** |

The upload/download interface is frequently overlooked, but it allows almost every user to export data from or import data into the SAP system. The user interface includes a generic function for downloading lists or reports. Many applications also offer their own download functions.

In the event of a download, users themselves are responsible for the confidentiality of data. Users must secure the data stored on their own computers (*see* section 2.7 on secure transmission of data with SNC). In most cases, SAP users find this a useful and desirable function for integration of Office products, for example. Users can download only the data for which they possess read-authorization. If the system forbids a download, a user can still share the data with a screen capture.

Both the use of SAP downloads and dealing with the files it produces are a large part of the security policies and guidelines on security for PC workstations at many companies. To protect against accidental errors, options are available to protect the upload/download functions with authorization objects (*see* the technical portion of this section).

Another important aspect of using upload/download is the potential spread of viruses. An upload might introduce virus-infected files into an SAP System (such as macro-viruses in Word or Excel files). Infected files are as unwelcome there as they are on the local workstation. Special user exits can link upload/download functions to virus-scanning programs [SAP-Scan].

Technical

Download protection

Authorization object S-GUI (activity 61) protects generic downloads of lists over the SAPgui.

Application-specific authorization objects protect download functions in various applications. An enhanced function module for checks and, in newer releasers, a user exit can be installed to run a customer-specific check routine for every download [SAP-Up/Down]. You can check the lists intended for download by transaction, report, and list title, and their contents, with these tools. If needed, you can also prohibit downloads completely.

3.5 REMOTE FUNCTION CALL (RFC)

The SAP remote function call (RFC) serves communication between distributed programs in the SAP system landscape. You use RFC to call function modules in remote SAP systems and to have the results transmitted to the requestor. RFC supports both synchronous and asynchronous function calls. In addition, transactional RFC operates with or without adhering to the sequence of calls. RFC is also used to communicate with external programs and for internal communication within an SAP system. RFC is the universal beast of burden in a group of SAP systems, and the security of RFCs is extremely important. RFC communication is also the basis for calling SAP Business Application Interfaces (BAPIs) and for SAP Application Link Enabling (ALE).

During communications with an SAP system or between SAP systems, RFC bridges several levels of system architecture. To provide effective protection of RFC communications, we must consider all these levels (*see* Figure 3.6). We will start at the network level and continue to the RFC environment on the SAP application server and the function modules that are called.

3.5.1 SAP Gateway

All RFC calls are routed over an intermediary, the SAP Gateway. A caller, or RFC client, addresses the Gateway on the network level. The Gateway accepts the function call and transmits it to the RFC server, possibly after some checks (*see* Figure 3.7). An SAP system or an external program can be both an RFC client and an RFC server.

The structure of the network and the settings of the firewall systems at crossover points in the network (*see* section 3.1) use address and port filters to determine how the SAP Gateway processes can be reached. An access control list (secinfo file) can regulate the RFC accesses permitted over an SAP Gateway (*see* the technical portion of this section).

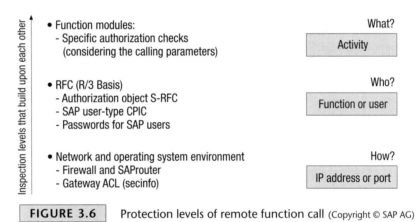

FIGURE 3.6 Protection levels of remote function call (Copyright © SAP AG)

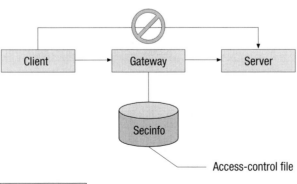

FIGURE 3.7 SAP Gateway (Copyright © SAP AG)

3.5.2 The RFC environment in the SAP system

To transmit remote function calls to an RFC server from within an SAP system, the RFC runtime environment needs information on the RFC server. To this end, an RFC destination is created in the SAP system for the target of each call (*see* the technical portion of this section). If the RFC client is an external system, the information is stored in a configuration file or transmitted directly with the call.

Remote function calls transmitted to an SAP system first undergo an authentication of the communications partner. Authentication can involve the simple mechanism of logging on with a user ID and password (*see* section 2.2 on user authentication). But authentication information should not be stored in files. Rather, users should enter their IDs and password interactively. Special protection for the file system or alternatives is required for automatic calls without user involvement.

As an alternative, you can use the trusted RFC, which sets up a trust relationship between SAP systems so that user authentication is forewarded from the trusted system to the trusting system. But this extremely practical mechanism should be used only between SAP systems that have a comparable level of security. Setting up a trusted RFC relationship between a development or test system and a production system would actually produce a significant security breach. Attackers who have rights to maintain RFC destinations in the development system can create users and RFC destinations to the target system. The attackers then know that these users exist in the target system and that they have extensive authorizations there.

SNC is another alternative that can authenticate a communications partner without passwords using cryptographic protocols (*see* section 2.7), available for RFC as of SAP R/3 Release 4.0.

After successful authentication of the caller, the RFC runtime environment checks the target system to see if the user who started the call has authorization for the function module (authorization object S_RFC; see the technical portion of this section).

3.5.3 RFC-enabled function modules

The SAP authorization concept applies at the level of the function module that was called (*see* section 2.3 on the authorization concept). For this purpose, the function module includes authorization checks at the application level. These checks occur independently of the general check in the SAP runtime environment, and according to the requirements of each application.

3.5.4 RFC Software Development Kit (SDK)

SAP offers a Software Development Kit (RFC SDK) to assist in the development of RFC client and server programs. In addition to an RFC communications library, the kit contains several sample programs with very general functions (such as programs that start other programs) that attackers can misuse easily. Accordingly, the RFC SDK should not be installed on production SAP application servers or frontend PCs. A production system requires only the RFC communications library, which is contained in the standard installation.

Technical

Security settings for RFC destinations

You use transaction sm59 to maintain RFC destinations. Use the menu path: *Tools • Administration • Network • RFC Destinations*. The transaction contains the appropriate maintenance functions for every type of RFC connection: R/3, R/2, and internal connections, logical destinations, and TCP/IP connections to external programs. Authorization object S_ADMI_FCD protects the maintenance of RFC destinations. As indicated in the sample in Figure 3.8, you can also store logon information when creating RFC destinations. You might even have to do so when setting up automatic business processes, such as ALE.

FIGURE 3.8   Security settings for RFC destinations (Copyright © SAP AG)

Storing logon information, however, should be kept at a minimum in productive operations, and then only in secure systems. You must never create RFC destinations with logon information for production systems in a development system. Doing so would create security gaps that can be detected with the Audit Information System (*see* section 2.5).

Better alternatives include the setting of options for the use of trusted RFCs or SNC.

Protecting the SAP Gateways and the secinfo file

To protect the Gateway, which is usually started with every application server, you must deactivate remote monitoring for the Gateway (profile parameter gw/monitor = 1).

You should create a secinfo file to protect executable external programs for each gateway (path in profile parameter gw/secinfo).

USER=<SAP user>, [USER-HOST=<client computer>,] HOST=<server computer>, TP=<server program>

This entry enables a user who calls an SAP system to execute the server program it contains on the server computer indicated. As an option, you can also include a client computer (in this case the SAP application server) from which the call must originate.

USER=<*>, HOST=<server computer>, TP=<server program>

This entry permits the server program to register its executable functions over RFC at the Gateway.

If the RFC server is an SAP system, the secinfo file is not needed. In this case, the required checks occur in the RFC runtime environment of the application server.

Authorization check with S_RFC

This authorization check is activated with profile parameter auth/rfc_authority_check. It checks the existence of an S_RFC authorization for the function group (of the function that was called) in the authorization profile of the authenticated user.

<hr>

3.6 CORRECTION AND TRANSPORT SYSTEM

The programs in use pose one of the greatest dangers to the security of an information processing system. The ultimate goal of many attackers is to place a manipulated program in another system. Of course, not only potential attackers develop new programs or modify existing ones. Those are typical tasks for any manufacturer or even any SAP customer. The protection of the development process and the secure transport of new developments and corrections into the productive system are central tasks of security in SAP systems.

Within the standard SAP system, the Correction and Transport System provides customers with a tool to organize their software logistics. This section treats the security aspects of the Correction and Transport System.

3.6.1 SAP system landscape with three systems

In a typical SAP system landscape (*see* Figure 3.9), development and customizing settings occur in a separate development system. Once they are mature, these programs and customizing objects are exported to a common transport directory. The developments are then imported into a QA system and inspected there. The import into the QA system can occur automatically. The QA system differs from the development system because it permits tests with sanitized (anonymous) or actual production data; only a few, selected persons have user IDs for the QA system. After the tests in the QA system, the transport is released for importation into the production system. The system administrator should perform the transport manually.

This system disposition should meet the following goals.

■ Development authorizations must be assigned only in the development system. For emergency repairs they can be assigned in the production system only for a short period and must be logged.

■ Developers do not have access to the current production data of the company.

■ Developments and changes must be done at a known location (in the development system) and checked in the QA system before they can be used in the production system.

■ The time at which developments and changes can be used in the production system is logged precisely in the transport log.

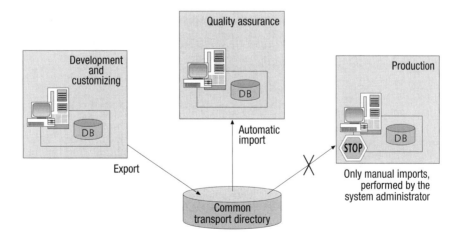

FIGURE 3.9   SAP system landscape with three systems (Copyright © SAP AG)

To protect the common transport directory, we recommend use of the network setup treated in section 3.1. For example, that structure would enable placement of the common transport directory only in the server LAN via NFS. The Transport Management System (TMS) within the SAP system also offers options for handing the transport data via SAP remote function call (RFC) and using different transport directories.

You can set the basic alterability of objects (programs, tables, and so on) in each SAP system. The gradations here (all objects alterable; all customer objects, but no SAP object alterable; only original objects alterable; and no objects alterable) can be set according to the security needs of each SAP system (development, QA, and production).

3.6.2 Transport process

As illustrated, the three-level SAP system landscape clearly defines the transport process. An appropriate division of roles in the development of new material and corrections rounds out the process.

A responsible project leader creates a change request in the development system with the Workbench Organizer (se09) and defines tasks associated with the request as well as the required QA steps. One or more developers perform the tasks that are released after work has been completed. The project leader then releases the change request for export into the transport directory. The QA team reviews the new development after it has been imported into the QA system and confirms its quality. Only then can the change request be transported into the production system. Appropriate authorization profiles can force developers to work with this division of roles (*see* the technical portion of this section).

Technical

Division of roles in the transport process

Table 3.1 provides an overview of the authorization profiles required for the division of roles discussed in section 3.6.2.

TABLE 3.1	Authorization objects for a division of roles during the transport process
Standard SAP profile	**Description**
S_CTS_DEVELO	Team members (process and release tasks)
S_CTS_PROJEC	Project leader (create requests, create tasks, and release requests)
S_CTS_ALL	System administrator (import requests)
S_CTS_SHOW	QA team (display requests)

Security with the Transport Management System (TMS)

You can use the Transport Management System (TMS) in the SAP system to organize transports and use RFC to perform transports even without a common transport directory. This heightens the security of the system landscape.

The TMS depicts transport groups for SAP systems. All the SAP systems administered from one system with the TMS create a transport domain. You can use a dialog transaction (stms) to make settings in both the controlling SAP system (the domain controller) and the SAP systems that form the domain. Use the menu path: *Tools • Administration • Transports • Transport Management System*. A graphical editor is also available to determine the transport paths. Figure 3.10 illustrates a sample.

The TMS sets up the required users (TMSADM) for all SAP systems and RFC destinations that have read access (TMSADM@<SID1>.<DOMAIN>_ <SID2>) or change access

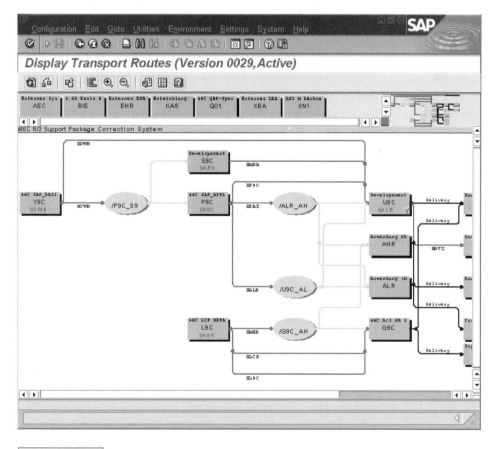

| **FIGURE 3.10** | Determining transport paths with the Transport Management System |

(Copyright © SAP AG)

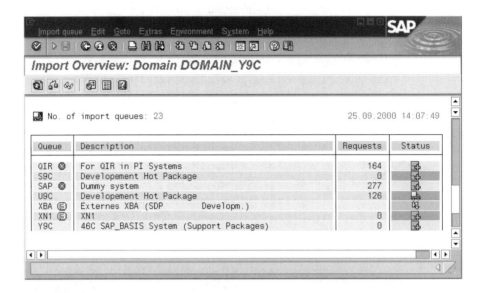

FIGURE 3.11   Import overview with the Transport Management System
(Copyright © SAP AG)

(TMSUP@<SID1>.<DOMAIN>_<SID2>) to the SAP systems in the domain. You can store logon information in the RFC destination for read-only access. We do not recommend this approach for change access: the logon screen appears during calls for this RFC destination.

The RFC connections established by the TMS transmit status information, transport files, and transport logs. You can also use different transport directories between SAP systems. And when you set up the transport paths, you can also configure virtual SAP systems that are connected to the domain for a brief period, and then disconnected immediately after a special transport between portions of the SAP system landscape. The Domain Controller System manages the imports centrally (*see* the sample in Figure 3.11).

3.7   APPLICATION LINK ENABLING (ALE)

SAP Application Link Enabling (ALE) allows you to set up cross-system business processes that can also include non-SAP systems [SAP-ALE]. Asynchronous input and output processing of messages and data creates the basis for distributed applications in an ALE system domain. To guarantee the security of the data and the systems involved, you must pay special attention to the distribution model, the required technical users, and the authorizations for the technical users.

3.7.1 Protecting the ALE distribution model

Within the ALE distribution model, RFC is used to inform the SAP systems in the ALE domain of each other and to define communications paths. To a large extent, security in ALE domains depends upon the security of the RFC calls (*see* section 3.5 on remote function calls). The ALE distribution model is used to make the necessary settings (*see* the technical portion of this section).

3.7.2 Users and authorizations

Most events in an ALE scenario occur automatically. The transmitting system must know the user and authentication data for the receiving system. We strongly recommend the use of trusted RFC or secure RFC communication via SNC (*see* section 2.7). Otherwise, you would have to store the password of the ALE user for the receiving system in the RFC destination of the transmitting system.

For this reason, we recommend setting up the corresponding ALE users with minimal authorizations in the target system. The only required authorization for ALE communication is the authorization to receive ALE messages (*see* the technical portion of this section). This authorization allows receipt of the ALE message, which then undergoes processing as an incoming message. Another user can handle the actual processing. The ALE user in the target system does not require any dialog communication and can have user type CPIC, which does not permit dialog connections (*see* section 2.1 on user administration).

For additional security recommendations for ALE, *see* [SAP SG].

Technical

Protection for definition of the ALE distribution model

The dialog transaction sale offers access to all the activities related to setting up an ALE scenario (*see* Figure 3.12). The activities include the definition of the distribution model and assignment of the required authorizations to users. You must also create the corresponding RFC destinations, BAPIs, and message types for the distribution model. Access to the transaction sale also requires protection.

ALE authorizations

The ALE environment also supports a distribution of roles with authorizations. Table 3.2 lists the ALE authorization profiles available.

TABLE 3.2 ALE authorizations

Standard SAP profile	Description
B_ALE_SYS	ALE/EDI: Maintenance of logical systems
B_ALE_MAST	ALE/EDI: Distribution of master data
B_ALE_MODL	ALE/EDI: Maintenance of the distribution model
B_ALE_RECV	ALE/EDI: Receipt of IDocs via RFC
B_ALE_REDU	ALE/EDI: Generation of messages

mySAP.com – security on the internet

With the internet, a global infrastructure for communication and collaboration between persons, companies, government agencies, and public agencies has developed. This infrastructure influences the life and work of many; it changes the business processes of institutions for which many work. The internet began as a communications tool between research institutions at the beginning of the 1970s, but it has quickly become an ever more important source of knowledge and information for those who can access it. The offerings of today's internet service providers (ISPs) means that participation is no longer limited to researchers, employees of technical companies, or employees of large enterprises. The medium of the internet is available to just about everyone today.

The rapid growth and continuing population explosion on the internet make it particularly interesting for commerce. The plans of the original internet community, not to use the new medium for commercial purposes and to keep its contents free of advertisements and other undesirable content, can no longer be realized. The internet has entered a new phase in which commercial use plays an ever larger role. This change offers companies and private individuals new opportunities that many have called a new industrial revolution. Companies that take too long to use the internet and its opportunities run the risk of falling behind the competition.

With the mySAP.com e-business platform in 1999, SAP turned all its new developments and products toward the internet (*see* Figure 4.1). The mySAP Workplace is an

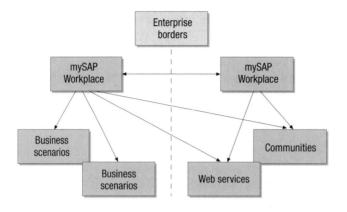

enterprise portal that can integrate all the available SAP systems by using a web browser as the user interface. From the Workplace, employees can access virtual marketplaces on the internet to gather information, issue quotations, or make purchases. The mySAP Marketplace handles these tasks. Business scenarios have been created for various SAP products. The products work together in the scenarios to perform various business processes on the internet. Many SAP services (web services) are being reworked to make them available over the internet. The services include availability and operation of SAP systems as a service to customers who access them over the internet.

This approach means that the technology of the internet can be used for more than external access to data and applications. Employees can work with the same technology within the enterprise (on an intranet), an approach that creates clear advantages with the integration of applications and user interfaces.

Security and data protection is an especially important topic here because the use of technology known throughout the world and the direct integration of company processes into a global infrastructure pose new risks. It's important for users of SAP software to recognize these risks and know how to mitigate them.

Accordingly, this chapter deals with security on the internet and on a company intranet with mySAP.com. We first treat the visions and fears of new technology that is now linked to the internet and from them derive the requirements and goals of secure use of internet technology with mySAP.com. We then treat secure use of individual components of mySAP.com.

4.1   THE INTERNET: VISIONS AND FEARS

You usually get your call through at about 10 in the morning, after a long wait for a connection that is often poor and subject to being lost. Entire regions are frequently unable to be reached on the telephone; they have left the service grid because criminal elements are working on the system. It's becoming harder and harder to learn the telephone number of someone you want to call because there are more and more telephone directories. Not one of them, however, is really up-to-date or complete [Riehm].

That's what the current situation looks like on the internet, if you compare it to the telephone service, which has long since passed this point. But the parallels to the telephone clarify that the teething problems of the internet will be overcome in a short time. After all, commercial use of the internet is just beginning: no one knows where it will eventually lead.

First, we treat the view of the future as seen by visionaries. Then we deal with the dangers and fears experienced by users. The dangers and fears clarify the desires and requirements of internet users, from which we derive our general recommendations for commercial use of the internet. We briefly discuss how the public and private sectors are joining forces to develop the internet further and we explain the security goals of mySAP.com. In conclusion, the technical portion deals with the security of internet technology.

4.1.1 Visions

Developments on the stock market in 1999 showed the great hopes for companies oriented toward the internet. The market prized the chances of these internet entrepreneurs even though most had not yet shown a profit. It's easy to get the impression that the market regards profit as a ban on future investment.

SAPNet, the SAP intranet, displays online media reports to SAP employees in a Workplace function. In 1999, you could detect the following trends, usually along with an explosive headline.

4.1.1.1 Spread of the internet

American and European estimates indicate that in 2003 some 170 million people will be connected to the internet. The British marketing research company, Fletcher Research, estimates some 121 million European internet users in 2004 – there were only 34 million in 1988. International Data Corporation (IDC) expects 177 million users in the US and 502 million throughout the world by 2003; there were 142 in 1998. IDC estimates that the percentage of internet users in this period will grow from 4 to 11 percent of world population.

4.1.1.2 The internet as a competitive advantage

According to figures provided by a German economics institute (IW), some 85 percent of internet-related jobs are to be found in the US. According to the Yankee Group, the volume of electronic commerce in the US will grow from $11.5 billion in 1998 to

$125.6 billion in 2003. And Forrester Research puts the figure at $184 billion in 2004. The European leader in 2000 was Germany, with a volume of 3.6 billion euro.

Forrester Research estimates worldwide e-commerce to involve $1.5 trillion in 2003, up from $1.5 billion in 1999.

4.1.1.3 Training and education

The internet will change every company and every country. Every nation must adjust its training and education programs accordingly. Future jobs will appear wherever employees have the most training. The roles of teacher and student will change dramatically. Teachers will become knowledge facilitators; students will select knowledge according to their needs and desires.

Government and industry in Germany have created Initiative D21 to give students, young adults, and, in particular, women, the opportunities of information and communications technology. The initiative foresees internet-enabled PCs in as many classrooms as possible. Sponsors are stepping beyond their marketplaces to contact schools.

4.1.1.4 Business portal

Online marketplaces offer production companies, their customers, and vendors a uniform communications and information platform. Newly invented, they have already become necessities. Portals for specific industries are being developed.

4.1.1.5 The internet and ERP software

According to IDC, only a few websites are fully integrated into business processes today. E-business that is not directly related to the core process runs into difficulties.

PricewaterhouseCoopers regards the linkage of the web interface with SAP functions as an opportunity to map complex business processes in the context of a very simple, user-friendly interface.

Up to now, e-commerce has occurred between business and consumers. We now see the beginnings of business-to-business (B2B) commerce in which integration of the company, internal prices, and the logistics chain come to the fore. The demand for SAP know-how and its 25 years of experience is in high demand here[1].

4.1.2 Dangers and fears

Most publications that treat the internet indicate its threatening dangers, and thus stoke the fears of users. The articles often make the risks (which obviously exist) their only message, and fail to note the means available on the internet to counter these risks. Truths and half-truths are promulgated in the media.

---

1 As reported in *Capital* 1.12. 1999, "Wir stecken im Umbruch".

▦ There's no confidentiality without encryption.

It's generally stated that unobserved communication on the internet is impossible. Every use of a customer card and every online shopping trip leaves data behind. And even with encryption, the traffic between individual users can be observed. When transmitting data, a user must be aware that the transmission can result in worldwide publication of the information.

The use of encrypted connections can offer a remedy here, providing that the recipient of the data treats it responsibly and observes the rules of data protection. Encrypted connections can be set up easily on the internet today (*see* the technical portion of this section). Strong encryption has become available in American products. These options must be used. To avoid surrendering to the network addresses being used, intermediate stations can be created at businesses, although doing so does complicate processing.

▦ Connecting to the internet enables a potential attack on the company's network to collect confidential information or to damage the system with viruses.

This risk is ultimately unavoidable and must be balanced with the benefits of an internet connection. We recommend the creation of firewall systems in any case, along with attention to access protocols and services. No firewall system can offer absolute security, but is one component of measures taken to mitigate risk. The firewall system itself requires careful management; company IT processes must be defined to ensure that no one can go around the firewall. Access protocols allowed by the firewall system must have appropriate security settings, and must be monitored regularly. Section 1.3 treated the creation of, adherence to, and continual monitoring of a company's security policies.

▦ It's as easy as pie to log on under a false name and shop on the internet at someone else's expense.

Many services offered on the internet actually do so. The global world of electronic communications has not yet developed means to determine the identity of persons and systems with any reliability. In this case, the retailers carry the actual risk. Most people are quite used to paying for a meal with a credit card in a restaurant, and hand over their credit cards without thinking about it. But when entering a credit card number on the internet, worries suddenly appear, even though the owner of the card can stop payment on the transaction at any time if no signature exists. Encrypted transmission of this kind of information is an effective countermeasure for misuse, as are trustworthy retailers who use the information entrusted to them properly. Most businesses also have a delivery address, or provide verification of an e-mail address. But commerce involving larger volumes must offer other mechanisms to identify the persons doing business: we treat this issue below.

- Illegal copies of software will lead to an epidemic spread of stolen intellectual property.

Internet piracy causes damage to the tune of $0.5 billion each year.

This problem does exist. Electronic identification of authors and digital watermarks are complicated endeavors and not always effective. Removal of an ID is, however, a crime and an infringement of copyright. Here, too, the risk must be weighed against the damage that will arise if nothing is offered on the internet. The production and spread of illegal copies is hardly limited to the internet.

- Bulk advertising mail is ridiculously cheap and therefore floods mailboxes throughout the internet community, even without prior contact between sender and receiver.

Persons on the internet do receive unsolicited e-mail with adult content or extreme political views, chain letters, and confidential company information that should not leave a firm. Sometimes the recipient is called to account before an official agency or upper management because of these e-mails.

These events seem unavoidable and are comparable to the flood of advertising brochures that appears in your mailbox every day. The use of signed and encrypted e-mails for formal and confidential communication has helped here, and must become more common in everyday work. Filtering and inspection software on the external firewall of a company can remove undesirable content from familiar sources.

- Internet banking is complicated and involves high risks. Banking institutions only pretend to offer their customers secure standards.

Banks have taken measures to make banking transactions on the internet secure. The measures include the use of encryption and authentication procedures, such as PIN/TAN and the HBCI standard. Users, however, must accept the need for their cooperation in these measures and not complain about user-unfriendly security procedures. Software errors in PC programs have been found and corrected. The authors are unaware of any losses to clients that banks did not refund completely.

- Marketing methods of online services and the lack of controls open the door to misuse.

Competition will quickly separate the wheat from the chaff here. As we argued above, security and adherence to data protection rules are an important competitive advantage. Internally developed rules in companies can fill the vacuum left by the lack of governmental controls and criminal statutes.

- The majority of European upper management doubts the security and performance of the web.

Technical innovation is seen as a threat; both employees and consumers wonder who can maintain an overview or be responsible at this speed.

Rapid growth will obviously not respect existing conventions. The battle for business on the internet will produce many losers and only a few winners. It's conceivable that latecomers will wash away the first wave of internet businesses. Companies that stand still and do not move with the evolution of the internet will lose market share and experience less growth. That will cost jobs in other companies and countries, unemployment, governmental outlays for unemployment payments, and the distribution of social costs over fewer shoulders. National isolation in the midst of global internet business is no way out.

4.1.3 Requirements and desires

Articles about the internet also clarify the requirements and desires of individual members of the internet community. We find it helpful to treat users in distinct groups: users, security professionals, and management.

4.1.3.1 Users

Everyone regards security as the central precondition for future use of the internet. Individual users demand complete disclosure of how their data is used and the risks they face. Users want to feel secure, content, and that all is well. The presence of security functions may not lead to lost user-friendliness and comfort when working with internet applications. Users want payment options: online, credit card, COD, invoice, or cash in advance.

Global companies must localize their presence on the web and consider the local language and culture so that they can react appropriately.

4.1.3.2 Security professionals

Companies increasingly have written policies that anchor security concerns, which gives security a valued place in companies.

A coherent security concept and its consistent application (with unbreakable encryption for data, passwords, and other authentication data) form the preconditions for a connection to the internet.

4.1.3.3 Management

Customer satisfaction means a high rate of return. Economic viability therefore depends upon building a comprehensive legal, quality, and security-conscious basis for activities. Those responsible for IT demand a company-wide policy to ensure the availability and confidentiality of all data.

4.1.4 Recommendations

Given the preceding facts, fears, and desires, the following recommendations are almost self-evident.

▦ Security must be seen as everyone's basic precondition for use of the internet. To be seen as a competent partner, availability and reliability must exist at all levels of a company. Outstanding service is the key to loyalty and long-term retention of customers.

▦ A company concept to ensure the long-term reliability and confidentiality of all data is absolutely indispensable. This concept has repercussions in company guidelines, its security policies, and in day-to-day security management. The concept should also include a procedure for self-regulation of internet contacts (net ethics and netiquette).

▦ Users' clarity about the use of their data and the potential risks involved will play a central role, particularly on the internet. Revelation of who stores, processes, and transmits what from whom, must become self-evident. The principle of self-determination for personal information must become a basic right. Information on all traces of data that is stored, transmitted, and analyzed (even when unnoticed) must be provided to users actively. It may not appear only in the fine print.

▦ Customer satisfaction must become the primary goal. Companies must consider the protection of privacy as one of their tasks. To provide internet users with the highest possible levels of security, it must become a matter of course to offer unbreakable encryption of data, passwords, and other authentication data along with the physical security of routers and firewalls. As a further part of a comprehensive authorization concept, data should be assigned to specific departments or areas in the company and linked to authorizations via roles or jobs.

4.1.5 Market and governmental measures in Germany

Both industry and the federal government see the D21 Initiative as a way to accelerate the change from an industrial to an information society. Unions have also signaled their willingness to collaborate.

Working groups have come to the following conclusions.

▦ Framework

Self-regulation in industry supplements legal proscriptions. A digital signature should have the same legal standing as a regular signature.

▦ Government in the vanguard

Government creates a portal for purchasing and procurement; information centers and discussion forums are created for citizens.

▓ Training and qualification

As many classrooms as possible should be provided with internet-capable computers. Sponsors contact schools via marketplaces.

▓ Women and IT

The percentage of women in IT should be increased, including opportunities for part-time and telecommuting positions.

▓ Founders

Competition and partnerships with large companies should encourage the foundation of new companies.

SAP is represented on the advisory board. It has already undertaken intense contact with institutions of higher education, placed students in practical and cooperative programs in addition to traditional training for IT, and encouraged company founders. Initiatives have been created at the federal and state level to bring local administration up to the standards of modern IT.

One essential task of Initiative D21 will be to overcome citizens' fears of Big Brother. Absolute security of privacy and transparency about the use of transmitted information will be the cornerstone of the success of D21.

4.1.6 Security goals of mySAP.com

A connection to the internet and the use of internet technologies run the risk of relinquishing already existing security standards. To avoid doing so, SAP has set high security goals for mySAP.com. But the high level of integration between intranet and internet applications at each user's workstation creates a new set of challenges and requirements. Users' web browsers become the generic interface not only to the applications users need to complete their daily work within the company, but also to sources of information and the products of business partners and competitors outside the company. All this is easy to reach – it's just one click away. Because transferring from one application to another becomes more fluid, users find it increasingly difficult to distinguish the sources of applications.

Accordingly, SAP has set specific security goals for the creation of the mySAP.com infrastructure and for the availability of applications with mySAP.com. The following sections treat these goals in more detail.

4.1.6.1 Use of confidential communications channels

Wherever it seems appropriate, data must have the ability to undergo transmission in an encrypted form. internet surfing with the HTTP protocol first occurs without encryption, but HTTPS enables establishment of encrypted communications links (*see* the technical portion of this section). The use of HTTP to access publicly available information (product catalogs, new products, quotations, and contact persons) does not yet pose any security problems. However, you should have a confidential channel available if users must enter passwords, if the connection transmits personal data (address, telephone number, banking information, or credit card numbers), or if business data (conditions on a quotation, prices, or delivery conditions) is involved.

All mySAP components that connect to internet technologies support the SSL protocol and therefore HTTPS as well (*see* sections 4.2–4.5).

4.1.6.2 Availability of strong authentication mechanisms

When it establishes a connection to the internet, an application must complete the important task of determining the identity of the person who wishes to use it. Publicizing publicly available information to unknown, and therefore anonymous, users is usually not a critical issue. In fact, it's often undesirable to identify such users. But access to personal services or to company applications and data should be limited to authorized persons. To ensure that this goal is met, the identity of potential users must be determined without any doubt – as far as possible. Passwords are the most common tool used to this end, along with digital user certificates that follow the X.509 standard (*see* the technical portion of this section).

The standard version of mySAP.com supports both a password procedure and digital user certificates that correspond to X.509 for authentication over the SSL protocol. Section 4.2 on the SAP Internet Transaction Server treats the basic operations of authentication here. mySAP Workplace and mySAP Marketplace (*see* sections 4.4 and 4.5) involve a single sign-on, so that the system does not repeatedly ask users to enter information for each authentication procedure.

4.1.6.3 Authorization according to roles

To simplify implementation of various authorizations for users with access rights, mySAP.com features a role concept as a consistent continuation of the SAP authorization concept. Users are assigned authorizations according to their roles in the company. The applications check the authorizations when they access the applications with their authentication. The definition of roles results from the potential activities or tasks that a user in that role might perform. The user interface (web browser) for that user then enables execution only of the tasks for which the user has authorization (*see* section 4.4 on the mySAP Workplace).

4.1.6.4 Provability of electronic business transactions

The ever-increasing amount of business transactions that are handled electronically means that many transactions in the future will not involve an actual person who can physically confirm an action with a signature or as an eye witness, for example.

According to its defined scope, business systems will process transactions automatically. Note that encrypted communication, authentication of systems, and access controls with authorization are all just as effective. Automatic processing involves technical users who represent systems, rather than actual persons. But electronic business transactions produce electronic documents and require appropriate security mechanisms to have the force of a legal action.

The rules for generally accepted accounting principles that already apply to IT systems face new challenges with the internet. The quantity and the effects of electronically automated fraud are much higher than what is possible when a written document is required at some point in the transaction. This problem made digital signatures (*see* section 2.8) important as a form of electronic security for data and transactions. SAP Basis also offers the functions needed to generate and check electronic signatures with mySAP.com as well, and plans to use a digital signature in an increasing number of mySAP.com applications.

4.1.6.5 Recording and logging all actions relevant to security

Logging of all security-relevant actions remains active in the infrastructure of mySAP.com. It enhances the options for recording and auditing offered by the SAP system itself (*see* section 2.5) with mySAP.com middleware for auditing and logging. Here, mySAP.com takes advantage of the web server in use, the SAP Internet Transaction Server, and the SAP Business Connector.

Technical

This section provides a short introduction to internet technology as it applies to security and data protection. The initial comments are general and do not apply to SAP specifically. Informed readers can skip these observations. Sections 4.2 through 4.5 treat the use of internet technology with mySAP.com.

Secure communications on the internet

Various levels of computer communications protocols in computer networks handle the communication of data between computers and the components of a distributed application. The protocols at the lower levels deal with transmissions over different physical media and with directing messages between sub-networks along the route from the sender to the intended recipient. The protocols at the higher levels use the services of the lower levels to establish communications links between application processes on the transmitting and receiving computers. The application processes comprehend each other over the higher-level protocols: partly because of how the data is presented, and partly because of its meaning.

Transmission control protocol/internet protocol (TCP/IP)

The internet protocol (IP) and the transmission control protocol (TCP) (TCP/IP) are used at the network level and to establish end-to-end connections between the application processes. *See* Comer (1991) for example.

To transmit data in a network, the IP protocol uses a packet design (network level). The data to be transmitted is divided into packets of a fixed size. Individual packets travel through the network independently of each other and are reassembled at the recipient's location. Each packet contains the address of the sender and the recipient as well as a sequence number. Routing protocols determine the route through the network; routers (intermediate stations) process the protocols. Routers work with address tables with a static configuration, but the configuration can also consider dynamic information on the network load and the best routes.

The TCP protocol builds upon the service created by the IP protocol and permit the establishment of end-to-end connections directly between the application processes (transport level). The phases here include the establishment of the connection, the actual transmission of data, and then the termination of the connection. The data transmitted over TCP therefore includes an identification of the assigned connection.

Hypertext transfer protocol (HTTP)

Higher internet protocols, such as those for file transfer (FTP), e-mail (SMTP), and remote login (TELNET, RLOGIN), are built upon the combined communications service created by TCP/IP. Tim Berners-Lee laid the foundation stone for the world wide web (WWW) at the beginning of the 1990s. The web considers the entire internet as a large hypermedia system. In this system, servers manage distributed resources (documents, images, audio, video, and so on) which are connected to each other by the hyperlinks that each contains.

The HTTP protocol (hypertext transfer protocol; *see* (Fielding et al. 1999) is used to request and transmit information on the world wide web. The HTTP protocol exists at the application level and works with a simple request–response paradigm (*see* Figure 4.2). An HTTP request addresses a document with a reference that can include the server name, the path to the document, and the parameters of the call. The standard internet format for this reference to WWW documents is called a uniform resource identifier (URI). If the URI also contains a server description, it is called a uniform resource locator (URL), which is now familiar to almost everyone (example: www.sap.com/security).

To transmit the request, TCP/IP is used to establish a connection to the server that manages the document. The first part of the URL contains the server name. The domain name service (DNS) maps the symbolic name of the computer to an IP address. The HTTP server process on the server listens to incoming requests at a specific port. HTTP usually works with port 80, but you can also use a different setting. The rest of the URL determines the target document on the server. The server process then returns the requested web page to the computer that initiated the request (HTTP response).

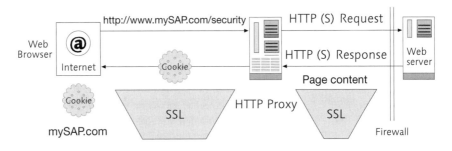

The standard for the HTTP protocol defines additional required and optional information for each request and response. This information is transmitted as a header (meta-information) transmitted before the actual body (contents) of HTTP messages. The header includes information on the type and format of the body. The HTTP protocol was first designed as a stateless protocol. That means that the HTTP server stores no information on an HTTP request at the protocol level; each request must contain all the information needed to make the request. If several HTTP requests follow each other, each must contain all that information. The HTTP protocol itself does not support the processing of several requests and responses in a common session.

The stateless characteristic of the HTTP server allows a simple and robust implementation. Given that the HTTP protocol was designed for performance, this type of implementation is not necessarily an advantage. Some optimizations to implement applications with a state were defined after HTTP 1.0. If several requests from the same HTTP client reach an HTTP server in rapid succession, HTTP 1.0 requires the establishment of a new TCP/IP connection for each request; the connection is broken as soon as the response is transmitted. With HTTP 1.1, however, the connection remains open after the response has been transmitted to see if the same web client has another request that can use the connection. The time that the connection remains open is adjustable.

Cookies

Another means of storing state information on web clients with the HTTP protocol involves cookies (Kristol and Montilli, 1999). The HTTP server can place cookies in the HTTP response it sends to the client's web browser (set-cookie header). Cookies are small units of information (the internet standard allows up to 4 Kb). After an HTTP server has generated cookies, the client's web browser manages them. The server application determines and interprets the contents of cookies.

The HTTP server can generate various attributes when it generates a cookie; the attributes determine how the cookie is managed in the web browser. One required attribute is the DNS domain for which the cookie is valid. If the domain attribute is not specified, a cookie is valid only for the server that generated it. This attribute can indicate an area, but then it must consist of two or more name components (such as company.com or mySAP.company.com). Cookies generated in a browser are sent along with every subsequent HTTP request to the server or domain (depending upon the type of domain specification) that generated the cookie. With this approach, the state stored in the cookie for a server or a domain is available at the next HTTP request sent to the server. HTTP requests to other servers or domains contain only the cookies valid for those servers and domains.

HTTP over the secure sockets layer (SSL) protocol (HTTPS)

Figure 4.2 illustrates the essential elements of the HTTP protocol and the essential components of secure communications on the internet. Communication with HTTP over TCP/IP does not support strong authentication and encryption of connections. To improve this situation, Netscape developed the secure sockets layer protocol (SSL) and submitted the protocol's specification to the Internet Engineering Task Force (IETF) for standardization in 1995. After some rework, SSL Version 3.0 was released in 1996; all popular web browsers and servers [SSL3.0] now support it. SSL 3.0 is also the basis for the current internet draft of transport layer security, version 1.0 (Dierks and Allen, 1999).

SSL operates between the two layers that build upon each other, the transport layer (TCP) and the application layer (HTTP). Building upon a reliable, connection-oriented transport service, SSL offers additional services for the strong authentication of communications partners with X.509 certificates (*see* the technical portion of section 2.8) and confidential communications with encryption.

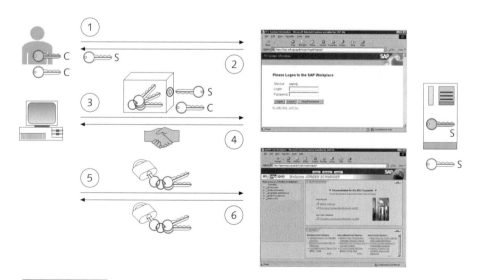

FIGURE 4.3   SSL protocol (Copyright © SAP AG)

Figure 4.3 illustrates the basic structure of the SSL protocol. *See* section 2.6 for more information on the terms used here. The client (web browser) first transmits a client-hello message to the server. The message informs the server of the cryptographic method used and the strength of the encryption (1). The server selects the desired cryptographic method (providing that the server supports it) and transmits it to the client along with its X.509 certificate in a server-hello message (2). The server can also optionally request an authentication from the client and inform the client of the types of certificate and certification authorities that it supports. The client then generates a symmetrical session key and transmits the parameters (pre-master secret) to detect the session key to the server (3). The public key contained in the server certificate is used to encrypt the information and make it secure. If the client must provide authentication, the client signs the authentication digitally and transmits it to the server with the client certificate.

The server needs the proper private key for the server certificate to decrypt the secret information in the session key. The server can also check the client's digital signature and know the identity of the client for sure. If everything is in order, the server transmits a confirmation that completes the negotiation phase (4). Both sides can now transmit encrypted messages between themselves (5 and 6). The SSL protocol includes several combinations of possible methods for authentication, key exchange, and encryption at various levels of strength (SSL cipher suites). *See* Esslinger and Müller, (1997) and the standards themselves for more information.

The SSL protocol can create secure communications at the connection layer if HTTP is used with SSL (HTTPS). For the user, the process is very simple: the URL here begins with https://.... The HTTP protocol is not changed here, it simply uses a connection established with SSL. HTTPS must, however, already be configured on the server, and the server must have an X.509 certificate. An encrypted channel can be established even with one-sided authentication (of the server). If the client possesses an X.509 certificate, the client can also be authenticated.

Experience with and studies of the SSL protocol have shown that it can produce a high level of security (Ellison and Schneider (2000)). But the use of short key-lengths (40 or 56 bits for symmetrical encryption) limits that level. Export laws have made this the case for the export versions of American products in the past. After the first approvals of exceptions for specific markets (such as healthcare and banking), the export laws in the US were significantly loosened. American products sold abroad now feature strong encryption.

Use of firewall systems

In addition to the SSL protocol, additional components can contribute to secure communications on the internet. As illustrated in Figure 4.2, most actual situations protect a company's access to the internet with a firewall system. These systems protect access to the internal network by granting access to the internal network only to specific communications services and protocols that are run by computers in a security zone, a demilitarized zone (DMZ: *see* section 3.1 on the network). In the ideal case, access is then possible only over HTTP or HTTPS, and the external network knows only the IP addresses of computers in the security zone. All outgoing internet queries are routed to an HTTP proxy server that functions as a stand-in. To avoid attacks, companies must conscientiously manage the firewall systems and the computers in the security zone. All unnecessary services must be deactivated. Attacks are always possible even for the permissible services, so that administrators must pay attention to improvements and corrections from manufacturers and update their systems immediately.

Internet information and security

Web clients use HTTP(S) to access information contained in web pages that are administered by web servers. The contents and structure of web pages is given in hypertext markup language (HTML; *see* Bornstein and Freed, 1996). HTML is a descriptive language that uses tags to describe the content and format of web pages. In addition to the content stored directly in HTML pages, the language can also include links to other web pages as hyperlinks. The feature and frame technology mean that you can create web pages that represent several documents in various places on the page. Each document has a reference to its origin, to the name of the server that provided it. The standards define a document domain security policy that prohibits viewing the contents of documents in other domains.

The recent development of extensible markup language (XML; *see* [W3C-XML]) has provided an expanded descriptive language that far exceeds the capabilities of HTML and has already found wide acceptance. XML can describe the syntax of various types of documents generically. XML parsers check the syntax and can correctly predict the structure of a document even before an application interprets its contents. XML cannot, however, describe the semantics, so that the application areas still require discussion and standards. The World Wide Web Consortium (W3C) is currently working on a standard digital signature for XML documents that will make security possible at the document level.

Active contents

If the contents of HTML and XML documents featured only static texts and images, there wouldn't be too much more to say about security. Active contents, however, commonly appear, and these contents pose a significant threat to security. A web page can have a program as a component that runs each time the page is accessed by a web browser. Java, JavaScript, or ActiveX can create such programs, but only Java has so far presented a dedicated security model for these active components. In a web browser, Java applets run in a limited environment, a sandbox, that does not permit access to the computer's local system resources (files, programs, or interfaces). Only trusted Java programs are granted this type of access. Users can turn on these programs individually by Java applet or by manufacturer (for Java applets with a digital signature). Although

ActiveX from Microsoft can also identify the manufacturer with a digital signature, it does not offer a sandbox model.

The use of JavaScript poses a particularly tricky threat because JavaScript programs can be built into and called from just about any web page. Although JavaScript has become extremely popular because of its flexible implementation of web pages with good appearance and functions, its effect on the security of web documents is only now becoming apparent. For example, several violations of the document domain security described above have recently been discovered in Microsoft's Internet Explorer. Each manufacturer's different implementation of the functional scope of JavaScript in each browser makes it difficult to judge the security of these active contents.

Users can turn off active scripting, Java, and ActiveX in their browsers, or turn them on only after confirming their desire to do so. In actual practice, however, this feature offers little help. Complete deactivation of active components would mean that many internet services simply become unavailable because they use these technologies extensively. Users who want to decide upon activation must have a good technical understanding of the issues involved. Surveys of users show that they easily become overwhelmed, which means that they often revert to making the components active all the time. Users cannot be expected to know how to distinguish between a dangerous situation and an everyday occurrence. It's up to the browser manufacturers to identify and plug existing security gaps and implementation errors in today's products.

4.2   SAP INTERNET TRANSACTION SERVER

SAP R/3 Release 3.1 created the possibility of linking SAP systems to the internet as early as 1996 with the SAP Internet Transaction Server (ITS; see Heckner, 1999). The first step on this path supported development of SAP internet and intranet applications as internet Application Components (IACs). IAC users worked with a web browser as the interface, and queries were sent to a web server over the HTTP internet protocol. An SAP enhancement on the web server, the Wgate, directed queries to a gateway computer that stood in front of the SAP system, the Agate. In turn, the Agate created the connection to the SAP system and called the SAP applications required for the query.

At first, the ITS did not automatically offer access to all the transactions and data in an SAP system, but only to those available as IACs. To provide access to all transactions and data, you must configure the Agate appropriately. Access over the internet to SAP systems is possible only over the Agate, a feature that offers security advantages for the systems.

4.2.1 Secure network setup with the ITS

To set up secure access from the internet to SAP systems with the ITS, the network level itself must be structured properly (*see* Figure 4.4). An access request occurs over the HTTP or HTTPS protocol (*see* the technical portion of the previous section) at the edge

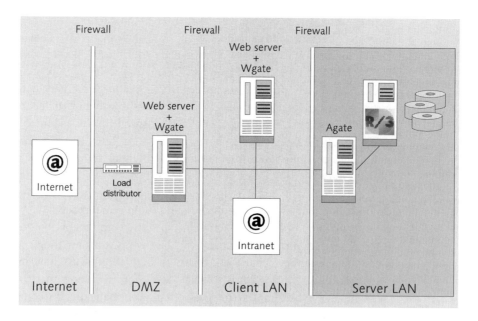

| FIGURE 4.4 | Network setup with the Internet Transaction Server (Copyright © SAP AG)

of the firewall system, between the external and internal systems. Other communications services are blocked. A load distributor sends access requests to a web server in the demilitarized zone. The Wgate component of the ITS is the only component installed on that web server. The Wgate establishes a communications link to the Agate in the internal network, which is installed on a separate computer. The Agate then sends the request along further. This action requires opening the ports for the SAP protocol between the Wgate and the Agate. The Agate creates a communications link to the SAP system and starts the desired application there. The results of the request follow the same route to return to the web browser. The same approach can be used in an intranet by setting up the web server and the Wgate in the server LAN.

Figure 4.5 illustrates how to set up a secure communications channel over the entire path between the web browser and the SAP application server. An encrypted connection is set up with HTTPS between the web browser and the web server. An SAP protocol is used between the ITS Wgate and ITS Agate. The SNC interface can use external security products (*see* section 2.7) to encrypt communications that occur via the protocol. SNC ensures strong authentication between the Wgate in the demilitarized zone (DMZ) and the Agate in the internal network. This approach fulfills an important requirement for communications that move from the DMZ into the internal network.

The Agate is usually within the server LAN along with the application servers. If the Agate is outside the server LAN, you can set up another firewall system between the Agate and the application servers (not illustrated in Figure 4.5). You can also use SNC to secure the communications between the Agate and the applications servers.

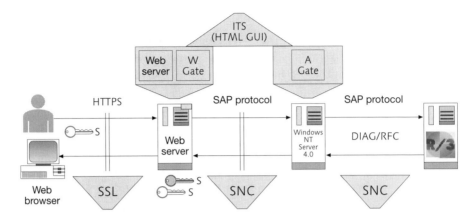

FIGURE 4.5   Secure communications channel with the Internet Transaction Server
(Copyright © SAP AG)

The strength of the protection offered by the communications link depends upon the web browsers and servers in use. As noted above, previous export restrictions on American manufacturers meant that they only supported weak encryption (40-bit variable key). Exceptions were permitted only for specific markets, such as banking. Now, however, American products offer strong encryption. The security reached with SNC depends upon the security product used at the SNC interface. The currently available SAP partner products ensure that it is practically impossible to attack the communications link successfully.

Because the communications channel between the web browser and the SAP application server is set up over routers, rather than end-to-end, the theoretical possibility of attacking the router exists. The web server in the DMZ offers a tempting target for attacks in this configuration. It's vital that everyone attends to the secure administration of the web server. The web server should be accessible behind the firewall only over the HTTP(S) protocol. Nonetheless, some attacks over HTTP(S) have come to light (*see* [MS-Bulletins]). Administrators must keep an eye out for new developments and install any updates from manufacturers that may result to maintain the security of the web server.

For access to the SAP system itself, it pays to provide the Agate with a great deal of security: this computer can store logon information for anonymous or automated access. Productive operation of an Agate computer demands different security settings than testing operation. You can select the security level you desire when installing the Agate. The value you select influences the setting in the Windows NT file system for the installation files and for the administrative capabilities of remote computers (*see* the technical portion of this section).

4.2.2 User authentication with ITS

When using HTTPS, the web server authenticates itself to the web client with a digital server certificate (*see* the technical portion of the previous section). Authentication of the user at the web browser can occur in two ways with the ITS (*see* Figure 4.6):

1 standard SAP logon with user ID and password

2 X.509 client certificates.

In the first method, the ITS asks the user to enter the SAP user ID and password in the web browser; it then transmits the information to the SAP system over the encrypted channel. Authentication occurs in the SAP system based upon the hash value stored in the database for the user (*see* section 2.2).

The second method can be used as an alternative in SAP R/3 Releases of 4.5 and above. In that case, the services offered by the ITS are set to have the web server demand a client authentication over the SSL protocol.

If the user has an X.509 client certificate available in the web browser, authentication occurs in the web server over the SSL protocol (*see* the technical portion of the previous section). The Wgate then sends the client certificate over the secure channel to the Agate, which then transfers it to the SAP system for logon. A user ID in the database maps the name of the user contained in the client certificate. The user master record must contain the entry for the mapping. If it does not, the user cannot log on with this method.

When logon occurs with an X.509 client certificate, the SAP system does not actually authenticate the user; it simply trusts the authentication provided by the web server when it established the HTTPS connection. The SSL protocol used for this purpose on the internet is regarded as very secure. Because this logon method means that users do

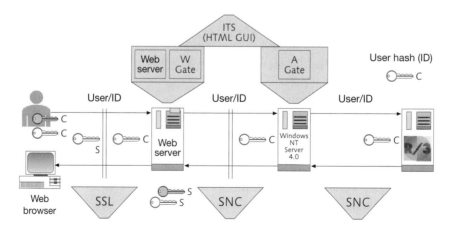

FIGURE 4.6 User authentication with the Internet Transaction Server (Copyright © SAP AG)

not need to enter a user ID or password, secure administration of the web server and a secure channel from the Wgate into the SAP system are vitally important. To use this logon method, you must set up SNC between the Wgate and the Agate and between the Agate and the SAP systems.

4.2.3 Security of the ITS applications

After successful authentication, the ITS applications (IACs) run under a user in the SAP system, and therefore under the control of the authorization concept (*see* section 2.3). This feature ensures that the SAP system logs all user actions, according to the settings in the system (*see* section 2.5).

In addition to IACs that perform user authentication, some IACs provide general services and information on the internet and on intranets. Such ITS applications do not require authentication of the user in the web browser; they merely give the user access to publicly available information. In this case, the ITS employs technical users to log on to the SAP system. The Agate stores the encrypted logon information for the technical users (*see* the technical portion of this section). Partly for this reason the Agate requires the special protection noted above.

A decision about setting up an ITS application with a technical user who has all the required authorizations in the SAP system or having the application perform user authentication and then logging on to the SAP system as that user demands careful thought. From a technical standpoint, the SAP system offers all the options necessary for personalized applications with a technical user. The application then must authenticate users at the proper time and check whether or not the user has the right to perform a specific action. To guarantee an audit trail for the system, the application itself must log all user actions – an even more critical consideration. The log must indicate the true user name for any changes to a change document, tables, and logs to prevent misuse and provide an audit trail.

That is enough reason to let personalized applications always run under a specific user and to save technical users for anonymous access. Of course, you can always limit the authorizations of technical users quite severely. Technical users with powerful authorizations always represent a significant security threat (*see* section 2.1 on user administration).

In addition to user authentication and the SAP authorization concept, IAC can also use additional security functions at the application level. An IAC can use a digital signature along with application-specific tools and information.

Technical

Wgate

The Wgate is an application that has been installed on a web server. Its essential tasks consist of establishing a communications link to the Agate and to send request and response data to and from the Agate. The Wgate is available for various web servers. An IS-API version exists for Microsoft IIS, an NS-API version for Netscape, and a CGI version for web servers under UNIX. You can set up a connection protected by SNC (*see* section 2.7) between the Wgate and the Agate.

The typical structure of a URL that requests an ITS service contains the server names. The URI portion of the URL also contains the path to the Wgate. The URI portion can also include parameters to execute a service directly, but not for certain parameters that affect security.

Example:

http://<servername>/scripts/wgate/<service>/
!?~parameter1=<value1>&... &~parameterN=<valueN>

Agate

The Agate is the actual gateway to the SAP system. So far, it is available only under Windows NT; a porting to Linux is under consideration. The Agate opens connections to the SAP system over the SAP protocols DIAG and RFC. It administers the connection contexts with the logon data it requests from the user. The logon data for technical users is stored in the file system of the Agate.

You can select one of three security levels when installing the Agate:

1 unlimited access for all users

2 access for the ITS system administrator and ITS users

3 access only for the ITS system administrator.

Level 2 permits access for the ITS administrator and a specific group of users to ITS files (HTML templates and service files). You can use this setting during development. Select level 3 during productive operations.

Service files on the Agate describe the services provided by the ITS. The global.srvc file contains valid entries for all services. The specific service files contain additional parameters or overwrite the entries in the global service file. Table 4.1 lists some examples of some security-relevant parameters. *See* the SAP documentation on the ITS [SAP-LIB] for further information.

Logon with X.509 Client Certificates

To enable user logon with X.509 client certificates, you must first configure the web server for HTTPS. The web server must have a key pair for SSL and the corresponding X.509 server certificate. You must also set the ~clientCert parameter in the service file

TABLE 4.1	ITS service file: sample parameters

Parameter	Value
~systemname	XYZ
~logingroup	PUBLIC
~messageserver	Xyzmain.wdf.sap-ag.de
~client	400
~login	Myservice
~password	********
~language	DE
~timeout	60
~usertimeout	60
~cookies	1
~clientcert	1

TABLE 4.2	Profile parameters for logon with X.509 client certificates

Parameter	Value
snc/extid_logon_diag	0/1
snc/extid_logon_rfc	0/1

on the Agate. You can set the parameter to make the X.509 client certificate optional (~clientCert 1) or required (~clientCert 2). SNC must secure the communications between the Wgate and the Agate and between the Agate and the SAP system. The use of SNC ensures protection for the X.509 client certificate for logon.

You must set the profile parameters for logon with X.509 client certificates (*see* Table 4.2). The user master record must map the correspondence between the user name in the certificate and the user ID in the SAP system for all users who can log on with X.509 client certificates over the ITS. For more details on the configuration procedure for logon with X.509 client certificates, *see* [SAP-X509].

4.3	SAP BUSINESS CONNECTOR

The SAP Business Connector is another new mySAP.com component to link SAP systems to the internet. The SAP Business Connector links systems between business partners – consumers and manufacturers, manufacturers and vendors, vendors and raw-material suppliers, and so on – over the internet to form a common infrastructure. Unlike the SAP Internet Transaction Server, the SAP Business Connector focuses on automatic processing by software systems without user interaction.

SAP Business Connectors exchange business documents, such as orders and invoices, described in XML among themselves or with other systems. Descriptions of documents in XML is increasingly becoming the standard on the internet (*see* the technical portion of section 4.1). The SAP Business Connector integrates processing of XML directly along with the functions of an HTTP client and an HTTP server.

The SAP Business Connector provides the infrastructure required to implement the logistics chain over the internet. The following sections teach the security functions implemented in the SAP Business Connector and any supplemental measures you must take.

4.3.1 Secure network setup with the SAP Business Connector

To enable other systems to reach the SAP Business Connector over the internet by using the functions of the built-in HTTP server, you must set up the system in the demilitarized zone (*see* Figure 4.7). For security reasons, you should configure HTTPS, meaning HTTP over the SSL protocol (*see* the technical portion of section 4.1). An SSL implementation makes it directly available with the SAP Business Connector (*see* the technical portion of this section).

The SAP Business Connector uses BAPI calls to redirect requests from the internet to the SAP system. To do so, the firewall system that protects the internal network area must permit RFC communications. The SAP Business Connector is therefore integrated into an ALE system (*see* section 3.7 on Application Link Enabling). SNC provides security for RFC communications entering the internal network.

Because of its location in the DMZ, the SAP Business Connector demands careful

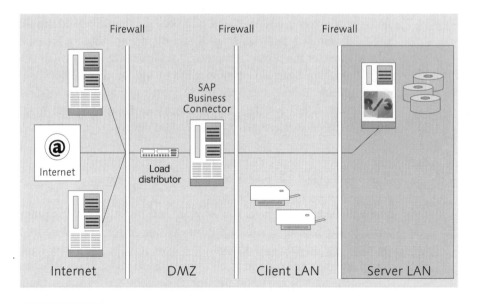

FIGURE 4.7   Network setup with the SAP Business Connector (Copyright © SAP AG)

administration. You should set up a special port for administrative tools, a port that remains unavailable on the other side of the firewall system. Be sure to change the initial password for the administrator after installation.

4.3.2 User authentication with the SAP Business Connector

To authenticate partner systems and the users of other web clients, the SAP Business Connector uses a simple password mechanism. The users must be set up in the SAP Business Connector; the passwords are stored in the file system of the SAP Business Connectors or in an LDAP directory. An alternative method uses X.509 client certificates over SSL to authenticate users from the internet, as the ITS does. We strongly recommend this approach when using the SAP Business Connector in a productive system because passwords do not offer optimal protection.

   The backend SAP systems are regarded as trustworthy, so no special authentication of users occurs. Outgoing requests from the connected SAP systems are transferred from the user in the SAP system and mapped to a user in the SAP Business Connector (and vice versa). We therefore strongly recommend the use of SNC to secure communications with the backend.

4.3.3 Security of SAP Business Connector applications

Access-control lists protect the individual applications that are set up on the SAP Business Connector. The list can contain entries for users who are allowed access to a particular service. When using the SAP Business Connector in a productive system, you must ensure that no unprotected services are available. SAP is currently working on another security mechanism for the SAP Business Connector, the integration of a digital signature. The SAP Business Connector captures all events in log files.

Technical

HTTPS settings

To set HTTPS for the SAP Business Connector, you must first configure an HTTP Listener. You can then make the required keys and X.509 certificate available to the administrative interface of the SAP Business Connectors: use the menu path *Settings • Security*. Table 4.3 lists the individual parameters. These settings are valid globally for all configured HTTPS Listeners.

   To initialize the security settings, you can use *Settings • Security • Setup Security* (*see* Figure 4.8). To generate the SSL key pair, the administrator of the SAP Business Connector enters the desired key length and the information needed for the X.509 server certificate. That triggers generation of the key pair. A certificate request for the key pair in PKCS#10 format [PKCS10] is created and displayed on the administrative interface (*see* Figure 4.9).

TABLE 4.3	HTTPS settings for the SAP Business Connector

Menu selection	Meaning
Server's Private Key	Private key of the SAP Business Connectors
Server's Signed Certificate	An X.509 certificate issued by a trust center
Signing CA's Certificate	The X.509 certificate of the issuing trust center
Require Client Certificates (y/n)	Determines whether or not the X.509 client certificate is required
Request Client Certificates (y/n)	Determines if a X.509 client certificate is required
CA Certificate Directory	Directory of X.509 certificates at the certificate authority
CA Fingerprint File	File containing the fingerprints of the certificate authority

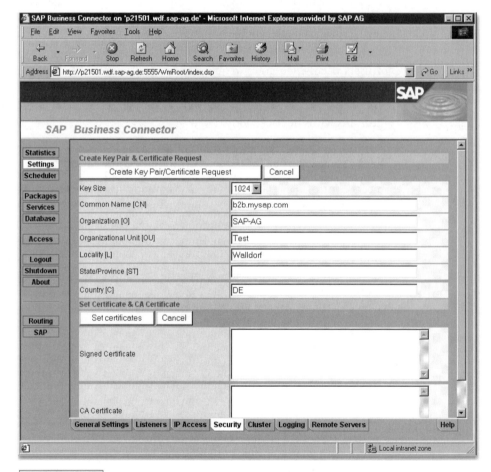

FIGURE 4.8	Generating an SSL key pair for the SAP Business Connector

(Copyright © SAP AG)

FIGURE 4.9   PKCS#10 certificate request for the SAP Business Connector
(Copyright © SAP AG)

The PKCS#10 certificate can be sent to the desired trust center that will issue the server certificate. Simply cut-and-paste the request into an e-mail. The signed certificate is imported into the administrative interface with cut-and-paste.

4.4   mySAP WORKPLACE

The mySAP Workplace portal is one of the new building blocks of SAP products that involves the internet. Users employ a web browser to access SAP and other applications that are listed in a personalized menu (*see* the sample in Figure 4.10).

The Launch Pad at the left of the screen lists the activities that users perform, based upon their roles in the company. The selections contain links (URLs) that can connect SAP applications, non-SAP applications, and information sources on the internet and intranet. Users can add their own favorites to this list. The right side of the screen displays the selected application. This portion of the screen can display several applications in different frames (MiniApps) that contain up-to-date information for the user as soon as they are displayed.

During everyday work with the mySAP Workplace, users hardly notice any difference between an intranet and the internet. Many links connect to other systems in the

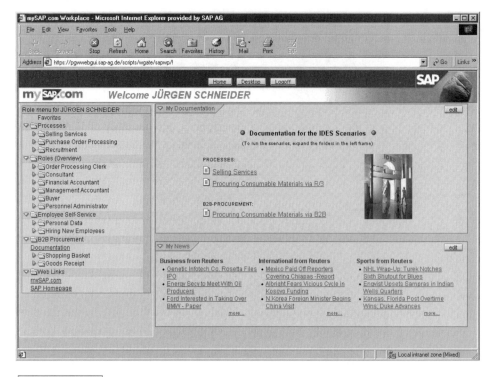

FIGURE 4.10 Workplace user menu (Copyright © SAP AG)

company's intranet; other links connect to web servers on the internet where they access current information, offers, and services from business partners. In this case, the security of communications and of business transactions must be guaranteed.

We have already introduced the essential components of the mySAP Workplace (*see* Figure 4.11). The Workplace server stores information on users and their personalized menus, role definitions, and other administrative data. When a user first logs on to the mySAP Workplace, the user is authenticated based upon the user data stored in the Workplace server. Access occurs over a web browser and Workplace middleware that consists of a web server, the SAP Internet Transaction Server (ITS), and the Workplace Engine. The latter is realized as a service over the ITS. The mySAP Workplace recognizes that the contents of an R/3 screen and the HTML page displayed in the web browser might change at runtime. Accordingly, you do not need to store conversion instructions for most applications on the ITS Agate. The ITS thus provides a complete SAPgui for HTML.

The comments made in Chapters 2 and 3 also apply to secure operation of the mySAP Workplace portal, the SAP systems the portal accesses, and how those systems are embedded in the company network. The Workplace server is not added to the backend area as a central system to administer the portal. Section 4.2 treats the secure configuration

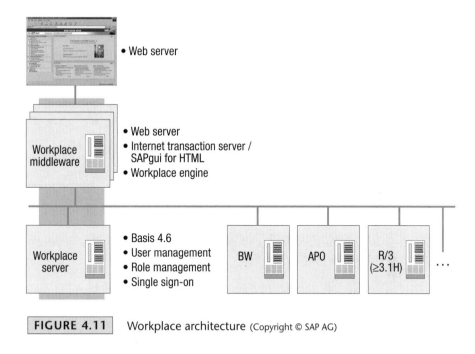

- Web server

- Web server
- Internet transaction server / SAPgui for HTML
- Workplace engine

Workplace middleware

- Basis 4.6
- User management
- Role management
- Single sign-on

Workplace server

BW   APO   R/3 (≥3.1H)   ...

FIGURE 4.11   Workplace architecture (Copyright © SAP AG)

of the SAP Internet Transaction Server. The web browser becomes the interface, but security settings for the browser depend upon the product being used. This chapter treats additional functions relevant to the security of the mySAP Workplace.

4.4.1 Secure communication

The network setup of a mySAP Workplace landscape is essentially the configuration illustrated in Figure 4.4 in section 4.2 on the SAP Internet Transaction Server for access from an intranet and the internet. You can set up RFC connections with or between the server LANs in the backend for communication between the Workplace server and the SAP systems to which it is linked. You can also protect the RFCs with SNC.

You must use HTTPS to secure communications between the web browser and the mySAP Workplace (*see* the technical portion of section 4.1). The release of strong encryption in American products as of January 2000 means a significant advance for the security of commercially available web browsers. Additional SSL proxies that used to complicate installation and administration are quickly becoming a thing of the past.

4.4.2 Central user management

SAP R/3 Release 4.5 makes central user management available for a group of SAP systems. The following preconditions usually exist when implementing this function:

- a system landscape with several SAP systems along with several clients in the systems (logical systems)
- the same users work in several logical systems in various roles
- it takes considerable effort to synchronize user data in all the systems.

This is exactly the situation that exists with the mySAP Workplace. It is therefore a good idea to set up central user management in the Workplace server to simplify administration of the Workplace.

Central user management involves the setup and maintenance of users for all SAP systems from one central SAP system. The central system automatically distributes the user data to the associated systems. Distribution includes addresses and fixed values, the user's state, assigned authorization profiles and roles, and check information for the initial ID.

Depending upon your wishes, you can configure the distribution of user information at the field level:

1 only central maintenance of the fields and distribution from the central system to local systems

2 only local maintenance of the fields without distribution

3 only local maintenance of the field after initial population by the central system

4 local maintenance of the field with retrograde distribution over the central system to other local systems.

Only setting 3 is permitted for passwords. Central user management also enables locking users globally, without a local system having the ability to release the lock. In all other aspects, the maintenance interface for the user manager remains the same. Individual dialogs for user and authorization management (*see* Figures 2.4 and 2.11 in Chapter 2) feature an additional system field in which you enter the logical system for which the user data is to be valid.

Distribution of user data occurs over SAP Application Link Enabling (ALE, *see* Figure 4.12). Transactional RFC is used for communications. In the central system, you first define the ALE distribution model and set up RFC destinations for all the connected systems. Section 3.7 treats security with ALE.

Setting up central user management in the Workplace server ensures that all users in the company can be authenticated in the mySAP Workplace and that roles in the enterprise can be assigned to them. The user ID for one user is identical in all the connected systems (although the passwords might differ). SAP development is currently working on storing user information in a directory service to enable the integration of user management, operating system, and other applications.

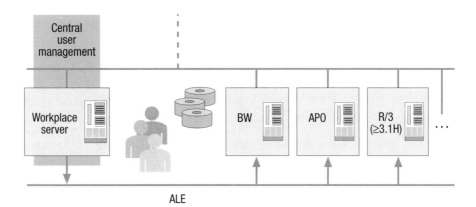

ALE

FIGURE 4.12   Central user management (Copyright © SAP AG)

4.4.3 User authentication and single sign-on

When started, the mySAP Workplace asks the user to supply authentication. The system authenticates the user based upon the user master data in the Workplace server system. As noted in section 4.2 on the SAP Internet Transaction Server, the ITS (a constitutive element of Workplace middleware) offers two options for logon:

▩ standard SAP logon with user ID and password

▩ logon with an X.509 client certificate.

The following treats both alternatives in more detail. The single sign-on offered by the mySAP Workplace does, however, demand responsible, security-conscious treatment of the PC at the workstation when the user logs on in the web browser (PC security and a screen saver with password). Other sections of this book have noted these non-SAP security issues several times.

4.4.3.1 Single sign-on with user ID and password

Standard logon (*see* section 2.2 on user authentication) requests that users enter a user ID and password (over the ITS). Workplace middleware transmits the user's entries to the Workplace server, where they are compared to the check value in the database (over an RFC call). If the check is successful, the Workplace middleware sets a mySAP.com single sign-on cookie in the user's web browser. *See* the technical portion of section 4.1 and Figure 4.13 for more information.

After logon, the cookie is sent along with every HTTP(s) request from the Workplace menu, as long as the query is directed to a web server in the same DNS domain to which the Workplace middleware belongs. The information in the cookie is used to log on the user in each target system. No other interaction from the Workplace user is required.

The use of cookies to authenticate users is a very simple procedure for single sign-on with the use of standard internet technology. Besides the SAPgui for HTML, users can also call the SAPgui for Windows, the SAPgui for Java, and the SAP RFC mechanism from the Workplace menu. As an additional advantage, existing SAP systems can be integrated into mySAP Workplace without any changes.

But there are also disadvantages. The logon information stored in the mySAP.com single sign-on cookie is valid only for connected SAP applications, and is transmitted only within a DNS domain because of the security model for cookies. The cookie is not transmitted along with requests from the Workplace menu that go to other DNS domains. If existing SAP systems are integrated into the mySAP Workplace without any changes, the single sign-on works in the SAP systems for which the user already has the same user ID and password (mySAP.com SSO Cookie Version 1).

As of version 2.10 of the mySAP Workplace, different passwords can be used in the associated SAP systems, since systems connected to the Workplace no longer need to request a password. This feature is based upon a ticket-based log-on procedure (mySAP.com SSO Cookie Version 2). Existing SAP systems require a kernel patch to use this feature. The authenticity of the logon ticket is secured with the digital signature of the Workplace server. Target systems use the public key of the Workplace server to inspect the logon ticket.

The following applies to security for Workplace single sign-on with cookies.

▨ The mySAP Workplace must use HTTPS. This approach ensures that logon data and SSO cookies are always transmitted with encryption.

▨ The SSO cookie is created in the web browser only in main memory; it is not stored on the hard disk. When the web browser is closed, the SSO cookie is no longer available.

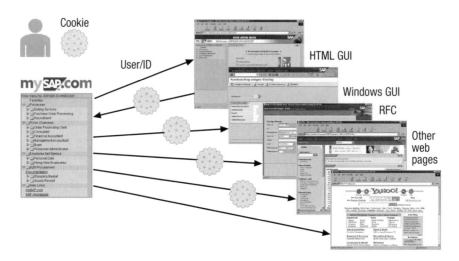

FIGURE 4.13   Workplace single sign-on with user ID and password (Copyright © SAP AG)

▩ The SSO cookie is valid only for a limited period (the default is 60 hours; customers can adjust the setting).

▩ The information in the SSO cookie has strong encryption (SSO Cookie Version 1) or a digital signature (SSO Cookie Version 2).

▩ The SSO Cookie is generated with the DNS domain specification of the Workplace middleware; it is therefore available only in this domain.

The use of passwords and SSO cookies for single sign-on to the Workplace creates only a specific level of security. Only careful management of the application landscape can largely counter most of the risks associated with that level of security. The applications available on the web servers that belong to the productive DNS domains require strong controls. Trojan horses that infect productive DNS domains in these applications can collect SSO cookies.

Web pages can easily contain attractive programs (*see* the technical portion of section 4.1); pages that appear quite harmless can easily read the cookies sent along with a query, without the user noticing anything. The SSO cookies can then be used to log on for a limited time, even without having to decrypt the logon information contained in the cookie.

In the past, several bugs were found in Microsoft Internet Explorer, for example, violating the cross-domain security policy outlined in section 4.1. Websites of other DNS domains were able to read information in other documents in the Workplace: a fatal error for cookies. Microsoft released a patch and these problems have been solved.

Apart from implementation errors, however, the problem here is general. Executable programs that can hide Trojan horses with unforeseen effects are hardly a problem that affects SAP alone. The risks that arise on the internet are increased because it's far easier to infect a web page with a Trojan horse or virus than it is to install an executable program in the file system of a company computer. System administrators must be aware of the risks and must have the knowledge to combat these risks. For example, a firm's bulletin board filled with individual, private notices from employees does not belong on the same web server as the one that runs the ITS and contains current business data.

4.4.3.2 Single sign-on with X.509 client certificates

The second alternative for single sign-on with mySAP Workplace creates a higher level of security. If users have an X.509 client certificate, they can make it available in the web browser and use it for logon to the mySAP Workplace. In this case, user authentication occurs via the web server and the SAP Internet Transaction Server in the Workplace middleware, as described in section 4.2. Here, users need do nothing special: authentication is handled by the SSL protocol (*see* the technical portion of section 4.1). No passwords are used.

After a successful logon to the mySAP Workplace, all additional calls can occur in the same manner with HTTPS (*see* Figure 4.14). This use of internet standards also enables the integration of other applications into the web, as long as they support certificate-based logon. Settings in the browser, such as a PIN, can reach the protection offered by an X.509 client certificate. You can also use smart cards. They offer the most secure solution for single sign-on, especially for users who are out of the office. It's preferable for employees to use their own devices (laptops or palmtops) rather than a PC in an internet café or an airport lounge.

SAP development prefers a highly secure alternative to the X.509 client certificate for future Workplace installations. To provide users with X.509 certificates quickly and easily, SAP offers the mySAP.com Trust Center Service. But users can also use the services of other trust centers and internal public key infrastructures.

4.4.4 Role concept

The mySAP Workplace consistently applied and enhanced the authorization concept treated in section 2.3 and the maintenance of activity groups to create the role concept. A role consists of all the authorizations associated with a specific role within an SAP system, as well as the resulting user menu in the Workplace. Roles defined in the Workplace server have significance beyond the system. These collective roles group together individual roles in individual systems.

Figure 4.15 illustrates the procedure for defining a role with the mySAP Workplace. Individual roles are first created for each target SAP system in each target system, since the systems feature different applications and various release levels. The profile generator is then used to generate the required authorization profiles locally, once the individual roles have been defined.

The individual role definitions are then imported in the Workplace server system

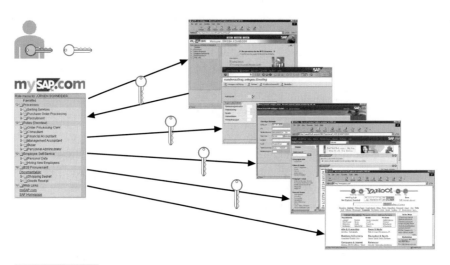

| **FIGURE 4.14** | Workplace single sign-on with an X.509 client certificate (Copyright © SAP AG) |

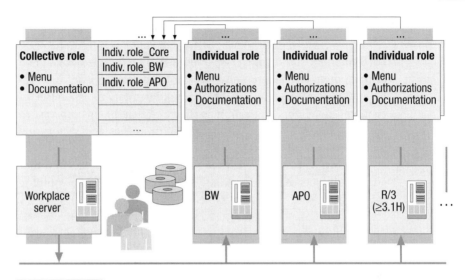

FIGURE 4.15   Role concept of the Workplace (Copyright © SAP AG)

and become available to create collective roles. A collective role can contain several individual roles and sets up the cross-system user menu. In the last step, the required collective roles are assigned to a user, who can also possess several collective roles. For example, one employee can function as a clerk in the sales department, an officer of the corporation, and a purchasing agent who deals with one of the company's vendors.

With the mySAP Workplace, SAP delivers predefined roles with comprehensive and industry-specific significance. Customers can use these role definitions as is, but it's best to check their contents carefully. Long experience with the authorization concept has shown that individual situations are quite specific to customers and can differ greatly. It's quite simple to use a role delivered by SAP as a template and make your own adjustments to it, large or small, depending upon your own needs.

The role concept gives users of the mySAP Workplace a comfortable environment for the creation and administration of various authorizations in the company. This ability applies across various SAP systems and, to a lesser extent, for other applications integrated into the Workplace user menu. The roles in mySAP Workplace can also contain links to other intranet and internet applications, if they are available over a URL. Some roles might permit access to such applications from the user menu and others might not.

The lack of an international standard for authorization in software systems makes it very difficult to use the fine granularity of the authorizations created in SAP role definition for other applications. We can only hope that common use of directory services by business applications can improve this situation. SAP development is now working on exporting the mySAP Workplace role definition to a directory.

mySAP MARKETPLACE

For e-commerce on the internet to succeed, suppliers of goods and services must be able to find potential customers and vice versa. The global infrastructure of the internet can help. Almost every company today can publicize its goods on the internet and look for economical vendors and suppliers there. To help in this process, virtual marketplaces are being created that focus on specific industries and sectors and offer regional or global services.

With mySAP.com, SAP also offers electronic marketplaces on the internet; a rapidly growing number of suppliers from various industrial areas are finding themselves in the marketplaces (http://www.mysap.com). The mySAP Marketplace is being enhanced as standard software for an additional SAP product upon which other service providers can create internet marketplaces. This section introduces the security functions of the mySAP Marketplace.

The mySAP Workplace as an intranet portal within a company and the mySAP Marketplace as an internet portal for industry solutions complement each other (*see* Figure 4.16). Users work at their workstations with a web browser and have access to internal and external applications over their user menu.

4.5.1 Secure communication

For the confidential communication of user and quotation information, the mySAP Marketplace can be reached via HTTPS: https://www.mysap.com. During access with

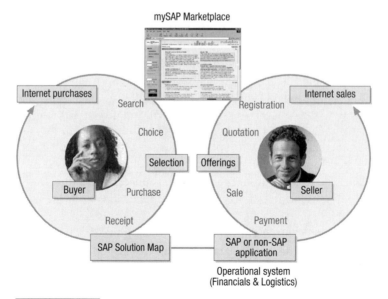

FIGURE 4.16   Marketplace (Copyright © SAP AG)

HTTP, HTTPS is activated on the server side (at least) as soon as user-specific data is transmitted. Commercial web servers and browsers handle this task. Now that American export regulations have been relaxed, products with strong encryption are available globally.

4.5.2 User registration and management

The first version of the mySAP Marketplace offered users the option of self-registration. Only a little data is needed to create a user (name and e-mail address). Entry of other information (address or telephone number) is optional (*see* Figure 4.17). The user ID can be chosen at will, as long as it does not already exist. Registration also requires selection of a password that contains at least six characters.

mySAP Marketplace uses a commercial directory product via LDAP as a standard interface to store user data.

When users register themselves, the e-mail address they enter is validated. Once the user is created, an e-mail is sent to the new user requesting confirmation of the registration. The e-mail contains a unique URL. The procedure can at least confirm that the user does, in fact, have that e-mail address. But this process cannot state anything else about the user. Users who have not confirmed their registration cannot yet use any services that require user data. They are deleted from the system after a period.

One more group of users enhances the user concept of the mySAP Marketplace:

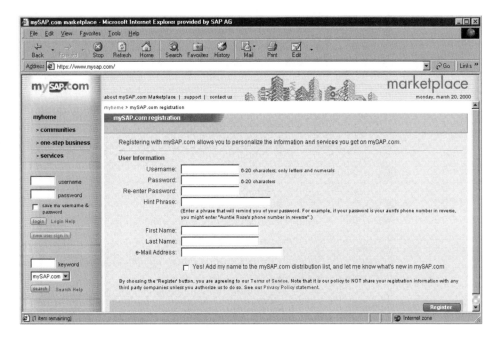

FIGURE 4.17   User registration for the Marketplace (Copyright © SAP AG)

company users. These users have a confirmed relationship with a company. A known person from a company creates these users. In such cases, the mySAP Marketplace also contains an entry for a business directory to register these users. When a company is registered, a specific procedure checks the validity of the entries: the Marketplace operator performs the validity check manually.

Entries can also be given (optionally) for persons from the company when the company is registered. These persons would then serve as administrators for additional users from the firm. The company administrators have greater rights in the mySAP Marketplace to perform management functions for the users assigned to them. In the future, registration of company users can take place automatically from the mySAP Workplace of the company. The Marketplace logs all transactions relating to user management. Administration of user data is subject to the rules for data protection treated in Chapter 8.

4.5.3 User authentication and single sign-on

Initial access to the mySAP Marketplace occurs anonymously. At this point, the user can access only general information on the home page. But the user can enter a user ID and password at any time (*see* Figure 4.18). The logon information is transmitted in an encrypted form via HTTPS. Here, too, however, an X.509 client certificate can be used for the logon. The user then arrives at a personalized home page. Users can enter an X.509 client certificate in user management of the Marketplace later.

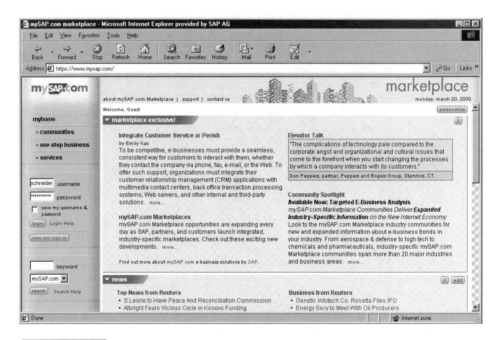

FIGURE 4.18   Home page of the Marketplace with logon option (Copyright © SAP AG)

After successful logon, a mySAP.com Single Sign-On Cookie is set in the user's web browser. The cookie does not remain in the web browser's main memory permanently; it is no longer available after the session ends. Generation of a persistent mySAP.com Single Sign-On Cookie that contains the user's logon information in encrypted form is offered as an option. But this option should be used only when security at the PC workstation is adequate.

The single sign-on function of the Marketplace continues to work when the user is directed to the web server of another service provider in the Marketplace (*see* section 4.5.4). An HTTP redirect passes the user ID authenticated in the Marketplace to the redirect URL. The entry in the URL has a digital signature to avoid counterfeiting. The service partner must then check the digital signature.

4.5.4 Service registration and circulation of user data

Logged-on users can personalize their pages in the Marketplace and register for additional services from other providers. Registration for additional services requires the entry of additional user information (*see* the sample in Figure 4.19). Each service can

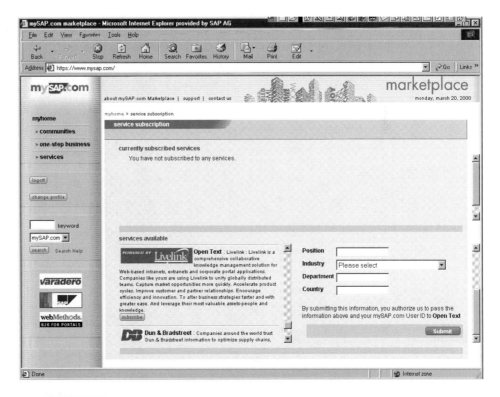

FIGURE 4.19   Service registration on the Marketplace (Copyright © SAP AG)

determine the contents of that information. At registration, the system displays all the fields of the user master record to users, so that they can decide if they agree with the service registration.

With a service registration, users declare that they agree that the Marketplace can transmit the information required for the registration (only the necessary fields of the user master record) to the service provider. Without this information, it would be almost impossible for service providers to do business. Service providers must ensure that the rules of data protection are observed over the Marketplace.

4.5.5 A look ahead

As this book was being written, the mySAP Marketplace was only a few months old. It integrates numerous security mechanisms described here to enable e-commerce over internet marketplaces. Experience will show if these measures are sufficient, but the need for some enhancements can already be seen:

- the use of digital signatures in Marketplace applications to secure individual business transactions
- the integration of electronic payment methods with limited liabilities.

Future developments in this area are sure to be exciting. Yet the lack of security will soon be no argument for not doing business over the internet.

Part 2

Data Protection

## CHAPTER 5

Basics and goals

This chapter on data protection must begin with an apology. The entire section on data protection focuses on law, but we are not legal experts. Where do we get the courage, as outsiders, to publish about an area ruled by jurists?

5.1　INTRODUCTION

5.1.1　A slightly different view

We see the problem of security and data protection from the perspective of developers of standard software. We are used to researching the wishes of our customers and implementing them in our products. But that does not mean that every customer-specific suggestion or project is immediately transferred to the standard product. That occurs only for the features desired by many customers and that can be implemented in a reasonable time. The same approach applies to desires for security that go beyond basic protection.

But we certainly do know about customer requests and desires. We learn about the real problems that responsible parties must deal with in day-to-day practice. These parties include not only security experts and data protection offers, but also system and application administrators, project managers, HR departments, union representatives, management councils, and users themselves.

We hear about the difficulties involved in installation and the problems security experts face in winning acceptance and enforcement of their efforts. We are asked to mediate confrontations that remind us of diplomacy missions: confrontations involving the design of a work environment between works councils on one side and HR departments and upper management on the other. We learn about problems involving bargaining agreements and the balancing act between strict control and effective collaboration with supervisory agencies. We also hear from so-called data protection experts. Many of them guarantee data protection in a company after just one day, and others provide the company with a register containing thousands of pages of rules and regulations. The latter group claims that the law requires a register, the law must be followed, and the law does not limit the quantity of rules or state how those responsible for data protection have to deal with all that information.

Our personal experience with the use of SAP software in our own company or its subsidiaries also gives us the courage to speak about data protection and security in a somewhat unusual medium.

5.1.2 Laws and compliance

Over and over we hear about efforts, particularly in Germany, to regulate every conceivable aspect of data protection with laws, the fullness of which are unknown to those affected by them. This observation also applies to the (German) Federal Data Protection Law and many employee regulations. Many well-educated employees have honed their skills over 20 years, and have hardly come into contact with legal matters, other than a theoretical understanding of constitutional law or a concrete experience with traffic law. Most people learn all they need to know about law from the Ten Commandments. Schools do not generally treat the penalties for violating data protection laws or for computer crimes, but luckily we're only a click away from this information in the internet age. Despite all the laws and threats of punishment, viruses wantonly manipulate or destroy millions of dollars worth of data. Intensive prosecution and quick trials are usually not the case, so that public confidence in the laws also suffers.

Since we assume that those responsible for data protection are sufficiently trained in the law, our observations concentrate on the importance of data protection from a company's viewpoint. We will treat information from online media, magazines, and data protection and security brochures because this material presents itself to those responsible for data protection as adequate and its influence in creating opinions in the business world is not to be underestimated. We will not shy away from referring to critical voices.

As noted, we cannot formulate any positions in cast iron. But we can describe our opinion from a business perspective, from that of a software manufacturer. We hope that this book contributes to a greater familiarity with the legal issues involved and how to implement them in practice.

5.1.3 Secure data transfer

We will plead for the free exchange of data.

We don't see those responsible for data protection as being able to slow or stop the flow of important information in and between companies. Rather, they can contribute to guaranteeing secure transfer. They also have the task of translating complicated and hard-to-understand laws into bulletins, regulations, or electronic manuals for normal, non-expert, staff. They must sell their expertise not only to other employees, but also to management. Data protection thus becomes a management task from two perspectives.

Those responsible for data protection cannot stop the trends toward global companies, inter-enterprise cooperation, and application hosting (even in the area of personnel). But the transmission of sensitive and private data may occur only with the existence of appropriate security measures formulated in the context of risk analysis and a cost–benefit analysis. Those responsible for data protection are not the only ones who must strive for secure and legal transmission of data as a company goal. Top management, as the party ultimately responsible, must do the same in its security policies.

Data protection officers are often lost. They face the pressures of management for quick implementation of innovative, absolutely essential projects that mean the company's survival, and the often unclear requirements of the law. They can always follow the suggestion of Wolfgang Strubel, a member of the board of the GDD (German Association for Data Protection and Data Security)

> Hold the Federal Data Protection Law firmly in both hands, and decide for yourself with good common sense. Then wait until someone proves the opposite.

You can probably already predict that the following treats data protection from the viewpoint of a functioning business.

The law itself does not occupy the foreground of our discussion. That place is taken by the questions of how a company or group of companies can enable and secure the optimal flow of information, even when considering basic rights, particularly the privacy of all participants.

5.1.4 The true danger

Using a press report as an example, the following shows the acute and emerging dangers of violating personal rights in the private sphere.

The world's largest online marketing agency, DoubleClick, and the market research company Abacus Alliance wanted to combine their profiles of usage patterns and personal data on consumers into one database. One company used advertising banners to place over 100 million cookies on consumers' computers, and the other administers 2 million customer profiles that it gathered from e-commerce purchases. The customer profiles include name, address, shopping preferences, and demographic information on the customer.

According to the German law on protecting data among remote service providers (TDDSG), DoubleClick's intentions are clearly illegal because usage and personal data cannot be combined. Such data may be combined only with the express consent of the person involved. In this case, however, the opposite holds true. Customers can make their cookies anonymous only at their own request.

The comment that closes the report is particularly interesting:

In any case, juridical consequences here [in Germany] seem unlikely. While it's true that DoubleClick has a German subsidiary, as long as the central office in the US collects and processes all consumer data, German consumers can't do much. Because it's generally unclear what server transmits an advertising banner, the potential for data collection usually remains hidden ([Heise] January 26, 2000).

This report highlights the true problems of data protection.

- Actions of users are recorded secretly.
- Cookies are used to store reusable profiles of users on their computers; the cookies are read and enhanced whenever the user visits the site.
- The recorders are mostly anonymous.
- The user cannot determine who or where something was recorded.
- Users are not informed about the data collected, its storage, and its use.
- Data is transmitted to third parties in secret.
- The data is routed to international servers, mostly in the US where they are not obligated to follow the EU standard for data protection and do not do so.
- Private data is collected over several years by various companies in different industries, joined into one database, and linked.
- No legal matter of fact regarding a user's permission exists. Neither clear permission from users nor a contract exists; the interests and the basic rights of users are abused.
- The prohibition against this procedure in EU and German law is simply ignored.
- Even experts think that users can hardly defend themselves against this kind of procedure. Neither the prohibition of recording nor the requirement to identify the source of the data can be enforced.

At the same time, the media often discloses private matters of some people to the public. Even presidents are not immune from such revelations: American or German. The required consideration of the rights of an individual to privacy and the constitutional protection for free speech does not occur. Since these revelations are a considerable business, paparazzi who peek through keyholes have long since become acceptable (Ehmann, p. 237, 1995). Values such as responsibility and morals are sold for hard cash. The pleasure, or to put it better, earning money at the expense of others drives circulation and advertising rates upward. Privacy does not pay.

From this perspective, the challenges that face those responsible for data protection are clear. They must recognize that companies collect data for contractual or legal reasons and must do so to reach goals that benefit both parties. The exchange of information between partners is the essential precondition that enables companies to face the challenges of doing business in the information and internet age.

5.2 SAP SYSTEMS AND DATA PROTECTION

Consultants advise companies on the use of SAP systems, even though they announce in advance that the material is very complex and they are only novices. Customers frequently do not implement a requirements check for individual data fields. This failure is often held against SAP because it must offer numerous fields as the manufacturer of an international standard. If communications with regulatory offices do not function even after extensive, clarifying discussions, the (German) government can make the following threats:

> The political discussion on the lack of data protection in SAP systems will last until all the stipulated shortcomings are corrected in light of privacy laws.

Here we must clarify that the letter clearly indicates that shortcomings were not stipulated, but objected to.

Others complained at one point about authorization problems involving downloads to PCs, although these problems were solved long ago. The solutions appear in R/3 notes, and were published in the guidelines on data protection for SAP R/3. The solutions even permit updating old release levels with the new improvements. Only after implementing the correction does the person making the complaint realize with surprise that it's not a matter of forbidding downloads in general for specific employees, but of limited downloads of a specific transaction or a special report list. These demands vary from company to company and can be arranged with customer modifications to the standard system. The SAP developers were lucky in this case. They offered both an authorization object and a program exit for this request.

Data protection officers among our customers often complain that SAP systems do nothing for data protection or cannot do anything for it. When we enquire further, however, it's clear that they have no idea of the security mechanisms in the SAP system. They are unaware of SAP documentation on the authorization concept, access control, encryption, remote maintenance measures, and guidelines on security, audits, and data protection.

The data protection officers who raise these complaints usually face the problems of security mechanisms and data protection only after the systems have gone into production. The officers had no opportunity to work alongside the implementation team, to learn together, and to design the system together. Their complaints would be better heard if they had worked along with the project to set up the system landscape, Customizing, the plan of modifications, the transport system, user management, and the authorization concept. Then they could claim that the project was so complex and the systems so multifaceted that only expert knowledge from several employees and consultants could guarantee the security of the system. It's also a truism that the protection of a system is a matter of balance. You cannot have a weak link in the chain, and the chain consists of the SAP system and its environment. That's why there's such a demand for specialists in the database, the operating system, the network, devices, and so on.

In conclusion, think of the greatest security risks: employees and administration. They need both expert training and an introduction to the problematics of security and data protection.

The security of a system depends upon its maintenance and how people work with it. The system itself cannot prohibit the storage, processing, and transmission of personal data. It cannot see if the contents of an individual field in a data stream are confidential or private and may not be transmitted over a given connection. But you can protect a system and keep others from having access to it.

5.2.1 International aspects

Inexorable structural change is revolutionizing traditional business practices. Globalization, ever-shorter production cycles, and increased demands arising from an awareness of the relationship between price and service all drive this change.

Departmental, company, and national borders all fall away from an international group's market orientation and organization setup. Legally separate subsidiaries must be linked to harmonized business processes, and grow through mergers and acquisitions. To meet current challenges head on, IT personnel see the rapid exchange of customer, market, and employee information within the group as a necessity.

Governmental restrictions on communications are regarded as stumbling blocks on the way to economic advances. Limitations on the free exchange of information, particularly within a group, hamper competition and are seen as injurious to employment. No one wants to admit that data protection laws, particularly in Germany, treat subsidiary firms like third parties.

Although headquartered in Germany, SAP has a vital stake in the global orientation of companies. Eighty percent of all SAP systems operate outside Germany. Large, international enterprises and groups use SAP products. Ninety-five percent of the fifty companies with the largest revenues in Germany and throughout the world use SAP solutions.

When we deal with questions of data protection in the context of SAP systems, a national view must take a back seat. A standard system with a global orientation must meet international requirements and enable implementation of special, national regulations in special cases.

Compared to most of its American competitors, a German software manufacturer has a definite lead regarding data protection. The strong German laws on data protection at the federal and state level are part of systems development, and the influence of works councils on recording employee data (HR systems and user data) is even stronger. Implementation projects feature not only discussion on data protection between customers, consultants, and partners, but also involve works councils in decision making that affects the processing and transmission of personal data. SAP Consulting often takes on the role of a mediator when employers and employees cannot agree on questions of participation in the project, the training of shop stewards, or performance evaluations of employees.

If you follow the European trend of establishing data protection as an inalienable, fundamental right, it makes sense to treat questions of data protection against the background of internal EU regulations, particularly regarding data transfers to countries with a low level of security.

It will be interesting to see how the flood facing the information landscape puts pressure on lawmakers. The increasingly visible shareholder-value principle, the trend toward mergers and global cooperation between corporate groups, and the unstoppable growth of the internet have all placed lawmakers under tremendous pressure to act. If laws are not adjusted to the new realities, they will be interpreted in favor of companies. If they are not, then companies will move their corporate headquarters, group offices, or IT centers into countries with more favorable laws. As a result, lawmakers will have to deal closely with economic demands.

Many questions will arise that this book cannot address in detail. The book was written during a phase in which the new media force massive changes in the economy, economic areas grow ever closer together, and lawmakers find it difficult to follow the global trend. Just think of tax law to grasp how long a road must be traveled. But because Europe is oriented toward an international division of labor, third-party countries must also be linked to the economy – according to the data protection laws of the EU: fairly and legitimately.

5.2.2 Terminology

The data protection portion of this book often speaks of companies. By that word we mean legally independent private companies and public agencies. Data protection laws see individual companies in a corporate group or a group of companies as third parties. It regards an exchange of data within the group as a transfer. Data protection laws do not recognize corporate groups.

Terms such as employee, person affected, data protection officer, and so on refer to persons of both genders. If the gender has significance in a given case, we speak specifically of a gender.

A data protection officer is an employee who holds responsibility for protecting the privacy of data.

Employee representatives mean works councils, shop stewards, or other representatives, such as the employee representative on the supervisory board.

5.3 THE EUROPEAN VIEW

The EU Commission had 20 years to react to the demands of governments and the European Parliament with its EU Directive for data protection. Member countries had previously passed their own laws. Germany, for example, has had a federal law on data protection since 1977 and state laws for public agencies in each federal state. For this reason, the new EU Directive could not be created in one go. They had to take the characteristics of national laws into consideration.

At the 18th DAFTA conference in 1994, Spiros Simitis referred to the difficulties involved in creating the EU Directive on data protection. Except for the Germans, no one understood what a data protection officer was, and no one in the German delegation understood what sensitive data was (GDD Business Report p. 10 [GDD 1994]). The Germans did not want an official, strict monitoring system, but self-inspection within companies through the functions of the data protection officer.

Because the Directive seeks to even out the interests of each country, they can serve as a solid and broad foundation to discuss the data protection requirements of an SAP system.

"Directive 95/46/EC of the European Parliament and of the Council of 24 October 1995 on the protection of individuals with regard to the processing of personal data and on the free movement of such data" (EU Directive in the following) was a compromise between the EU Commission and the European Parliament. The Commission seeks to foster a free market within the EU. It regards every new legal limitation as an obstacle to the free exchange of goods. Special regulations on personal data were dismissed as equally counterproductive, along with other exceptions for marketable goods [Dammann, p. 61 (1997)].

In the end, individual governments that went their own way with data protection laws forced the Commission to act if it did not want to lose sovereignty over data protection in the EU.

After issuance of the EU Directive, the member states had three years in which to convert the directive into national law. By mid-1999, only Belgium, Finland, Greece, Italy, Portugal, and Sweden had implemented the directive fully; Denmark and the UK had done so partially. In 1999, nine EU countries received warnings: the UK, Denmark, Spain, and Austria reacted to the warnings. In January 2000, the EU Commission threatened to bring Germany, France, Luxembourg, the Netherlands, and Ireland before the European Court. According to the press, a lack of data protection is the popular reason behind the action.

Incomplete implementation occurs in the midst of efforts by the European Commission to introduce data protection provision in the US quickly – at least by individual companies if not by the government. The Americans are playing for time and refer to the incomplete implementation in Europe. The US looks toward self-regulation in the economy and wants to give companies a free hand in the collection of private data. The market will regulate itself because consumers can decide for themselves which companies they trust with their data.

When individual states join together to form a large internal market, integration of the states plays a far-reaching role. Even data protection must be seen in the context of the free exchange of goods, information, and persons. On one side of this equation, national concerns for data protection come up short. On the other side, SAP offers standard business software that encourages international exchange of goods. It is only logical that SAP considers market forces when evaluating the EU Directive. Those responsible for security and data protection must always keep an eye on the desire of the market for a free exchange of information when they evaluate security measures. This preamble is prefixed to the reasons for considering the EU Directive.

This section first examines the basic ideas behind the EU Directive that appear in the 72 preambles to its 34 articles. The next section offers a detailed study of the demands made by the directive and the options available for implementing them in an SAP system. We hope that this initially SAP-neutral overview will provide readers who are unfamiliar with data protection with some information on the European laws affecting data protection. That information is the precondition for a company to judge or implement protective measures.

5.3.1 Free enterprise (Preambles 1–6, Article 1)

Although the Directive must be understood more as a restrictive regulation, it is noteworthy that the first six preambles clearly support a free market economy. It is given as the basic precondition to improve the living conditions of members of the Community.

As this point is so important for data protection, we find it worthwhile to quote the first six preambles of the EU Directive.

(1) Whereas the objectives of the Community, as laid down in the Treaty, as amended by the Treaty on European Union, include creating an ever closer union among the peoples of Europe, fostering closer relations between the states belonging to the Community, ensuring economic and social progress by common action to eliminate the barriers which divide Europe, encouraging the constant improvement of the living conditions of its peoples, preserving and strengthening

peace and liberty and promoting democracy on the basis of the fundamental rights recognized in the constitution and laws of the Member States and in the European Convention for the Protection of Human Rights and Fundamental Freedoms;

(2) Whereas data-processing systems are designed to serve man; whereas they must, whatever the nationality or residence of natural persons, respect their fundamental rights and freedoms, notably the right to privacy, and contribute to economic and social progress, trade expansion and the well-being of individuals;

(3) Whereas the establishment and functioning of an internal market in which, in accordance with Article 7a of the Treaty, the free movement of goods, persons, services and capital is ensured require not only that personal data should be able to flow freely from one Member State to another, but also that the fundamental rights of individuals should be safeguarded;

(4) Whereas increasingly frequent recourse is being had in the Community to the processing of personal data in the various spheres of economic and social activity; whereas the progress made in information technology is making the processing and exchange of such data considerably easier;

(5) Whereas the economic and social integration resulting from the establishment and functioning of the internal market within the meaning of Article 7a of the Treaty will necessarily lead to a substantial increase in cross-border flows of personal data between all those involved in a private or public capacity in economic and social activity in the Member States; whereas the exchange of personal data between undertakings in different Member States is set to increase; whereas the national authorities in the various Member States are being called upon by virtue of Community law to collaborate and exchange personal data so as to be able to perform their duties or carry out tasks on behalf of an authority in another Member State within the context of the area without internal frontiers as constituted by the internal market;

(6) Whereas, furthermore, the increase in scientific and technical cooperation and the coordinated introduction of new telecommunications networks in the Community necessitate and facilitate cross-border flows of personal data.

As noted in section 6.1.1 in more detail, the EU Directive does not necessarily offer us protection for all personal data. Instead, it contributes to human economic and social progress by safeguarding fundamental rights – including privacy.

5.3.2 The proper level of protection within the EU (Preambles 7–13)

Up to now, the transfer of personal data within the EU could fail because of the differing levels of protection of personal freedom in individual countries. The EU Directive aims at an equal level of protection within the Community, although the member states do have some leeway in the design of their laws.

5.3.3 Data categories (Preambles 22, 33–34, Articles 6, 8)

As noted above, not all personal data can be treated the same way. For example, the protective measures and their costs can depend upon the data category.

With only a few exceptions, the EU Directive prohibits the processing of sensitive data on race, religion, politics, health, and sex life.

Those responsible for data protection within a company must carefully decide what categories of data can affect an individual's right to privacy and are therefore particularly worthy of protection. An expectation of handling all data that refers to persons in the same way would overwhelm those responsible for data protection. As we will see later, thousands of fields (such as those in a HR system) can relate to one person.

Since the literature rarely contains hints on how to separate the broad range of personal data into categories or types, Section 6.2.4 offers a possible distribution, based upon an SAP HR system.

5.3.4 Basics of data quality (Preambles 28–29, Article 6)

Article 6 treats the principles of data quantity.

Article 6

1. Member States shall provide that personal data must be:

(a) processed fairly and lawfully;
(b) collected for specified, explicit and legitimate purposes and not further processed in a way incompatible with those purposes. Further processing of data for historical, statistical or scientific purposes shall not be considered as incompatible provided that Member States provide appropriate safeguards;
(c) adequate, relevant and not excessive in relation to the purposes for which they are collected and/or further processed;
(d) accurate and, where necessary, kept up to date; every reasonable step must be taken to ensure that data which are inaccurate or incomplete, having regard to the purposes for which they were collected or for which they are further processed, are erased or rectified;
(e) kept in a form which permits identification of data subjects for no longer than is necessary for the purposes for which the data were collected or for which they are further processed. Member States shall lay down appropriate safeguards for personal data stored for longer periods for historical, statistical or scientific use.
2. It shall be for the controller to ensure that paragraph 1 is complied with.

Processing must be fair and lawful, it must be performed for a specific purpose, and may not occur for any other purpose. The data must be current and correct; otherwise it must be deleted or corrected. After the purpose for which the data was collected has been realized, the data must be deleted or made anonymous.

5.3.5 Responsibilities, rights, and obligations (Preambles 18–21, 25 and Articles 4–6)

Responsibility toward subjects must always be maintained. The laws of Member States apply in the countries where data is processed. Processing in a third country requires measures to ensure that the rights and obligations laid down in the EU Directive are also maintained there.

Those dealing with data in member states have the following responsibilities:

- guarantee of data quality
- provision of technical security
- notification at control points
- maintenance of the requirements for processing.

The subjects of the data being processed have the following rights:

- information on the processing involved
- an opportunity to access the data
- an opportunity to rectify the data
- an opportunity to raise an objection to the processing.

5.3.6 Validity in law (Preambles 30–33 and Articles 7–9)

The basic principles of data quality indicate that personal data is processed in a legal manner and collected for clearly defined and legal purposes.

Validity in law requires the express consent of the data subject, the conclusion of a contract or legal requirement, vital interests of the data subject or for tasks related to the public interest.

5.3.7 Information on the data subject (Preambles 38–45 and Articles 10–12, 14–15)

Data subjects must always remain masters of their own data. They must always know who is processing their data. They must be informed if personal information is being transmitted to a third party.

All persons have a right to information, particularly the ability to verify the accuracy of the data and lawfulness of the processing. As noted in Art. 6, data subjects have the right to dispute and rectify data. They can lodge a complaint against processing and demand the rectification, erasure, or blockage of incorrect data.

5.3.8 Appropriateness of measures (Preamble 46 and Articles 16–17)

The EU Directive mirrors the appropriateness of measures found in German law. Rectification, erasure, or blockage of data is to occur even for data transmitted to third parties, unless doing so proves impossible or involves disproportionate efforts (Art. 12c).

Technical and managerial measures must be taken to protect the rights and freedoms of the persons involved. Germans know these as the Ten Commandments of information processing.

Security measures need not be infinite: they must be appropriate and dependent upon the following criteria:

- level of technology
- costs associated with the measures
- risk of processing
- the type of data to be protected.

5.3.9 Disclosure and advance control (Preambles 48–54 and Articles 18–21)

Notification should disclose the purpose of the processing.

The French, who are used to centralization, prefer a general obligation of companies to notify a government agency. The Germans regard that approach as unenforceable bureaucracy and prefer the self-regulation of the market. But the German approach is not uncontrolled, as it is in the US Instead, it requires hiring a data protection officer in companies of a specific size. The data protection officer reports directly to management and exercises the tasks involved completely independently.

Notification must be made to a public agency or to the data protection officer, before any processing occurs.

A disclosure notification must contain the following information:

- name and address of the person responsible
- purpose of the processing
- description of the data subjects and categories of data
- recipients of the transmission
- planned transmission to third countries
- description of the security measures (does not apply if a data protection officer has been appointed).

The EU Directive lets member states choose between the two forms.

5.3.10 Supervisory authorities and investigations (Preambles 55, 62–66 and Articles 28–30)

If the rights of data subjects are violated, national law must create the opportunity for an investigation. Sanctions must be available as a remedy for any damage created by illegal processing.

Independent public supervisory agencies in each member state must have the means and rights they need to inspect, investigate, and initiate legal proceedings. All agencies in the EU must assist each other to ensure that the protection rules apply throughout the EU. All individuals can turn to the supervisory agency to protect their rights.

Individual member states must establish their own data protection groups to advise the Commission and ensure that the requirements of the Directive find uniform implementation. Group 29, named after Article 29, is the most familiar of these groups because of its working papers, especially its recommendations on the transfer of personal data to third countries.

5.3.11 Appropriate level of protection in third countries (Preambles 56–61 and Articles 25–26)

Once again, the Directive emphasizes that cross-border traffic in personal data is necessary for international commerce. The protection guaranteed in the EU does not hinder transmission of data to other countries that show evidence of an appropriate level of protection.

If the third country does not have an appropriate level of protection, transmission is prohibited.

The following are exceptions:

- the data subject unambiguously agrees with the transfer
- fulfillment of a contractual relationship between the processor and the data subject
- maintenance of public interests, such as taxes, duties, and social security
- special measures indicate proper security, particularly clauses in contracts or codes of conduct.

5.3.12 Liability and sanctions (Preamble 55 and Articles 22–24)

If the rights of a data subject are violated, restitution must be made for any damage caused by prohibited processing. Those responsible for processing can be freed of liability if they can show that the damage arises from another party, particularly by misbehavior of the data subject or actions by a higher authority.

Member states are to specify sanctions that apply to violations.

5.4 CORPORATE CULTURE

To arrive at the best form of practical data protection in a company, you must first examine the relationships between people in the company, with partners and with customers. The living corporate culture indicates the value placed on privacy and how the company will deal with the personal data of employees and customers. If employees can ignore any sense of responsibility and care, then simple, internal measures for data protection will be insufficient to guarantee the company's adherence to data protection laws.

The attitude in the company is an important contribution to human capital. Besides ability and creativity, loyalty, motivation, team spirit, and identification with the company are a firm's most important factors for success. The attitudes of employees and management and their relationships with each other indicate if the firm must order data protection from above by decree and monitor it closely, or if it can rely on self-responsibility and gentle pressure.

Consider the answers to the following questions.

- Is there an open exchange of information, independent of hierarchies and departments?

- Are the employees teachable and ready to learn and master new technologies?

- Does management trust employees and foster the individuality of each one?

- Can employees work as a team?

- Do employees practice ongoing knowledge transfer?

- Are employees used to taking on responsibility?

- Are partners treated fairly?

5.5 GUIDELINES FOR DATA PROTECTION

We would like to supplement the general guidelines on security made at the beginning of the book with some special considerations for data protection.

These guidelines depend to some extent upon the preambles to the EU Directive, but also summarize lessons learned by experience in the area of data protection.

- Improving economic conditions by respecting basic rights

   Borrowing from the demands made by the EU Directive, SAP products must also contribute to social and economic advancement and an increased quality of life. The free exchange of goods, persons, and information across all borders is the precondition for achieving this goal.

   This free movement can be achieved only when the basic rights of each individual are respected. Whether they be citizens, contractual partners, or other data subjects, all individuals must be able to assume that the authorities are storing and processing their data operate fairly, in accordance with their stated purpose, and according to law.

■ The challenge of innovation in IT

The rapid development of the Information Society must not become a specter for individual groups of persons. Progress must be mastered, and innovators must be able to transfer their expert knowledge credibly. The mastery of new developments and transparency for those affected are preconditions for their acceptance.

Quality, reliability, availability, security, and good documentation may not take a back seat to functionality.

At the same time, lawmakers must adjust to the new context dynamically and close to the fact. They need not regulate everything with laws: most responsible persons will gladly accept guidelines and practical hints on security and data protection. Laws should be building blocks that are valid from one generation to the next. Software development, however, runs through several, often contradictory change cycles before it is ready for the market. And even then it must be able to react flexibly and quickly to the changes in the market and in law.

■ Rights and obligations of those responsible

One person can hardly gain an overview or master the overall scope of modern IT. The board of directors and those responsible for data protection and security must delegate individual tasks and responsibilities.

When tasks are delegated, rights and obligations must be clearly defined for all those involved. Those responsible have taken on positions of trust: they must also be reliable, loyal, and beyond reproach.

Particularly in the area of administration, those delegating responsibility must know that administrators have many rights and authorizations to execute their tasks. Both system and R/3 administrators, as well as developers, can manipulate an application or system. The only help here comes from a division of labor and responsibility or strict monitoring.

■ Dealing fairly with employees and customers

Anyone who wants to retain customers and employees over the long term must deal with them fairly, as partners. As stated by the European Council in 1981 and repeated in Article 6 of the EU Directive, personal data must be processed fairly. Here, too, reliability, trust, and lawfulness are the guidelines. Partnership means give and take. Dealing with the available data fairly, whether it be confidential or personal, must be self-evident.

■ Data protection must be managed

When performing their tasks, data protection officers are not bound to any directives and they are often unable to issue directives. They are single combatants and not specialists in every area.

The law primarily demands juridical and organizational stability for such persons. Nonetheless, a certain amount of programming and system administration knowledge is essential to deal with system administrators and to hold one's own with application specialists.

Data protection officers must manage data protection. That means not only delegating responsibility to administrators, system specialists, and application specialists, but also coordinating certain tasks with other departments or even letting other departments (security, human resources, legal, training, and internal auditing, for example) perform the tasks.

Responsibility for weighing interests

Companies and those responsible for data protection have a great deal of responsibility when dealing with personal data. They must decide which data is stored and processed, and who, inside and outside the company, may receive the data. In some unclear cases, various interests must be weighed.

A German law requires weighing the interests of the processor or a third party against the protection rights of the data subjects (§ 28 BDSG). Article 7 of the EU Directive also gives companies the opportunity to weigh the interests of data subjects and to consider their basic rights and freedoms.

According to Article 9, reconciliation must be reached between the right to privacy and the right to freedom of expression for personal data used in journalistic, artistic, or literary purposes.

Company management must also find the right balance between its goal of maximum progress and growth, respect for basic rights, and the social responsibility of companies demanded by politicians and unions.

Limited data

Everyone should adopt a basic approach of storing only as much personal data as required and as little of it as possible.

The potential danger of misusing protected data increases with every technical advance in IT. Capacity bottlenecks used to force programmers to handle every bit and byte of data parsimoniously. Today's storage media have an almost infinite capacity and quick processing times. Previously inconceivable amounts of data can be stored online or quickly accessed from an archive. The technical need to delete superfluous data no longer exists.

Data warehouse systems collect data from varied applications in a network and sometimes even supplement that data with information from public databases. The ostensible goal is to provide management with the links to the information it needs to run the company successfully.

The requirement of data protection laws regarding the linking of data collection to a specific purpose may well be ignored.

- Project work

  The decisive settings for data protection and security arise during an implementation project for an SAP system. Poor planning, unfamiliarity with new technology, and unrealistic expectations can delay or destroy a project.

  If the project simply forgets to deal with the responsible instance in the company for personal data, uncomfortable delays can occur when the system is scheduled to go into production. In Germany, for example, elected employee representatives have more rights than data protection officers and security experts to sanction violations of law.

  From the very beginning, a project must involve employee representatives, data protection officers, and security experts. It must inform and train them to exercise their authority responsibly.

## CHAPTER 6

Data protection law

SECURE DATA COMMUNICATION

This chapter treats the demands of the market for the free, international exchange of information. This freedom can exist only when all countries require and maintain a uniform level of legal protection.

6.1.1 Open borders in the European market

As noted in section 5.3, the introductory preambles to the EU Directive place the human person and human welfare at the center of its concerns. A free market and the unrestrained exchange of goods, persons, and information are preconditions for economic and social prosperity. The EU emphasizes the advantages of continuing internationalization along with innovative information technology for the common market. The Directive on data protection must be seen against this background.

6.1.1.1 Context

The document mentions the context for the free exchange of goods and information almost parenthetically:

- to maintain peace and freedom
- to advocate democracy
- to protect fundamental rights and maintain the rights of the human person
- IT must respect fundamental rights and freedoms, particularly the right to privacy.

To secure long-lasting peace, freedom, and prosperity, Europe needs an economic area without borders and restrictions, an area about as large as the United States. This freedom should also apply to personal data. National or egotistical limitations on data transfer must be repealed within the Community and shifted to a common border for the Community as a whole.

6.1.1.2 Sticking with old habits

Countries with a long internal history of data protection, such as Germany and France, find it difficult to implement these principles. Why do we have to walk away from previously successful policies? Why can't we just keep to the course we're already on? Of course, these questions assume that first-class data protection works because of first-class laws and compliance.

Both Germany and France have a long tradition of data protection, albeit with very different approaches. The question revolves around central monitoring or self-regulation. These countries, in particular, have found it difficult to bring their traditional methods in line with the EU Directive.

As world leaders in exports, the Germans are particularly dependent upon their competitiveness in international commerce for goods, services, and information. All the more reason to wonder why they did not gratefully implement the EU Directive immediately and become the first champion of free and secure information transfer. Instead, they used a two-phase approach. Only the second phase included a revision of the Federal Law on Data Protection (BDSG according to its German abbreviation). The first phase, threatened with EU sanctions, will deal only with the most necessary changes to the BDSG, and will occur in 2001.

6.1.1.3 Free movement of data exchange in the EU

Let's return to the free movement of data in the European Union. According to Dammann, there was a reason for adding the phrase "free movement" to the title of the Directive. The Directive does not deal exclusively with data protection, but also strives to strike a balance between data protection and the free movement of data that is so eminently important for the single market (Dammann, pp. 66–67, 1997).

Article 1, section 2 of the Directive strengthens this interpretation, as it expressly emphasizes that data protection cannot serve as an argument for limiting the exchange of personal data within the Community.

Article 1 of the EU Directive reads as follows:

1. In accordance with this Directive, Member States shall protect the fundamental rights and freedoms of natural persons, and in particular their right to privacy with respect to the processing of personal data.

2. Member States shall neither restrict nor prohibit the free flow of personal data between Member States for reasons connected with the protection afforded under paragraph 1.

In other words, laws that implement data protection may not prohibit the exchange of personal information in general or between nations. Instead, the law must weigh the interests of the company that processes the information against the interests of the persons involved. Even by way of example, laws, regulations, or interpretations cannot reflect this comparison from an external source to public agencies or to companies. It demands that decision makers operate with the highest possible levels of responsibility and farsightedness.

Companies in the Member States play the decisive role in all these considerations. They perform a part of the processing at their own cost and risk.

Companies do more than provide employment. They are also the basis that enables free commerce to function in an open market. They must adjust to market forces, recognize risks and opportunities, and realize their very best. They do not desire strict regulations on the movement of personal data.

6.1.1.4 Classic free market economy

To understand the demands of the market better, we must turn to Adam Smith. The father of national economics, Smith pleaded for free markets more than 200 years ago in an attempt to free England from the tightly regulated economy of an absolute state. According to Smith, the distribution of resources by the state must give way to a free market economy; state paternalism of individual participants in the market will no longer be tolerated. Smith saw an international division of labor as the foundation of economic development and social prosperity.

The theory states that the common good is better served when people follow their own, individual interests, than it would be when the common good itself is the original goal.

In Smith's view, everyone should act according to the principles of maximizing profit. The state guarantees liberal order by not creating barriers and restrictions and by removing those that already exist as quickly as possible. The loser in this competition between the strong and the weak is at fault and cannot blame anyone else. Many people today still share the view of the English poverty laws of that period: poverty is the just punishment for laziness and unemployment should be made as uncomfortable as possible.

6.1.1.5 Social market economy

The social component of a free market economy was developed much later and is noted in the EU Directive. Technological progress and economic prosperity contribute to social well-being when the state avoids creating conditions that limit efficiency. The left-leaning political parties are also redefining a social market economy today. In their view, the state should no longer provide security for all social risks, but guide people toward self-responsibility. A strong economy is the precondition for social justice.

The economic growth of the 1990s in the US is a result of liberalized commerce. Domestic manufacturers and the labor market benefit from increased competitiveness. In a continuing distribution process, it's much easier to distribute pieces of a dynamically growing cake than it is to benefit one group at the expense of another in a weak economy.

6.1.1.6 Self-responsibility and innovation among employees

A modern company must place the human person, the employee, in the center. Employees are part of the company, a part that promotes innovation and progress – even with their personal data.

To develop new ideas, the almost infinite knowledge stored in the minds of employees must be coordinated and made available to the company as corporate knowledge. The use of new technology influences the growth of a political economy much more strongly than capital and labor. Technologies are themselves the product of good ideas, new discoveries, and the implementation of knowledge (Wildemann, 1999).

Companies must adopt the model of a learning company and display interest in the systematic evaluation and targeted sharing of the available knowledge. Employees contribute in two ways. They make their data available and recognize important information and ideas in the material available. In a well-functioning communications network, individual employees must help to ensure that information gets to decision makers, who then recognize and interpret it properly.

Employee self-responsibility plays a crucial role here. It directs the intensity of the regulations and controls implemented by the company. An ideologically created lust for regulation can create a context that hinders performance among employees and for the company as a whole. Non-lawyers – in most cases those responsible for a company – see an incomprehensible forest of laws, regulations, legal opinions, guidelines, and rules.

But what good is a plethora of regulations in the area of data protection when those affected by them are unaware of them or do not understand them? What's the benefit when short-staffing in supervisory authorities makes it impossible to monitor compliance? Nor can a company police itself if it does not create a position that holds responsibility for security and data protection or simply uses the position as a cover to protect itself.

6.1.1.7 The current challenge

In the internet age, companies and their employees no longer have a problem getting information. The amount of information available is growing both qualitatively and quantitatively, so that no one really has an overview of it any longer. It has become increasingly difficult to see what affects one personally and to recognize its importance. The current challenge is to differentiate important from unimportant information, and therefore to create optimal structures and filters in internal networks. The options here include using employees as information brokers, intelligent systems that filter the information available, or in-house search engines tailored to a company's needs.

But all these rapid developments in mass communications must not leave behind the confidentiality of the information exchanged. All the more so because individual networks coalesce, and private and public communications run along the same routes. All sorts of different service providers, each strongly competing with the others, offer the routes and are primarily interested in profit. A company cannot decide upon a provider solely because of a low price. It must also consider security criteria: validity, confidentiality, completeness, and the ability to identify the source.

6.1.1.8 Contractual partnership

A thoughtless transfer of the rules governing the relationship of government to citizens to the relationship between companies and their contractual partners does not recognize that the close relationship of the latter works toward a common good. It is to be expected that both parties cooperate mutually. In an environment of global suppliers and customers, only partnerships can lead to a competitive position. The rules of fairness, trust, reliability, and mutual respect must apply here. The rules are the precondition for the success and quality of long-term cooperation. The companies involved in a partnership must regard all partner data as an economically important good that they must maintain in confidence and protect. In most cases, however, only important business data is captured; purely private data remains taboo.

6.1.1.9 Non-contractual relationship

In addition to the differentiation between the relationships of government to citizens and companies and contractual partners, a differentiation must be drawn for the relationship between a company and a private person when no contract between them exists. These companies are subject to registration in Germany, and not without reason. They include address brokers; information services; detectives; warning services; credit information services; market, opinion, and social research institutes; and telemarketing companies (Bergmann et al, RdNr. 41–43 on § 27).

These companies collect and transmit high-quality business and personal data to interested parties. The value of personal information depends upon the level of categorization. In particular, private data, such as income, property, shopping patterns, family structure, mobility, leisure-time activities, and so on, can be combined into a comprehensive pattern of behavior.

Those affected usually know nothing of these one-sided relationships. They also remain ignorant of how it is stored and evaluated, merged with other material, and transmitted to other unknown parties. The right to informational self-determination is often ignored in many cases. The full scope of the prescriptions for data protection must be applied and implemented here. Those affected must be informed about the use of their data. Companies must ask for clear permission and they must provide information on the scope of the data they store, who is authorized to access it, who receives it, what it's being used for, and how they can correct it.

6.1.2 Relationships to third parties

The internet will radically change the traditional business model of suppliers and customers. Individual companies will no longer add value exclusively, but do so in a community of kindred spirits: business partners and competitors. To bring profitability in international business to the level desired by investors, companies can supplement mergers, friendly takeovers, and unfriendly takeovers with common purchasing, production, and sales.

In this approach, application processes are distributed and run over a network. The location and country of the system are immaterial to the company.

And personal data will also cross company borders. Customer data and some personal data will be exchanged with third parties among corporate groups and within partnerships. As is typical in a network of networks, those affected will enjoy neither transparency nor security regarding the transportation paths involved.

6.1.2.1 Conflict of interest in healthcare

Healthcare will also experience strong pressure to win the race against space and time. Close cooperation can offer improved chances for recovery in cancer treatment, for example. University clinics, research institutes, hospitals, and medical practices are already joined into competence networks. Nonetheless, Article 8 of the EU Directive specifically prohibits the processing of healthcare-related data. Yet, if the subject gives specific approval or the situation involves life-threatening interests, the EU prohibition has no force.

The example of healthcare illustrates the dilemma for legislation on data protection. On the one hand, the law wishes to limit the storage of personal data to a minimum and its transfer to third parties outside the company. Those with access rights to the data should also be limited, the rights themselves should be minimal and limited to one's own patients, and, in the best case, every change to a data record (or even field) should be logged. Spain and Denmark insisted on these special development requests.

On the other hand, those with access to such data belong to a group that enjoys high confidence among the general population. They are also subject to medical non-disclosure and privilege.

To maintain life and health, the medical industry must have an optimal information structure. It must be able to exchange patient data completely and directly among the different parties responsible for a patient. When the person responsible changes during treatment, there must be an opportunity for immediate access. An emergency patient would have little understanding of the need to jump bureaucratic hurdles for the sake of data protection laws.

Although clear, irreversible procedures to make the data anonymous are recommended before any data transfer occurs, doing so can be difficult in many cases. Experts must often have access to specific information about an individual person: birth date, place of birth, medical history, and blood group.

Here too, the responsible parties must act in accordance with the law, but they must also act according to common sense, or responsibly. Employees and their own sense of responsibility should also be respected.

6.1.2.2 Transfer within a corporate group

All monitoring of adherence to data protection laws and regulations must recognize that companies and corporate groups guard their own employee and customer data as a corporate secret – in their own self-interest. The data represents a substantial amount of revenue and its disclosure to external parties could lead to significant material and immaterial losses. Global groups often require transfer of data within the group for specific purposes. Self-regulation enables a company to guard personal data as a corporate treasure and decide for itself if employee data improves information exchange within the company or if it can be offered to customers after discussions with employees. In this case, those responsible for data protection must coordinate the interests of the company and the employee, and consider the appropriate provisions of the labor contract regarding the protection of personal data.

The provisions of existing data protection laws regard independent parts of a corporate group as third parties, which makes transfer of data within the group rather difficult. As early as 1992, European business associations requested a better definition of third parties in the second draft of the EU Directive and for an exception to be made for transfer within a corporate group. Such an exception is needed to satisfy the economy's need for the free exchange of information (Schleutermann, 1995).

The special needs of corporate groups still remain unfulfilled.

6.1.2.3 Virtual economic area

The mySAP.com e-business platform presents a new, virtual economic area or market on the internet to foster integrated collaboration in the economy. Processes that used to consist of several transactions handled by disparate companies will be handled in the future in one step over the internet and the mySAP Marketplace. SAP customers can form economic communities and become business partners. This approach could create a huge community of 12,000 companies and over 100 million people.

See section 4.5 for a treatment of security in the mySAP Marketplace.

6.1.3 Data exchange with third countries

Placing the highest regard upon a free market and human prosperity creates a bridge to the attitude toward data protection in the US. *See* section 6.6.3 for a discussion of third countries outside the EU. That section uses the US as an example.

6.1.4 Rights and obligations during the transfer of data

Even companies have the right to work with data of the contractual partners (such as employees and customers) as long as their rights to privacy are not violated. The data stored in an SAP system overwhelmingly consists of business contact information for customers or vendors, and data for employee management or for fulfilling legal requirements, such as the calculation or payment of benefits. Data that applies to evaluations of employees (whether collected for this purpose or garnered from use of the system) is subject to co-determination by management and employees. The labor contract, employee representatives, and the human resources department regulate the use of such data. A well-run company ensures that this information is never and cannot be abused.

A free market not only grants rights to, but also demands responsibilities from those involved. These duties include the observance of governmental limitations, issued as laws, regulations, guidelines, and so on, to protect individual companies or persons or to regulate the market.

Naturally, the free market has its limits, especially when some basic preconditions are missing, such as complete market transparency and legally equal and independent participants. Just imagine a situation in which anyone could open a medical practice, in the belief that the market would ultimately sort out the bad doctors. Even liberalized approaches still foresee some regulation that guarantees and fosters human prosperity.

Restrictions for data protection help to protect fundamental rights, particularly the right to privacy. But laws can cover only general guidelines.

The highest responsibility remains with a company, which must undertake the detailed work. If a company processes and transmits personal data, responsibility within the firm plays a leading role.

6.1.5 Appropriate level of protection

Current legislation permits the transfer of personal data to a third country (still within the EU) only when the data enjoys as much protection in the target country as it does in the originating country. The EU Directive aims at creating a uniform level of protection in the Community. Once this has been achieved, all the countries in the EU could be regarded as one country, and there would be no problem in transmitting personal data between them.

Transfers to third countries that cannot guarantee the corresponding level of protection are not permitted. The EU Commission is charged with categorizing these countries, with creating black and white lists. Companies can enter into contracts with third parties that guarantee protection. This provision applies especially to transfers within a corporate group.

Note that the Directive does not generally speak of the creation of a comparable level of protection for personal data, but for the protection of privacy:

- protection of the rights and freedoms of natural persons, especially of privacy (Preambles 7, 9, and 11)
- protection of human rights and basic freedoms and the right to privacy recognized as a fundamental right in EU law (Preamble 10).

Categorization of data is a basic precondition to mastering the different types of data in standard software. This requirement must be observed when checking the reliability, legality, and purpose of data, authorizations, and any required protective measures.

See section 6.2.4 for a more detailed discussion of categorizing data.

6.2   LEGALITY OF PROCESSING

The primary topics of this section include the legality of processing, the right of each person to self-determination, the basics of data protection, and the need to categorize personal data.

6.2.1 Permission

Any processing of personal data must proceed according to law. According to Article 7 of the EU Directive, the legality of processing is present when the following preconditions are met.

- The data subject has unambiguously given consent.
- Processing is necessary for the performance of a contract to which the data subject is party or in order to take steps at the request of the data subject prior to entering into a contract.
- Processing is necessary for compliance with a legal obligation to which the controller is subject.
- Processing is necessary in order to protect the vital interests of the data subject.

- Processing is necessary for the performance of a task carried out in the public interest or in the exercise of official authority vested in the controller or in a third party to whom the data are disclosed.

- Processing is necessary for the purposes of the legitimate interests pursued by the controller or by the third party or parties to whom the data are disclosed, except where such interests are overridden by the interests for fundamental rights and freedoms of the data subject which require protection under Article 1 (1).

These requirements correspond to those of German legislation.

6.2.2 Right to informational self-determination

The literature offers a rich reservoir of opinions on balancing the valid interests of the processor and the protective interests of the data subject. Some regard the comparison as giving free, unbridled permission for data transfers; others state that the company must be on the edge of ruin before its interests can take precedence over the interests of an employee.

As noted, one goal of the EU Directive is to foster the free exchange of goods and information, even personal information, within the Community while protecting fundamental rights. This fundamental approach makes the decision of the German Federal Constitutional Court regarding census data rather relative. That decision formulates the right to informational self-determination: each individual has the right to determine the exposure and use of personal data.

The EU wants to include the right to data protection in the EU Charter of fundamental rights since the constitutions of some member states already contain it or because courts have recognized it [WP-26].

A German court decision about the proper use of census data illustrates the relationship of a state to its citizens. This relationship differs from that of contractual partners as is typical in a free market and in the use of standard business software such as SAP systems. Private business demands additional clarifications. Does the contractual relationship between a company and an employee mean that the company may process personal data without any additional permission? Does the lack of a direct contract mean that a company may collect personal data without the subjects knowing about it explicitly?

In the latter case, German law requires registration. Germany registers and monitors companies in the business of storing data for later transfer or that process data as service providers. These firms include address brokers and service, outsourcing, marketing, and advertising companies.

We believe that the person responsible for data protection plays a crucial role in weighing the valid interests of processors and the data protection interests of data subjects. To guarantee the ability of a company to protect data, that person must make the necessary decisions. That person must weigh each side's interests neutrally and contact representatives of both groups when dealing with global questions. Those affected –

both management and supervisory authorities – must also accept, respect, and implement the decision. The position can be strengthened only in this manner. The person responsible for data protection in a company must have the authority to implement decisions throughout the company or else become a meaningless figure in the firm who simply appears to perform a task.

To weigh the interests of two or more parties, the following questions should be clarified in advance.

- What are the interests of the processing company?
- What data protection interests does the data subject have?
- Should the data be available to a specific group, company, or division within a corporate group?
- Is there a contractual relationship between the parties?
- Does the contract regulate processing and transfer?
- Did the subjects submit the data personally?
- Have the subjects been informed about storage, processing, and transfer?
- What categories of data have been stored for this purpose?
- Have the appropriate protective measures been taken to protect the interests of the subjects?
- Are there comparable guarantees in third countries if data is to be transmitted there?

6.2.3 User data

Users of any software system leave considerable traces of user data. The database can do more than re-create integrated entries from documents or logs. A system can also store and evaluate accounting information on transactions, the date and time of entry, the time taken to enter the data, the number of peripheral inputs and outputs, and the number of printed lines.

Normally, accounting information is needed to calculate costs, and should not permit references to individual persons. But, if a user has a unique account number, all data can be related to that person.

If an employee is informed in advance, labor contracts permit recording employee data, even to monitor performance and behavior, in agreement with representatives of the works council.

6.2.4 Data categories

Not all personal data can be handled in the same manner: the need for specific protective measures depends to a large extent upon the category of data. The security and protective measures taken for day-to-day communications differ from those required for extremely confidential or private data.

The business data (telephone, e-mail, mail drops, and areas of responsibility) needed for optimal internal operations in a company are stored and must be available to all employees. Optimal access to the right information can be a tremendous advantage when making decisions. Global companies also need to have up-to-date and available information from all companies within the group. In many cases they need to make specific data available to current and potential customers as a guarantee of optimal service.

This kind of data is treated openly in companies. The parties involved expect that they can trust the data. As do the subjects, the parties require that the data is correct and current and does not exceed the use for which it was collected. They expect it to be used fairly, explicitly, adequately, and not excessively (*see* section 6.2.5 on data quality for a discussion of these terms). Modern employee self-service systems allow subjects to maintain and monitor their own data. In this case, modern technology supports data protection: subjects remain masters of their own data and decide for themselves what information is stored and transmitted. They are informed of the use of their data and are responsible for its correctness and currency.

We need to draw a clear distinction between business data and private data.

Business data is used for business purposes. It may depend upon a particular person, but is not related to a person's privacy. As used in legislation, the term personal data does not make the jobs of those responsible any easier. In actual practice, they must decide what categories of data might affect a person's privacy and therefore need special protective measures. Handling all the data that relates to a person in the same way would far exceed the capacity of those responsible for data protection.

6.2.4.1 Definition of personal data

Article 2 of the EU Directive defines personal data very generally:

> "Personal data" shall mean any information relating to an identified or identifiable natural person ("data subject"); an identifiable person is one who can be identified, directly or indirectly, in particular by reference to an identification number or to one or more factors specific to his physical, physiological, mental, economic, cultural or social identity.

Article 25 of the EU Directive refers to the type of data when it treats the transfer of personal data to third countries:

> The adequacy of the level of protection afforded by a third country shall be assessed in the light of all the circumstances surrounding a data transfer operation or set of data transfer operations; particular consideration shall be given to the nature of the data, the purpose and duration of the proposed processing operation or operations, the country of origin and country of final destination, the rules of law, both general and sectoral, in force in the third country in question

and the professional rules and security measures which are complied with in that country.

Working Paper 12 recommends measures for sensitive data:

> If sensitive data in the sense of Article 8 is involved, additional security measures are required: the data subject must agree explicitly to processing [WP-12, chap. 1]

6.2.4.2 Sensitive data

Article 8, section 1 grants special protection to sensitive data. Processing is essentially forbidden: the following quotation lists a series of exceptions. Member Sates might see exceptions for important public interests. Regulatory agencies are responsible for processing criminal acts. Data that can negatively affect a person's fundamental rights or privacy (because of its nature) may not be processed without the subject's express permission.

> Member States shall prohibit the processing of personal data revealing racial or ethnic origin, political opinions, religious or philosophical beliefs, trade union membership, and the processing of data concerning health or sex life.

6.2.4.3 Privacy as a special goal of protection

Article 1, section 1 of the EU Directive highlights the aim of data protection to secure fundamental rights and freedoms. Protection of privacy is highlighted here.

> In accordance with this Directive, Member States shall protect the fundamental rights and freedoms of natural persons, and in particular their right to privacy with respect to the processing of personal data.

6.2.4.4 Privacy as an essential, fundamental right

Full-page advertisements for a private bank in Geneva stress Swiss know-how and the structures it has put in place to guarantee privacy as the locus of independence and self-responsibility. Privacy is regarded as an essential and fundamental right.

> Privacy is as important for human beings as oxygen is for nature.

These comments indicate that we cannot reasonably implement data protection in business without categorizing the data. We cannot equate data for business communications with highly sensitive personal data and institute the same protective measures for each. In addition to a company's self-interest in protecting its data, the EU Directive also requires technical and organizational measures to protect data and prevent unlawful processing (Article 17). The effort required here should be in relation to the stated protective goal. The measures taken must form part of the company's security concept and be directed toward the sense of quality in the company and among the subjects.

We often hear demands for the registration of all data (in individual systems) that have any relation at all to a person. This usually involves human resources data related to an employee number: several thousand fields in hundreds of tables. The file register produced from such a source would not provide the overview required by the BDSG: it would simply offer a huge amount of incompressible data that is rarely up to date. *See* section 7.3 for a discussion of tools for data analysis.

Those responsible for data protection must also consider categorizing data when it moves across borders.

Borders between business and personal data are fluid, depending upon the company and the laws of each country. We recommend involving employees or their representative in the process that decides which data belongs to which category. A consensus on the categories and company-wide communication on how the data is handled nips any mistrust and fault-finding in the bud.

Technical

A working group of the German Association for Data Protection and Data Security (GDD) and SAP have developed four categories of employee data. To understand the categories better, we present the following tables from Human Resources (infotypes) in an R/3 System. The borders are not static between various companies. Competent authority in each firm should make the appropriate determinations and communicate its decisions understandably.

We are convinced that only the differentiation of data gives those responsible for data protection the opportunity to introduce specific security measures to achieve an appropriate level of security for each type of data.

You can use the ABAP Dictionary to determine the individual fields from tables. *See* Chapter 7 for additional information. Figure 6.1 illustrates an excerpt of infotype 0002, personal data.

Employee-related data for business communication

This data appears in a company address book. It is frequently stored electronically and the subjects maintain the data themselves. Corporate groups usually offer the data to a group of companies. The data is linked to individual employees, but is also part of the working utilities of the company, so it is also linked to the company. The corporate culture and level of open communication in a company might well consider salary part of this category. Other firms would be horrified at that idea.

This data needs a low level of protection. Abuse causes relatively little nuisance to the subject.

HR infotypes also contain organizational data (Table 6.1).

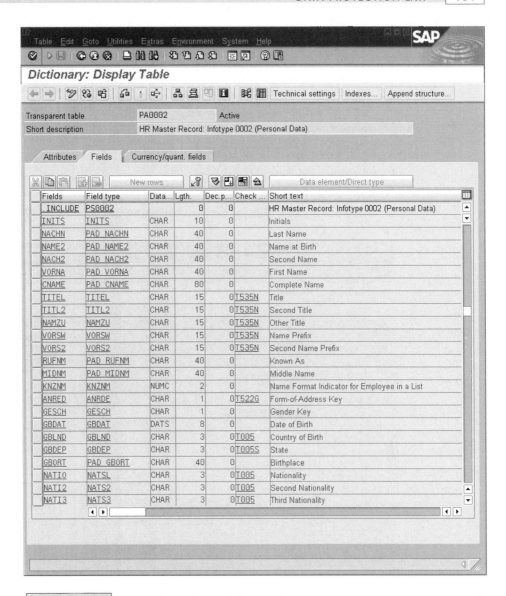

FIGURE 6.1   Sample fields from infotype 0002 (Copyright © SAP AG)

TABLE 6.1   Business contact information

Description	Infotype	Fields
Organizational assignment	0001	Organization, business area, and cost center
Personal data	0002	Name

Business contact information is usually maintained in address books. In SAP R/3, central address management stores the data in its own tables. All applications can use the data; system users maintain the data with transaction su3. Each employee decides which of the following data is available in the system for communication:

- salutation, family name, given name, and academic title

- position and department

- telephone number, fax number, and e-mail address

- building, floor, and room number

- company address and mail drop

- telephone and fax number for the administrative support group.

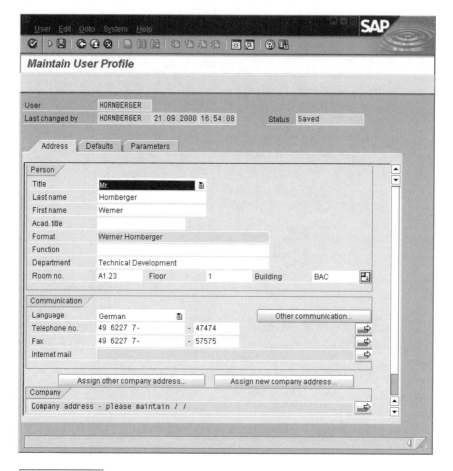

FIGURE 6.2 Maintenance of user data with transaction su3 (Copyright © SAP AG)

Personal business data

This data (Table 6.2) is related to the company, which must store it. The data is needed in many cases to implement legal requirements of contractual obligations. This data should not be transferred without permission of the subject.

TABLE 6.2	Personal business data	
Description	**Infotype**	**Fields**
Organizational assignment	0001	Position, job
Leave entitlement	0005	Start, end...entitlement accounted
Addresses	0006	Distance in kilometers
Planned working time	0007	Hours, days...employment percentage
Basic pay	0008	Payscale group, currency key, wage type...unit of time/measurement
Bank details	0009	Bank key, account number...check digit
Capital formation	0010	Amount, payment date...account number
Fiscal data (Germany)	0012	Tax card, tax class...persona; exemption
Education	0022	Branch of studies, duration, course fees...certificate
Qualifications	0024	Qualification key...proficiency
Appraisals	0025	Name of appraiser, date, criterion...affects remuneration
Workers' compensation	0029	Name of association...hazard pay position
Corporate functions	0034	Function...start date
Company instructions	0035	Instructions...date
Insurance	0037	Type, number, total, rate...premium
Company loans	0045	Interest rate, annuity installment...exemption for interest rate advantage
Maternity protection	0080	Expected/actual date of delivery
Military service	0081	Service type, date, unit...rank
Garnishment/Cession – D (to 0117)	0111	Type, status, repayment, court/official authority...creditor

A sample of infotypes outside of Germany is given in Table 6.3.

Private data

This data is private to employees: it is unrelated to the employer. It can be required to communicate with an employee at home or reach relatives in case of emergency. Some of this information is available publicly.

Much of this information is made available to a limited group of staff in service companies or for telecommuters.

This data (Table 6.4) can become more important if it is combined with and transferred along with a person's employment data.

TABLE 6.3	Personal business data for special countries	
Description	**Infotype**	**Fields**
Family allowance in Austria	0043	Tax office, family allowance…child number (within the family)
Sickness certificates in Austria	0056	Doctor key, date…leave
Commuter rate in Austria	0058	Distance…time
Social fund in the Netherlands	0063	Start of application processing (date)
Court orders GB	0070	Protected earnings…issuing authority
Work incapacity periods in GB	0085	Date and notification of leaving
Residence tax Japan	0142	Tax year…tax office assignment
Unemployment insurance USA	0209	Work site for unemployment tax
Company cars in GB	0222	Car list price…expected business mileage

TABLE 6.4	Private data	
Description	**Infotype**	**Fields**
Addresses	0006	Address…telephone number
Personal data	0002	Date of birth…marital status
Family	0021	Date and place of birth, nationality…children

This category of data also includes:

- private fax number and mobile telephone number
- personal physician
- auto plate number.

Sensitive data

According to Article 8 of the EU Directive, Member States are prohibited from processing sensitive types of personal data (Table 6.5) without the express permission of the subject.

TABLE 6.5	Sensitive data	
Description	**Infotype**	**Fields**
Sensitive data according to Article 8	–	Racial or ethnic origin
Sensitive data according to Article 8	–	Political opinions
Sensitive data according to Article 8	–	Religious or philosophical beliefs
Sensitive data according to Article 8	–	Trade union membership
Sensitive data according to Article 8	–	Health or sex life

This data requires a high level of protection. Abuse can have significant economic and social effects. This data is usually subject to professional or official privacy privileges.

No infotypes exist for this category of data, unless legislation requires storage of special data.

Infotype 0002 stores an employee's confession (religion) and number of children for accounting purposes (church tax in Germany). But this information may not lead to conclusions about the employee's religious stance or sex life. Infotype 0004 can be used to store data on handicaps, such as group, type, level, accounting factor, employment office, or on services for severe handicaps.

A mobile telephone used for business illustrates how an employee's privacy is endangered if around-the-clock availability is expected and implemented. Many who first thought of a mobile phone as a privilege soon cursed it, but nonetheless felt that the company should always be able to contact them. A mobile phone can easily spoil a vacation.

Protection of the employee requires conversations, rules, industrial agreements, or a good corporate culture. Even with these features, a company should check if it wants to publish a mobile phone number without the employee's permission. Different companies will reach different conclusions. In this matter the employer, employee representatives, and those responsible for data protection weigh the interests of the employee and the company. Legislation should not get involved.

6.2.5 Data quality

The following summarizes the basics of data quality according to Article 6.

The following must be observed when processing personal data:

- fair and lawful processing
- only for specified, explicit, and legitimate purposes and not subject to further processing
- adequate, relevant, not excessive, accurate, and kept up to date
- kept in a form which permits identification of data subjects for no longer than is necessary for the purposes for which the data was collected.

The requirement of fairness is known throughout the world by the term fair play. It means dealing fairly with a partner and includes other conditions.

- Collect only the data that you absolutely need.
- Use the data only for its intended purpose.
- Inform your partner about the reason and purpose of processing.
- Transfer the data to others only when doing so follows the sprit of the partnership.
- Be prepared to provide information on the status and whereabouts of the data at any time.

- Keep the data up to date; correct obsolete or erroneous data.
- Let your partners be the masters of their own data.
- Make sure that processing avoids anything that could harm your partner.

The adjectives clearly indicate the essential concerns of the Directive, which are taken from Article 5 on data quality from Convention 108, issued by the European Council on January 28, 1981. All EU Member States and other countries such as Norway, Switzerland, and Hungary have ratified the convention. It can also serve as an indicator for third countries considering an appropriate level of data protection.

In our opinion, Article 6 should introduce every employee handbook. It is short, to the point, and clear to a normal user.

6.2.5.1 Fair partnership

The history of SAP has always included partnerships with hardware and software manufacturers and with its customers for implementing and maintaining productive systems. The R/3 System significantly expanded hardware and operating system platforms; database and network suppliers strengthened the operating systems. In addition to technology partners, SAP found other partners for sales and customer implementations. The complementary software partner (CSP) program and mySAP.com partner programs offer supplemental applications, certified by SAP, for SAP systems. SAP is currently working with partner companies on the basic technologies to integrate mobile and portable devices with mySAP.com.

Such collaboration can succeed only when the partners deal fairly with each other. Obviously, each partner wants to realize its own goals, but it should not do so at the expense of the other partner. Cooperation can work well only when both partners share a good portion of the goals. Any partnership should therefore examine the common goals at the very start.

Like all partners, employees entrust their personal data to a company in the hope that the company will use the data only in their own and the company's interest. If both interests move in the same direction, there is no reason to start out mistrusting an employer. Mistrust should arise only when the company represents interests that run contrary to those of its employees. These situations often occur when those responsible lack knowledge or are inattentive.

6.2.6 Data austerity

Today's storage media offer almost infinite capacity and quick access time. A limited storage capacity no longer applies as a reason to limit the quantity of data.

Data austerity offers one option that respects technical innovation:

The discussion on technologies that support data protection should initiate a changed trend here for specific application areas. Information technology should help in the following areas:

1   some applications can avoid the collection of personal data without affecting the goals of data processing (data austerity)

2   in other cases, the scope and spread of personal data can be circumvented without calling the goal of the processing into question (data frugality)

3   personal data should be referenced to an individual person only where required; it should otherwise be stored, transferred, and processed anonymously or under a pseudonym [Berlin].

Data that has not been collected cannot be manipulated or reused illegally. The same holds true for data that is limited to the absolute minimum or is stored anonymously or under a pseudonym. It's easy to forget unnecessary data once it has been stored, and the data can take on a life of its own. Superfluous fields at the record and table level are simply passed on without undergoing a check and might even end up in external systems. Such data appears in database backups, recovery files, help files, and archives. It can also appear in Office products because of a download or cut-and-paste operation.

A policy that requires comprehensive logging of user actions contradicts this principle. The spirit of data protection would be perverted if, in the name of data protection, user-specific, detailed information were recorded for monitoring purposes that would ultimately expose the employee. Data protection is understood too literally if all data is protected with complete logs but not the people involved.

Examples of technology that protects fundamental rights include cryptography, digital signatures, and prepaid telephone or bankcards that cannot be traced back to the purchaser.

Technical

A central basis exists for the data of an R/3 System. Infotypes, for example, store personnel master data. These tables store similar data fields. These include address (infotype 0006), working time (0007), basic salary (0008), banking information (0009), and social insurance (0013). National requirements are stored in separate infotypes. The following lists the countries that have special infotypes for this purpose: Switzerland (0036), Austria (0044), Spain (0061), France (0064), UK (0069), and South Africa (0150).

The infotype level can therefore enable compliance with national legislation.

If needed, you can block infotypes or create new ones. You enter the data online or later in a background job. Entries are based upon screen fields formatted for each infotype. User-friendly table control lets you display or hide infotype fields without having to change the program.

We recommend that during a project, those responsible for data protection and employee representatives determine any improper infotypes and block or hide them.

Predefined processes are available for personnel actions. For example, a series of screens handles a new hire or a promotion. Companies can tailor these processes to their individual needs.

Those responsible for data protection and employee representatives should also participate in customizing the processes.

6.2.7 Responsible persons in the company

The company itself has the highest level of responsibility. It must undertake the detailed work. If a company processes and transfers personal data, the responsible persons in the company play a crucial role.

Such persons determine in-house rules for dealing with data, approve the data for processing or transfer, ensure transparency, and inspect the selections. They should perform these tasks by creating a consensus with the organization units involved. The information is just as important to the subjects. They should always be informed of the use of their personal data. Of course, the degree of information depends upon the level of sensitivity possessed by the data.

6.2.7.1 Company management

Company management carries the ultimate responsibility for the firm.

Company organs are liable for damage that results from non-compliance of IT security if they are not well informed about the IT security in the company and the risks involved, and if they have not taken the measures appropriate to the technology and costs that the firm could reasonably handle.

6.2.7.2 Data protection officer

A contact person for data protection, a data protection officer, should exist in a company. That person should report to company management and not be subject to other areas. The tasks here involve guaranteeing the basics of data protection, teaching employees, and inspecting programs, authorizations, data austerity, and data transfers. This person is the contact for all questions and complaints and must be involved in all projects that include personal data from the very beginning.

German law (BDSG) requires that companies have a data protection officer and enumerates the officer's tasks. The EU Directive sees a data protection officer as an alternative to self-regulation in a company. The existence of the data protection officer can simplify negotiations or even make it unnecessary. The following uses the term data protection officer (DPO) for all persons responsible for data protection.

The DPO should be integrated into projects that involve personal data just as

TABLE 6.6	Responsibilities in a company	
Area	**Question**	**Status**
Responsibility	Who is responsible for what?	
	Has the person responsible been informed of the responsibility and its scope?	
	Is there a description of tasks and functions?	
	Are there targets?	
	Who supervises the activities?	
	Are there preconditions related to the area?	
	Is there enough time?	
	Is the space sufficient?	
Decision-making ability	Does this person have the authority to make decisions?	
	Do superiors agree with the decisions?	
	Does this person know the organization and responsibilities?	
	Do other responsible persons know this person?	
	Is the person generally accepted in this position?	
Project involvement	Is the person responsible automatically informed about all projects?	
	Is this person involved in projects?	
	Are other decision makers, such as employee representatives, involved?	
	Can this person influence projects according to the area of expertise?	
	Does this person need to approve projects officially?	
Internal support from:	Management, supervisors, work directors?	
	IT director?	
	Security director?	
	Human resources department?	
	Employees?	
	Employee representatives?	
	Internal audit?	
	Specialists, administration, and development?	
Internal communication with:	Regular meetings?	
	Data protection or security authorities?	
	Publications on data protection on the internal network?	
	Electronic security and data protection handbook?	
External communication	Within the corporate group?	
	As a service?	
	How is the external depiction?	

employee representatives are. The project plan should include basic training for the DPO. However, the DPO does not need to become a specialist in SAP applications or the R/3 System itself. The DPO can rely on the assistance of contact persons, administrators, and SAP consultants.

6.2.7.3 Person responsible for the system

Project management must also set up a person with responsibility for individual applications and systems. These employees hold responsibility for the security of the overall system (see the SAP Security Guide); those responsible for applications serve as contact points for the DPO. They must have the necessary SAP training to perform their tasks.

Technical

The DPO can use the checklist given in Table 6.6 to inspect the responsibilities in the company. The list can also serve as part of the data protection audit.

6.3 RIGHTS OF SUBJECTS

The current management trend toward a return to core competencies has led companies to outsource functions to external service providers. In a similar way, employees can now perform tasks that used to require paper, mail, and the involvement of a specialist.

Employee Self-Services (ESS) give new meaning to data quality. Employees get closer to the idea of self-determination regarding their own data and become the masters of their own data – because they manage it themselves. When employees work directly with their own data, they implement the right to information and redress for subjects noted in Articles 10–14 of the EU Directive and their rights to correct, delete, and block their data.

Another section of this chapter deals with SAP self-service scenarios because we believe that this generation of standard software contributes the highest level of technology that respects data protection.

6.3.1 Information

Subjects should always be masters of their own data. They must always know who is processing their personal data. They must be specially informed about transfers of their data to third parties. Only when subjects are adequately informed about the storage of their data are they in a position to claim their rights.

The EU Directive intends that subjects can learn that processing is occurring and have comprehensive knowledge about the conditions under which it was collected.

Those responsible for processing must provide the following information as a minimum (Articles 10 and 11), except when it is already available:

- identity of the controller responsible for processing
- purpose of the processing
- categories of recipients
- voluntary or obligatory nature of questions with a reference to the consequences of a failure to respond
- existence of the right of access and the right to rectify personal data

The notification obligation does not hold if the subject is already familiar with these rights. If the data was not collected directly from the subject, the categories of data to be processed must also be named.

6.3.2 Access

Every person has the right to access, especially to inspect the correctness and propriety of the data. In particular, Article 12 mandates communication of the following information to the subject without excessive delay or expense:

- purpose of processing
- categories of data concerned
- recipients to whom the data is disclosed
- the data undergoing processing and information as to its source.

Technical

The SAP R/3 System features reports and transactions to help subjects access their data. This section treats some aspects of the Audit Information System. We recommend that those responsible for applications learn all the options for this kind of access so that they will be prepared should the need arise to use them.

Conversations with DPOs and surveys of our customers have convinced us that requests for this type of access are rare. A GDD survey in 1996 confirmed this finding: half of the respondents had no requests at all in the previous six months [IT-Sicherheit].

This finding may well result from the fact that the subjects themselves enter the data: employees, customers, and vendors. The subjects are therefore very well informed about what data is stored where. This is especially true when the processing company makes a great deal of the data directly available, such as data on wage accounting, time accounting, delivery notes, invoices, or online communication. In the case of wage accounting, information on address, time worked, vacation, banking, and so on should be expunged.

Accounting

You can use the Audit Information System (AIS) to find information on vendor and customer data. Use the following menu path: *Information Systems • Audit Info System.*

▨ Report RFDKVZ00 Customer master data with variant SAP&AUDIT_STAM

Menu path:

Business Audit • Financial Statement Oriented Audit • Assets • Receivables • Customers • Master Data • Overview • Account Detail Information

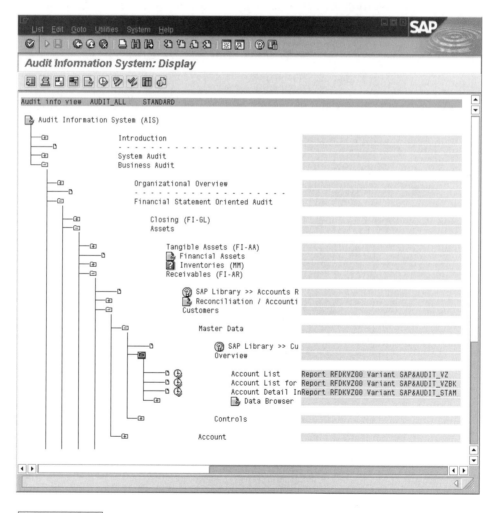

| **FIGURE 6.3** | Tree structure in the AIS (Copyright © SAP AG) |

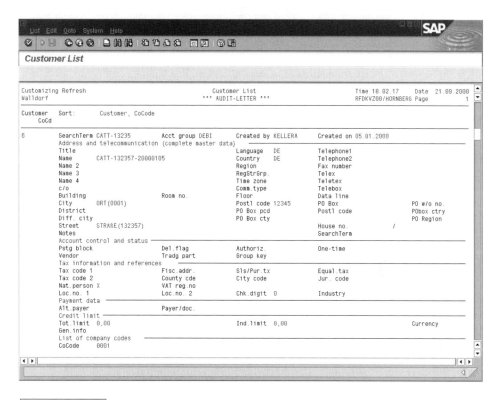

FIGURE 6.4 Output of report RFDKVZ00 (Copyright © SAP AG)

▨ Transaction fbl5n for document display

Menu path:

Business Audit • Financial Statement Oriented Audit • Assets • Receivables • Customers • Account • Line Item Display

▨ Report RFKKVZ00 Customer master data with variant SAP&AUDIT_STAM

Menu path:

Business Audit • Financial Statement Oriented Audit • Liabilities & Equity • Accounts Payable • Vendors • Master Data • Overview • Account Detail Information

▨ Transaction fbl1n for document display

Menu path (see Figure 6.5):

Business Audit • Financial Statement Oriented Audit • Liabilities & Equity • Accounts Payable • Vendors • Account • Line Item Display

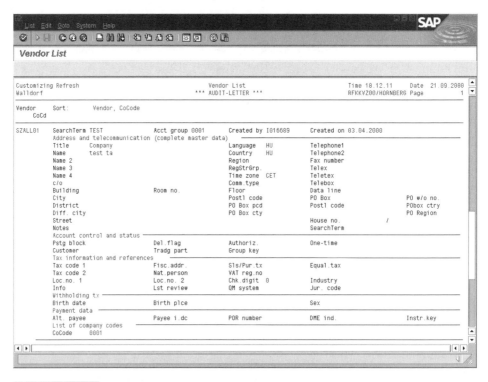

FIGURE 6.5   Report RFKKV200 with vendor's master data (Copyright © SAP AG)

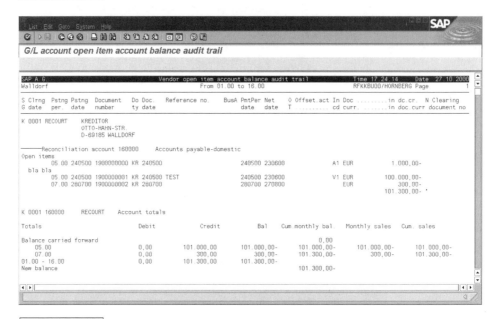

FIGURE 6.6   Display documents with report RFKKBU00 (Copyright © SAP AG)

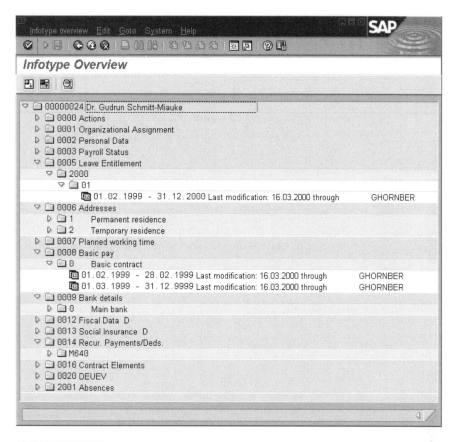

FIGURE 6.7   Overview of infotypes for an employee with report RPLINFC0
(Copyright © SAP AG)

You can also use RFKKBU00 or RFAUSZ00 to display documents, but only in the background (see Figkure 6.6).

Human resources

Personnel master sheet with report RPPSTM00 and country-specific adjustments

Overview of infotypes for an employee with report RPLINFC0 (see Figure 6.7)
You can use the employee number and infotypes to limit the report. Individual parts of the menu tree can be hidden or expanded.

Personnel file

The personnel file is behind transaction pa10. Each employee can analyze the populated infotypes and subtypes in detail. Two sample infotypes are illustrated in Figures 6.8 and 6.9.

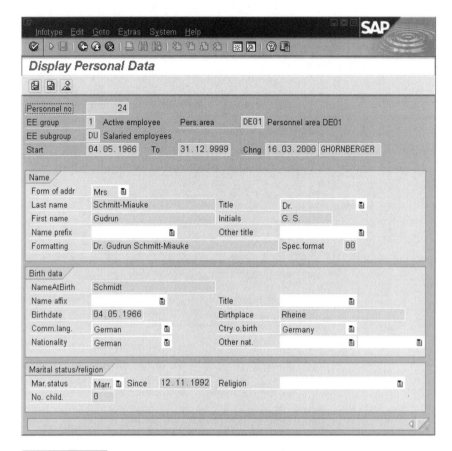

FIGURE 6.8   Personnel file with data on the person (infotype 0002) (Copyright © SAP AG)

Industry Solution Healthcare (IS H)

Report RNLAUS00 creates patient information.

Change documents for tables

▓ Report RSSCD100 (see Figure 6.10)

Menu path:

System Audit • Repository/Tables • Change Documents • Display Change Documents (Overview)

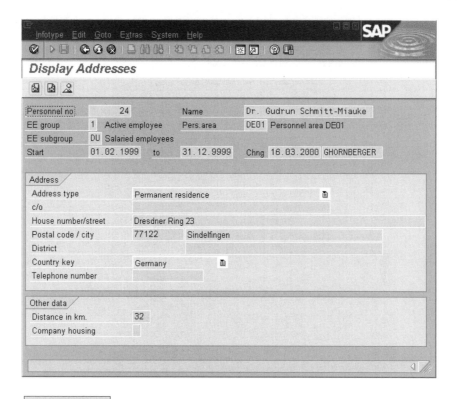

FIGURE 6.9   Personnel file with address (infotype 0006) (Copyright © SAP AG)

6.3.3 Rectification

Subjects have the right to rectify incomplete or incorrect data, to block it, or to delete it. The same holds true for data that does not comply with the Directive or the law. Any changes must also be communicated to any third parties who have received the data.

Technical

Employee Self-Service (ESS) in mySAP HR lends a new quality of data to SAP systems. Employees are requested to manage their own data. Employees decide which personal data is stored and administered. Employees accept the responsibility for the currency and correctness of the data. They can rectify inappropriate or incorrect data.

6.3.4 Cooperation with employee representatives

Employee representatives (works councils or personnel councils in Germany) should be integrated into projects that deal with personal data from the very beginning, as are DPOs. To ensure that they function from a knowledgeable perspective, they should have the same SAP training opportunities available to other project members.

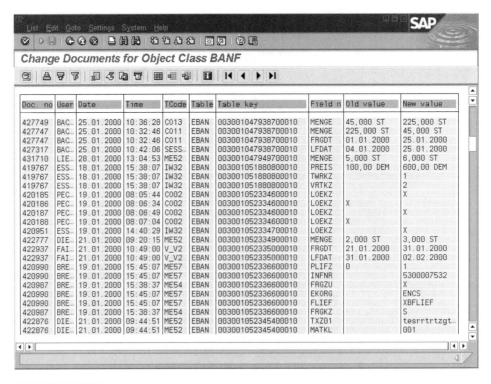

Doc. no	User	Date	Time	TCode	Table	Table key	Field n	Old value	New value
427749	BAC...	25.01.2000	10:36:28	C013	EBAN	003001047938700010	MENGE	45,000 ST	225,000 ST
427747	BAC...	25.01.2000	10:32:46	C011	EBAN	003001047938700010	MENGE	225,000 ST	45,000 ST
427747	BAC...	25.01.2000	10:32:46	C011	EBAN	003001047938700010	FRGDT	01.01.2000	25.01.2000
427317	BAC...	25.01.2000	10:42:06	SESS...	EBAN	003001047938700010	LFDAT	04.01.2000	25.01.2000
431710	LIE...	28.01.2000	13:04:53	ME52	EBAN	003001047949700010	MENGE	5,000 ST	6,000 ST
419767	ESS...	18.01.2000	15:38:07	IW32	EBAN	003001051880800010	PREIS	100,00 DEM	600,00 DEM
419767	ESS...	18.01.2000	15:38:07	IW32	EBAN	003001051880800010	TWRKZ		1
419767	ESS...	18.01.2000	15:38:07	IW32	EBAN	003001051880800010	VRTKZ		2
420185	PEC...	19.01.2000	08:05:44	C002	EBAN	003001052334600010	LOEKZ		X
420186	PEC...	19.01.2000	08:06:34	C002	EBAN	003001052334600010	LOEKZ	X	
420187	PEC...	19.01.2000	08:06:49	C002	EBAN	003001052334600010	LOEKZ		X
420188	PEC...	19.01.2000	08:07:04	C002	EBAN	003001052334600010	LOEKZ	X	
420951	ESS...	19.01.2000	14:40:29	IW32	EBAN	003001052334700010	LOEKZ		X
422777	DIE...	21.01.2000	09:20:15	ME52	EBAN	003001052334900010	MENGE	2,000 ST	3,000 ST
422937	FAI...	21.01.2000	10:49:00	V_V2	EBAN	003001052335000010	FRGDT	21.01.2000	31.01.2000
422937	FAI...	21.01.2000	10:49:00	V_V2	EBAN	003001052335000010	LFDAT	31.01.2000	02.02.2000
420990	BRE...	19.01.2000	15:45:07	ME57	EBAN	003001052336600010	PLIFZ	0	1
420990	BRE...	19.01.2000	15:45:07	ME57	EBAN	003001052336600010	INFNR		5300007532
420987	BRE...	19.01.2000	15:38:37	ME54	EBAN	003001052336600010	FRGZU		X
420990	BRE...	19.01.2000	15:45:07	ME57	EBAN	003001052336600010	EKORG		ENCS
420990	BRE...	19.01.2000	15:45:07	ME57	EBAN	003001052336600010	FLIEF		XBFLIEF
420987	BRE...	19.01.2000	15:38:37	ME54	EBAN	003001052336600010	FRGKZ		S
422876	DIE...	21.01.2000	09:44:51	ME52	EBAN	00300105 2345400010	TXZ01		tesrrtrtzgt...
422876	DIE...	21.01.2000	09:44:51	ME52	EBAN	00300105 2345400010	MATKL		001

FIGURE 6.10   Change documents with report RSSCD100 (Copyright © SAP AG)

6.3.4.1 The power of employee representation

If employee representatives do not participate in the implementation of an R/3 System from the very beginning, problems with acceptance and incalculable delays can result. A works council in Germany can actually hinder the introduction of application software.

6.3.4.2 An opinion favorable to employees

This section represents the thoughts of the technology information center of the German Association of Trade Unions [TBS].

It believes that the implementation of an R/3 System primarily represents an important part of a company's strategy. Company management expects efficient information management with current key figures and improved options for directing the company and lowering costs. SAP R/3 colors working conditions for years: it is a formative opportunity.

Hours spent at the computer will increase, and shorter processing time will cost jobs. But the situation will also require new and qualified tasks, and therefore create opportunities for employees to take on highly valued and future-oriented tasks.

Recording data in a database could lead to monitoring the performance and behavior of employees. But costs are rationalized along with employees and companies will also appropriately consider employee strengths, experience, and competencies.

The use of R/3 affects other areas, such as qualifications, groupings, hiring, workload, performance, and behavior monitoring. But the effects are not significantly different than those triggered by other programs. The R/3 System offers multifaceted opportunities to control how employees work. But the experience of the information center shows that companies generally do not use these features systematically. These evaluations must be prohibited or regulated precisely. Users should be evaluated only for the purposes of data protection, data security, and the technical analysis of programming errors. Agreements should call for deletion of this data within a few days.

The technology information center recommends that the works council form its own project group, that its members attend training, and that it formulate a project plan with the assistance of a union secretary or consultant. Members of the works council should be part of the project team and hold responsibility for the following subprojects: data protection and security concepts, training, and ergonomic and healthy design of computer workstations.

6.3.4.3 An opinion favorable to employers

Laws on labor contracts have given too much power to unions, at least in Germany. They have created a type of labor and social rights that threatens to ruin Germany as an industrial nation. Unions have shown themselves as enemies of technology regarding new IT methods, and at the beginning of its development even demanded prohibition of the use of an electronic HR system in companies (Ehmann, 1995, § 235).

Critics of unions see the power of works councils as a threat to Germany. They fear that co-determination will be used to implement interests that do not foster the good of the company and (therefore) its employees. Leaders of companies should consider whether the strong criticism by Horst Ehmann even remotely describes the situation.

He believes that current German industrial law subjects every capture of employee data to the right of co-determination of the works council. This could create the danger that processing employee data is permitted only when the continued existence of the company would be in danger. This would also mean that foreign companies would shy away from creating German subsidiaries because works councils would hinder the transfer of performance data to the parent company. In countries without works councils, the right to data protection is generally only a theory. In Germany it's the sacred cow of works councils, which frequently use it as a dead end that prohibits trading in cows (Ehmann, 1995, p. 242).

6.3.4.4 Summary

Information technology is to be implemented only in consultation with employee representatives, never against their will. That is true of all systems in which it is even theoretically possible to record user behavior. It need not explicitly be a system designed to store and process personal data. Modern systems store user data not only for accounting purposes, but also to monitor performance and abuse.

One task of employee representatives involves working with project management to determine what data can be recorded, what data may not be recorded, and what evaluations may be performed with the data. The decision should be contained in a single-plant bargaining agreement with the works council; in other cases we recommend formulation of an operating agreement between the employer and selected employee representatives.

We also recommend that you follow the principle of data austerity. Record only absolutely necessary data. Ensure that only administration can view the data and evaluate it only according to predetermined criteria. The R/3 System supports management of accounting data with an account number. Assignment to cost centers can create the desired anonymity.

In the past, we have heard several reports of conflict between employers and employee representatives during the implementation of an SAP system. In particular, disagreements about the formulation of industrial agreements require the use of SAP consultants as arbiters. We recommend that consultants discuss the recording and evaluation options neutrally. Missing information on the functions of SAP systems and the goals of a company is the main reason for mutual mistrust.

6.3.5 Self-service scenarios

An increased desire to involve employees is one of the largest and continuing trends among companies. Self-service applications and access to company data over an intranet and the internet implement these policies.

Why shouldn't employees be able to maintain their personal data directly in the HR system, submit orders themselves, or create their own salary plans with the sensitive HR system?

In the public sector, mayors can foresee bringing the city hall to the citizens' computer screens. Files will be created for computer storage, citizens will complete requests and forms online over the internet, and the appropriate office will process the data. Citizens will be able to pay fees automatically and query the data currently stored about them.

Self-service applications and access to citizen or employee data over an intranet or the internet makes these ideas a reality.

Electronic tax filing has been possible in Germany since 1999. Everyone with an internet connection can send tax information online to the local revenue department, as long as the department is connected to the system. Here, too, the user (taxpayer) is responsible for the quality of the data, which does not need to be read from illegible handwriting, interpreted, entered, and validated. Once it's entered here, it's here for good. There's no need for additional, time-consuming inspections and monitoring with pocket calculators: programs make sure that the math is correct.

6.3.5.1 Self-service in human resources

Employee Self-Services applications in mySAP HR are easy-to-use internet programs that enable employees to display and update their own personnel data. The applications free the HR department from time and cost-intensive tasks that simply provide information or update records; they enable it to work on decisions of strategic importance for the company. The applications also increase the quality and currency of information in the company, an important byproduct for data protection.

Another argument for data protection arises regarding the location of data previously processed by a third party. In this case, the persons responsible can no longer inspect and monitor the legality of the transfer and the processing.

R/3 Human Resources offers the following self-service components:

- address and dependants
- vacation request and information
- information on employee contributions
- travel costs and travel information
- employment certificates.

Employee Self-Services also operates with the typical SAP authorization and security concepts. The applications offer employees access only to their own data, for which they need a system-issued user ID and a password.

Users do not log on to an SAP R/3 System directly, however. The data flows over an RFC interface and is transferred to a fixed, predetermined sequence of programs that process it. The user can then navigate in specific menus or transactions. User activity is limited to the functions of the selected services. The RFC or CPIC user has the authorizations typical of every dialog user. The authorizations must be sufficient to access the desired user information.

Ultimately, the company decides if employees may display or change data on their own. Even when the firm uses this approach, a Workflow can direct any changed data to a supervisor for review and approval.

6.3.5.2 Role-specific access

SAP delivers the mySAP Workplace with predefined user roles that enable access to all SAP software components with a click of the mouse. As an open, flexible portal, the mySAP Workplace can be enhanced and connected to legacy systems, the company intranet, the internet, and other external and internal systems. The information available in the mySAP Marketplace can be tailored to individual needs and automatically implemented and updated in the Workplace.

Server-controlled administration of the mySAP Workplace enables role- and task-specific access: the Workplace presents only the individually required information to the user. Employees can also connect to the Workplace from remote locations and computers, and still call the made-to-order information. Each user is unique.

After it accepts a user logon, the Workplace displays links to applications and sources of information that users need to perform their jobs. There's no need to enter IDs repeatedly or change to other applications: all tasks can be performed in the Workplace environment.

6.3.5.3 Danger of transfer

Whenever data travels along the internet, the danger exists that someone can eavesdrop on the transmission, counterfeit the data, or that the data has no clear force in law.

To ensure secure data transmission, the data must be encrypted or given a digital signature.

6.3.5.4 Danger of access

Granting employees and customers access to systems that were previously sealed off can create all sorts of dangers for the data. To allow users to display and change their own data means that physical isolation with network configuration, firewalls, and routers must be lessened and that access authorization must be regulated in preconfigured security systems. Please note the security measures treated in Chapters 2–4.

Employee Self-Services can be accepted and used in companies only when the security of the data is guaranteed to subjects. A company must provide complete transparency on access authorization, further use, and transfers.

6.4   SECURITY AND CONFIDENTIALITY

Data protection attempts to guarantee confidentiality with special obligations for specific groups. You must implement both organizational and technical measures for the security of the data.

6.4.1 Obligations

Companies that use real-time workflow or have significant contact with external firms because of service or consulting should obligate all their employees to non-disclosure. The scope of the obligation should include confidential material within and external to the firm and observance of copyrights.

Technical

Obligations at SAP

SAP obligates all employees and partners working for or with SAP to main data protection and confidentiality (non-disclosure). An appendix contains the text of this declaration; it is also available in R/3 note 35493 and the White Paper on remote maintenance. *See* Chapter 10 on remote support for more detailed information.

In addition to a general obligation, specific duties for individual groups are also possible.

All obligations pertaining to data protection and security are maintained and kept current in an electronic data protection handbook on the intranet.

SAP distinguishes between the following documents.

- Obligation to data protection and non-disclosure

  New hires must sign the declaration, which becomes part of an employee's personnel file.

- Data protection booklet

  The booklet deals directly with an employee's work and obligations. It, too, becomes part of an employee's personnel file.

- Administrator's obligations

  Given the wide-ranging competencies of administrators, a special obligation was developed in consultation with area directors and appeals to the self-responsibility of administrators. This obligation applies especially in the areas that SAP regards as sensitive: recording data relating to the telephone, to internet access, or to physical access. Special agreements, negotiated with employee representatives, signed by a board member and the DPO, and published, apply to records of this data. The booklet on data protection refers to this obligation specifically.

- Booklet for employees in the HR department and for project employees

  A special, comprehensive booklet is available for departments whose employees regularly deal with personnel data (such as those in the HR department itself) or for employees who come into (even remote) contact with personnel or customer data. The booklet informs department heads of their responsibilities in dealing with confidential data and helps them adopt a uniform, group-oriented procedure.

6.4.2 Technical and organizational measures

Member States shall provide that the controller must implement appropriate technical and organizational measures to protect personal data against accidental or unlawful destruction or accidental loss, alteration, unauthorized disclosure or access, in particular where the processing involves the transmission of data over a network, and against all other unlawful forms of processing.

Employers must also guarantee the measures treated here in Article 17 of the EU Directive. Article 25 provides that the security measures in force in a third country are part of the evaluation of the security level.

6.4.2.1 The Ten Commandments of data protection

The technical and organizational measures are known as the Ten Commandments of data protection in Germany. The reworking of the BDSG tightened the Commandments so that they meet the requirements of the Directive and reflect the current state of information and security technology.

Through the relationship of the previous section to the annex to section 9 of the BDSG, we wish to illustrate the implementation options available in an SAP system. The options have been tested in practice and are much more concrete than those of the EU Directive.

The new annex to section 9 reads as follows:

> Where personal data are processed automatically, internal agency or internal company measures suited to the particular requirements of data protection are required. Special measures must be taken suited to the type of the personal data or data categories to be protected.

6.4.2.2 Admittance control

1. To prevent unauthorized persons from gaining access to data processing systems with which personal data are processed or used.

Organizational requirements:

building security, closed-shop computer centers, setup of security zones, logging entries and exits with rules for evaluation (control of abuse), and information for those affected.

6.4.2.3 User control

2. To prevent the use of data processing systems by unauthorized persons.

Organizational requirements:

- locking PCs and documents; securing the network
- minimizing the number of users for sensitive systems.

Technical requirements:

- user control with authentication of users, single sign-on, and chip cards
- logging users and controls.

Technical

- *See* section 2.1 on user management.
- *See* section 2.2. on user authentication.
- *See* section 2.5 on recording, logging, and auditing.
- *See* section 4.4.3 on user authentication and single sign-on.

6.4.2.4 Access control

3. To ensure that persons entitled to use a data processing system have access only to the data to which they have a right of access (access control), to prevent personal data being read, copied, modified or removed without authorization.

Technical requirements:

- authorization concept, user profiles, and monitoring authorized users
- limited access by persons and to specific times
- logging and monitoring
- limiting access to specific transactions or programs.

Technical

- *See* section 2.3 on the authorization concept.
- *See* section 2.5 on recording, logging, and auditing.
- *See* section 4.4.4 on the role concept.

TABLE 6.8	Sample roles from human resources
Administrative assistant	**Time-entry specialist**
Employer contributions specialist	Scheduling clerk
Salary specialist	Scheduling specialist
Department supervisor	Settlement clerk
HR manager	Settlement specialist
Organizational management specialist	Hiring clerk
Incentive wage clerk	HR system administrator
Incentive wage specialist	Training and development clerk
Time-entry clerk	

Transfer control

4. To prevent data from being read, copied, modified or erased without authorization during the electronic transmission of personal data or the transport of storage media and that it is possible to verify and determine the points at which the transfer of personal data is intended over data transmission facilities.

Organizational requirements:

- documentation of transfer programs and procedures, determination of transfer routes and recipients.

Technical requirements:

- secure network structure, encryption, and identity checks
- monitoring of uploads, downloads, and external calls
- logging of transfers and recipients
- evaluation logs.

Technical

- *See* section 2.5 on recording, logging, and auditing.
- *See* section 2.6 on external security products and cryptography.
- *See* section 2.7 on external user authentication and protecting network communications.
- *See* section 2.8 on digital signatures and encryption.
- *See* section 3.1 on networks
- *See* section 3.4 on uploads and downloads
- *See* section 3.5 on Remote Function Call.
- *See* section 3.7 on Application Link Enabling.
- *See* Chapter 4 on mySAP.com and security on the internet.

6.4.2.5 Input control

5. To ensure that it is possible to check and establish which personal data have been entered into, changed in, or deleted from data processing systems by whom and at what time.

Organizational requirements:

- determination of responsibilities

- documentation of entry programs
- logging of entries (documents, organization, storage medium, and archive)
- evaluation process for logs.

Technical requirements:

- efficient user management with identification, authentication, password rules, and audit logs
- tools for re-creation.

Technical

- *See* section 2.1 on user management.
- *See* section 2.2 on user authentication.
- *See* section 4.4.3 on user authentication and single sign-on.
- *See* section 2.5 on recording, logging, and auditing.

6.4.2.6 Order control

6. To ensure that, in the case of commissioned processing of personal data, the data are processed strictly in accordance with the instructions of the principal.

Organizational requirements:

- checks when selecting outsourcers
- written agreements with attachments for non-disclosure, security measures, and contractual penalties for not observing the wishes of the principal
- checking the identity of the principal.

6.4.2.7 Availability control

7. To ensure that personal data is protected against accidental destruction or loss.

Organizational requirements:

- protecting buildings housing the IT infrastructure (computer center, PCs, and network), and personnel
- protecting against viruses and penetration (distributed denial of service attacks)
- guidelines for programming, testing, and acceptance
- inspecting the data for correctness, clarity, and completeness.

Technical requirements:

- make and store (externally) backup copies
- fast backup.

Technical

See section 3.3 on the database.

Initiatives with hardware manufacturers have enabled SAP to document interest in secure and reliable installations. The main points include the high availability of SAP applications and backup/restore procedures that do not cut into productive time. The use of a second instance as a copy of the productive system is supported. mySAP.com further increases the demand for the highest possible performance and availability in e-commerce – as fast as the internet itself.

6.4.2.8 Segregation control

8. To ensure that data collected for separate purposes can be processed separately.

Organizational requirements:

The GDD clarifies the type of segregation. This point does not require a physical separation of the data, but only a logical separation created by user profiles and authorizations (*see* sections 2.1–2.3).

6.4.2.9   The Ten Commandments of security

Consulting firms that specialize in security indicate in their Ten Commandments of security that there are no upward limits to the organizational measures [Mühlen]:

1 determination of the need for protection based upon the risks

2 the principle of prevention

3 early involvement of security planning in all phases

4 principle of completeness and equivalence

5 principle of economy

6 strict tightening and broadening of the overall matrix of security measures

7 reduction of external, physical relationships

8 principle of consistency

9 principle of acceptance

10 anticipation of developments.

Those responsible for security and data protection should check their security concepts against these rules and orient the policies accordingly.

6.4.3 Appropriateness of measures

The EU Directive also speaks of the appropriateness of security and data protection measures. According to Article 12, the Member States guarantee each subject the right to receive the following from those responsible for processing data:

> . . . notification to third parties to whom the data have been disclosed of any rectification, erasure or blocking carried out in compliance with (b), unless this proves impossible or involves a disproportionate effort.

Article 17 of the EU Directive demands that measures consider the risks and costs:

> Having regard to the state of the art and the cost of their implementation, such measures shall ensure a level of security appropriate to the risks represented by the processing and the nature of the data to be protected.

One would expect that the persons responsible enjoy generous elbowroom when evaluating the measures. There are undoubtedly enough commentaries on this provision that provide a cost–benefit analysis as a basis for making a decision.

6.5   COMPLIANCE AND LIABILITY

Data protection legislation is effective only when complied with. Compliance requires effective instances that clarify the practicability of regulations to convert them into internal company guidelines and that have the time and authority to monitor the situation and punish abuse.

6.5.1 German data protection legislation

The state issues data protection legislation to regulate the gap between the economy's need for information and the need to protect the privacy of individuals. The treatment of informational self-determination in section 6.2.2 discussed in detail the demands of data protection as a fundamental right. This fundamental right already exists in the constitutions of some European countries.

Many legal regulations fail to account for the fact that while modern individuals demand an inviolable right to privacy, they are also dependent upon communications and the exchange of personal data.

No one can contribute to a flourishing economy and expect its financial and social rewards while excluding personal data from the flow of information upon which the economy rests. In many cases, the law forces subjects and companies to store and process data. But the same legislation often ignores this forced collection of data and appends the ideal of data frugality. And legislation also ignores the fact that companies not only function as deputies of the state in collecting tax data, but must also apply significant resources to protect the data.

6.5.1.1 The abundance of laws

Would you believe that 70 percent of the laws and requirements that apply to privacy come from Germany (Seidel, 1998) and that 98 percent of the data stored in an HR system is mandated by laws, regulations, and export rules?

This abundance of laws has made HR tasks and forced tax collection as agents of the state, the church (in Germany), and social agencies unthinkable without IT support. The medium-size and small software companies cannot keep pace with the tax regulations they must observe; regulations are issued with no concern for the effort it takes to implement them. Particularly in HR development, legal innovations appear at year-end and require implementation at short notice.

The slow and dragging implementation of legal requirements is often an advantage for the consumer. The international discussion on an internet tax has shown European politicians, in particular, that a national policy can end only in additional bureaucracy. A harmonized approach to taxes would actually be a prerequisite for any taxation of e-commerce. Or will someone come up with an idea of how to implement harmonized taxes with a new, uniform EU tax on the internet and bring it in through the back door? The internal and international discussions required here will take several months, especially because the US must also become involved, even though it has sworn off an internet tax for the present.

Particularly on the internet, it is easy to get the impression that laws on communications and the media are simply ignored in Germany. Many of those involved in the situation, particularly politicians wrestling to create new jobs, find that it is preferable to outsourcing technology jobs to foreign oases. Supervisory authorities accept violations of the data protection laws in silence. *See* Chapter 8 for more information on use of the internet.

6.5.1.2 Redesign

In programming we often see how continual innovations make it impossible to maintain an overview and can ultimately lead to a quality and security risk. Even this author finds it difficult to muster the will to repair programming when a customer's employee or a consultant causes inestimable damage with even a minor modification. The only result is a complete redesign.

Public opinion in Germany clearly feels that the 1990 version of the BDSG was incomprehensible and could be implemented only with the help of jurists. Moreover, the important information was not summarized, but was lost in general legal parlance. The required design of the BDSG will occur only in phase II, which will take place in this legislative period, that is by 2002. Given previous experience, does anyone really believe that everything will be solved by then?

Critics complain that the two-phase model has already meant five years of corrections to the BDSG to bring it in line with the EU Directive. Only philosophical thought has been given to the needed general reworking or design of the law.

Data protection regulations can be effective only when they replace obsolete technical rules and consider recognizable developments on the internet, globalization of the economy, and the exchange of data without borders.

6.5.1.3 Demands of the economy

The development history of the EU Directive shows that it inadequately considered the needs of the economy. From the perspective of a Swiss attorney, the legal regulation of the processing of personal data developed as follows (Schleutermann, 1995).

European economic associations demanded a new directive that permitted as unrestricted a flow of information between companies as possible. In actual fact, exact observance of the Directive prohibits processing personal data because the EU regulations are too difficult, cumbersome, and expensive.

The EU recognized the existing self-discipline and self-regulation in companies. Commercial considerations give companies a vested interest in data protection measures that do not need to be mandated by law. Competition between companies meant that transfers to third parties were always handled very restrictively. Companies also placed great value on having correct contents in its data.

These remarks resulted in the following demand:

> Given the broad disinterest in questions of data protection in many segments of the population, comprehensive bureaucratic regulation of private data processors is hardly justifiable. Not only data processing, but also data protection must consider the principle of proportionality. For data processing by the subjects of private law, a fundamental freedom of data processing and transfer must be anchored in law. Only gross violations must be forbidden (Schleutermann, p. 585, 1995).

As we noted in section 6.1.1, the very title of the EU Directive reflects the demand for the free transfer of data, but the Directive treats violations like a stepchild.

The attorney suggested the Swiss data protection law as a solution. It recognizes the fundamental right to process information by private persons. The data protection regulations should be liberalized in the private area; the state must strengthen protection for citizens in the public area. This demand comes close to our remarks in section 6.2.2.

6.5.2 Compliance

What good is a comprehensive set of rules in companies and legal proscriptions and regulations when they are neither accepted nor complied with?

For example, an Italian pornography provider published the names, address, e-mail addresseses, and credit card numbers of almost 1,000 of its subscribers on the internet. During safe-harbor negotiations with Gerard de Graaf, the EU representative, the US media asked with relish what good the EU Directive was, especially when it had already been implemented as law in Italy. After all, Italian companies are bound to comply with Article 17 and are bound to protect the personal data of their customers.

De Graaf's answer? The Member States are obligated to act in such cases. If they do not, the EU Commission can take measures against governments that fail to implement the Directive. Besides, publications of this sort not only violate the Directive, but other laws as well *[Wired]*.

The implementation of all rules must consider if the rules will be observed. If no one is observing the old rules, what's the point of creating new ones?

The opinion of critics of German legislation is clear:

> Sound and reasonable behavior is mostly possible because data protection rules are not being observed or are being interpreted very broadly (Ehmann, 1995, p. 23).

Ehmann believes that works councils are already making sure that data protection regulations are being observed strictly in Germany. A uniform level of data protection in EU countries that corresponds to the German model is next to impossible, unless German industrial laws and works councils were exported to neighboring countries.

You rarely see victories in the battle against viruses. If anything, you get the impression that the internet is a playground for virus developers, who do battle with anti-virus programs. Reports rarely indicate that a government or company has used every means at its disposal to fight those who spread viruses by finding them and prosecuting them to the fullest extent of the law. German penal law calls for two- to five-year imprisonment for illegal changes to data or computer sabotage. The worst possible punishment for such hackers would be a lifelong prohibition against surfing the internet at all. In the US, the most famous computer hacker was punished with a three-year prohibition of PC use (*see* section 6.5.6).

The reports of success in fighting the Melissa virus were therefore most welcome. The FBI was able to identify and arrest the developer. It will be interesting to see what American lawyers posit as appropriate restitution. After all, some 1.2 million PCs were infected in the US alone. Ironically, the means used to track down the hacker are the same tools that an honest data protection official fights. The hacker was convicted with the controversial serial number of Word that is secretly attached to users [IT-Sicherheit, 3/99, p. 3].

One future option for publishing and monitoring the observance of regulations can be seen in the development of marketplaces, which unite several companies. Marketplaces must observe security guidelines and a privacy policy. Just as they must do in the case of the EU Directive, participants in the marketplace obligate themselves to implement the rules in their companies, make them transparent, and guarantee compliance. Just as is the case in international contracts, marketplaces offer guarantees and legal remedies to companies if the employees of another company violate the regulations. A firm takes the initial responsibility for its employees. *See* section 6.6 for a further discussion.

6.5.3 Control instances

The EU Directive means official control organs here. Especially in Germany, these exist in droves. Given Germany's federal nature, its 16 states are responsible for monitoring and control. Many states have separate instances for the public and private sectors. Other states place the responsibilities at a local level.

Control instances in companies include the DPO, who must perform the required inspections. An internal audit can help here. Inspection methods must be agreed upon in advance.

6.5.4 Controlling abuse

6.5.4.1 Recordings for system controls

Before we examine individual options for inspections, we need to treat the problem that all-encompassing recording of data poses to data protection efforts. To enable the inspection and control of abuse, the optimal approach calls for very detailed and somewhat secret recording. But system administrators may expose the recordings only under previously determined criteria.

Nonetheless, recording employee activities can be abused. If the data is used to monitor performance, employee representatives must become involved. In Germany, the works council has the right of co-determination. At the very least, the subject is to be informed of recording and how it is evaluated.

Recording that checks the proper operation of an application and prevents abuse is often not completely transparent. Everyone must strictly observe the requirement that data may be used only for its intended purpose. Once every record is published, the road to abuse is open.

Example. In a case involving a hospital, patient master data in an R/3 System was deliberately falsified with the intention of abuse. The user name could be identified because the system automatically kept change logs. It had to be clear who was responsible for what changes. The system creates change documents or records the user, date, and time of the last change at the record level. In this case, an unknown person who had a password sneaked into user identification. At the time of the crime, the actual user was not in the hospital.

To identify the criminal, the administrators had to know what other (if any) activities the user performed in the system at the same time, such as:

- all changes performed by the user
- logon and logoff times
- the front end used and its location
- visits to other systems
- downloads and printed reports
- reports and transactions used
- e-mail sent.

Accounting data and the PCs used can also help in the case of discovering the person behind the abuse. The transaction profile can also let you know how well informed the person is about the system.

Many compliance regulations are ignored when trying to comply with the law and look for an abuser. For example, the sense of data protection makes it best to forget everything that a user has done on the internet. However, administrators must also ensure that employees always work in accordance with the law and that personal data is protected against external access.

SAP systems offer a variety of logging functions: *see* the discussion in section 2.5.

We believe that the person responsible for data protection points the way when it comes to recording. The DPO must recommend measures to management that correspond to Article 6 of the EU Directive: measures that are fair and legitimate to employees and customers.

The DPO and system administrators must plumb the options for recording and logging. In consultation with management and the HR department, the DPO prepares suggestions and arranges for the publication and implementation of the measures.

The level of recording and publication depend upon the corporate culture and the security requirements of a company. The system administrator is responsible for any data recorded. Exact regulations are required for the evaluation of the data in the event of abuse. Management is obligated to adhere to these rules. A written, single-plant bargaining agreement covers the process and the evaluation in Germany. In case of doubt, consultation with a supervisory authority can be valuable, particularly when the in-house legal department wants to interpret regulations on abuse to the best advantage of the company.

6.5.5 Sanctions and damages

The EU Directive states that every person has the right to demand damages from the person responsible for any illegal processing of data (Article 23). The Member States are to use the appropriate means and impose sanctions to ensure applications of the EU Directive (Article 24). The BDSG threatens fines and prison sentences of up to two years.

Although Europe claims to have the strongest data protection laws, the penalties in the US are actually tougher. When hackers attacked and shut down major e-commerce sites in February 2000, the US government and the FBI were involved immediately.

Those who attack and purposely damage open systems must feel the full effect of existing law. The firms under attack advertise their openness, authorize every user, and have minimal chances to defend themselves against hackers who have a different code of conduct and juggle multiple addresses. It's similar to the situation in a stadium. Everyone advertises for fans. Every fan is welcome, but the franchise wants to keep out undesirable hooligans. But when they slip in like friendly fans and abuse their guest privileges, they deserve merciless application of the law, including a ban on entering any stadium. If this approach were applied to hackers, they would be forbidden to communicate over the internet. A general prohibition on the use of computers could also be considered as a preventive measure to block further crimes with viruses.

6.5.6 Penalties

After almost five years in prison, the most well-known American computer hacker, Kevin Mitnick, was released. He is forbidden to touch a computer that can connect to the internet for three years or to use mobile telephones. He regards these mandates as forbidding him to work.

At the beginning of the 1990s, he was the most sought-after criminal in the US because of his attacks on large corporations and military computers. Although arrested in 1995, he did not face trial until four years later. It was difficult to trace his tracks. Attacks on military facilities were clearly seen as a major threat in a country that places its national security above all else.

China proceeds without mercy toward criminals. An appeal court upheld the death penalty for a hacker who broke into a bank and diverted $90,000 to his own account. But the penalty here does not seem specific to a hacker: the same fate would befall a bank robber.

The penalties for data protection crimes in Germany are milder. Although the maximum penalty involves a fine of DM 50,000 and two years in prison, penalties so far have not exceeded DM 10,000. The new BDSG increases fines to DM 500,000. Fines appear to be the last means used against the unteachable, who refuse to provide information or ignore legal requirements after repeated efforts to do so.

It will be interesting to see if the maximum penalty is applied against the alleged criminals who copied data from an external payroll accounting system. The data included 190,000 addresses with birth dates, number of children, and highest salary. The information is worth reading because the "crime" committed by a pizzeria owner seems to be regarded at the same level. The owner noted the usual information (address, amount, and so on) on the delivery slip and then added that the customer was impolite and should be excluded from other further deliveries. Wouldn't it have been fun to be around for the discovery of this crime by the supervisory authorities?

6.5.7 Summary

Particularly in the case of data protection laws, it is crucial to consider if and how they can be implemented. As long as many companies work around or simply ignore the current regulations, there's little point to supplementing current law. And most people recognize that legislation cannot keep pace with innovation in the internet age, and that the dichotomy between the two grows ever larger.

Many voices demand simplification of the laws and making them comprehensible to lay readers. The demands do not arise only from the data protection and communications sectors.

If Europe is to unite, legislation must follow suit. All sorts of EU Directives already exist that are already implemented in national law. The European Court is working on the basis for a catalog of fundamental rights for Member States and the European Human Rights convention. From now on, a constitutional convention is to develop a European charter of fundamental rights that includes the essentials of data protection as contained in Article 6 of the EU Directive. Yes, the rights are rather old (European Council, 1981), but they are oriented toward the future with their treatment of globalization and unity among nations. These fundamental rights should become part of EU contracts and thus part of enforceable, valid community law.

Existing penalties must be used for criminal abuse that involves significant damages. For example, eavesdropping on secure data is an abuse and can be punished, according to German law (§ 202a of the penal code), with a prison term of up to five years.

This appears to be the only right answer to hacker attacks. The internet is developing into a commercial venture worth billions. Providers must be open and count on mutually trustworthy relationships. A merciless battle must be declared against the gaming mentality of hackers. We are convinced that the FBI and Justice Department in the US will do everything possible to show quick success in fighting computer crime. They will identify hackers and impose exemplary, deterrent sentences. Damages in the millions will also contribute to helping hackers understand the damage they have caused.

The advantage here belongs to the US, where recordings of user data may be made to prevent abuse. The data can be stored for a long period and studied in fine detail, with the same energy used by criminals. The US will not only be the forerunner in commercial use of the internet, but also do everything it can to protect this fountain of economic prosperity.

In Europe, and particularly in Germany, both law and labor agreements prohibit the recording of most user actions. Informational self-determination and protection against performance monitoring have the highest priority; monitoring for abuse usually remains unmentioned.

Here those responsible for security and data protection must convince employee representatives that they will use recording only to monitor abuse. Exact agreements must be arrived at to evaluate this information, as is often the case in German single-plant bargaining agreements.

6.6   TRANSFERS TO THIRD COUNTRIES

Once the Community has implemented the EU Directive, you can assume the presence of an equal level of protection throughout the EU. Transfer of personal data within the EU thus becomes possible, as it does to third countries that show evidence of an appropriate level of protection.

6.6.1 Appropriate level of protection

The EU data protection Directive seeks to eliminate most limitations to the international transfer of personal data within the Community. Article 25, however, prohibits transfers to third countries without an appropriate level of protection.

Article 26 does permit exceptions, for example when the subject gives consent (section 1a), to fulfill a contract between the subject and the person responsible for the processing (section 1b), or when contractual clauses guarantee the protection of privacy. This contractual situation references section 2, according to which a Member State can approve the transfer of personal data when no appropriate level of protection exists.

> . . . Where the controller adduces adequate safeguards with respect to the protection of the privacy and fundamental rights and freedoms of individuals and as regards the exercise of the corresponding rights; such safeguards may in particular result from appropriate contractual clauses.

6.6.2 Contracts

A working group on the protection of personal rights during processing of personal data, called Group 29 for short, issued Working Paper 12 [WP-12] to treat its position on the transfer of data to third countries.

The Group places special value on the practical implementation of regulations: they must be implemented. Negotiations with the US had significant problems on this point.

A contract offers a means to provide for adequate guarantees by the person responsible for processing that involves transfers to a third country with an unacceptable level of protection. The Working Paper from Group 29 suggests that companies require contractual observance of the following basics from the EU Directive.

- Limitation of purpose (according to Article 6 section 1b)

  Data may be processed only for a specific purpose.

- Data quality and non-excessive nature (according to Article 6, section 1d)

  Data should be accurate and, where necessary, kept up to date. The data should be adequate, relevant, and not excessive in relation to the purposes for which it is transferred or further processed.

- Transparency (according to Article 10)

  Individuals should be provided with information as to the purpose of the processing and the identity of the data controller in the third country, and other information in so far as this is necessary to ensure fairness.

- Security (according to Article 17)

  Technical and organizational security measures should be taken by the data controller that are appropriate to the risks presented by the processing.

- Right to rectification, access, and objection (according to Articles 12 and 14)

  Subjects must have the right to receive a copy of all their personal data that has been processed and the right to correct the data if it has been proven incorrect.

- Limitation of further transfers to non-contractual partners (according to Article 25)

  Further transfers of personal data from the original recipient in one third country to another third country are permitted only when the new recipient can prove that an adequate level of protection exists there.

Group 29 sees efficient contractual solutions as a clear option for data transmission within global corporations. When those involved in a transfer belong to the same corporate group, an investigation is more likely to result if the contract is not observed, especially given the close relationship between the recipient in the third country and the corporate unit headquartered in the EU.

Transparency of purpose and processor aims at providing the subject with adequate information. Subjects cannot always deduce from a contractual relationship that their personal information will be transferred within a corporate group. Exceptions might include a service-provider contract that is valid around the clock and that mentions international contact points. The contract should therefore mention transfers within the corporate group.

See Däubler (1998) for a sample industrial agreement that refers to transferring data across borders and EUL (1998) for a sample agreement on data protection across areas.

The sample given by Däubler assigns the DPO far-reaching controlling rights for companies in a corporate group. The R/3 System of an American parent company stores personal data that originated from a German subsidiary. The contract states that the German employees have the same level of protection (in the US) that the BDSG grants them in Germany. If the German DPO suspects abuse, an inspection can take place at the parent company.

Eul also refers to a discrepancy in the literature, especially the possible right of a third-country government to execute a warrant. He treats previous contractual solutions that have closed the gaps in the level of data protection in third countries.

No one should think that only government agencies in third countries examine commercial communications. Members of the EU have long been suspected of being henchmen of the American National Security Agency (NSA). The suspicion is that the ECHOLON system eavesdrops on telecommunications satellites and underwater cables to find evidence of economic espionage. On February 23, 2000, the EU Commission organized hearing "attacks on privacy outside the sphere of police and judicial cooperation: the problem of the interception of telecommunications" [ECHOLON]. A former CIA director justifies outside economic espionage among European countries, to search for evidence of their "national culture" of corruption in international agreements [Heise].

6.6.2.1 Agreement on cross-border data traffic in the SAP Group

In consideration of the literature noted above, SAP has developed a contractual agreement that will apply to SAP and all its subsidiaries in the future. The IT security group, the legal department, employee representatives, and the DPO have all worked on the agreement.

A precondition for global implementation and compliance is the inclusion of all data related to security: confidential business data and personal data. Management and the team of those responsible for security must be convinced of the general need for this approach and involved in its implementation. In most cases, the DPO has neither the organizational opportunities nor means to conclude binding international treaties and monitor their observance. But those responsible for IT have issued rules for individual areas and know the contact persons who are responsible for global IT security and who are likely to become the official contact persons according to the agreement.

The agreement contains points that we think will continue to be important in the long term. An appendix indicates the dynamic changes in implementation methods. The methods are published on the SAP intranet as part of an electronic security manual and are always kept up to date. In general, the contract is only a way to package the legal requirements that the law will demand and that already reflect the security procedures in the SAP group.

The agreement consists of the following points.

Preliminary remarks   The secure and unrestricted transfer of data within the corporate group is an absolute precondition for the success of any global company. Such transfers move both confidential business and personal data across international borders.

The meaning and purpose of data protection is to protect the persons whose data is being processed. This goal is reached by a combination of rights granted to the subjects and obligations imposed upon those who perform or are responsible for the processing of the data.

To ensure the security and data protection of information that moves across borders, the parties have reached this agreement. It ensures the existence of a uniform level of security and data protection within the SAP group, a level that meets the requirements of the EU Directive of October 24, 1995. The agreement also follows the recommendations of the EU working group on the transfer of personal data to third countries.

Definitions   The following uses the term sensitive data to mean both business data and personal data.

Confidential business data includes information of the SAP group itself, its partners, and its customers that, if published (prematurely), would case harm to these or other individual persons. In particular, this category includes the following types of information:

- data that ensures the ability to compete
- internal reports
- draft contracts
- access information for systems (network addresses, user IDs, and passwords).

Personal data includes individual entries that contain personal or factual references to a specific person or a person who can be identified from the data. The processing company means the firm that processes data it receives from other companies in the SAP group. When processing employment data, the company that offers employment is always the responsible company.

Obligations during processing of personal data   The parties to the contract agree that personal data must be:

- processed fairly and lawfully
- collected for specified, explicit and legitimate purposes and not further processed in a way incompatible with those purposes
- adequate, relevant, and not excessive in relation to the purposes for which it is collected and/or further processed
- accurate and, where necessary, kept up to date; every reasonable step must be taken to ensure that data which is inaccurate or incomplete, having regard to the purposes for which it was collected or for which it is further processed, is erased or rectified

▓ kept in a form which permits identification of data subjects for no longer than is necessary for the purposes for which the data was collected or for which it is further processed.

The obligations that arise from data collection are derived from the principles articulated in Article 6 of the EU Directive.

Data security   The parties obligate themselves to handle sensitive data confidentially and protect it from access by unauthorized persons. The costs of the protective measures must correspond to the sensitivity of the data and the risks involved. The group-wide security standards must be observed here (*see* appendix A).

The company responsible must be informed immediately in the event of any violation of these rules or other irregularities during processing.

The following technical and organizational measures must be taken for sensitive data.

▓ Controlled admittance

Rooms that offer access to sensitive data must be secured according to SAP policies.

▓ Controlled entry

Only authorized persons can log on to the IT system. SAP policies require proper execution of appropriate measures.

▓ Controlled access

Users receive authorizations that correspond to their roles. When employees take on a new position, the authorizations must be adjusted immediately. If an employee leaves the company, the authorizations must be deleted immediately.

▓ Transfer control

This agreement prohibits the transfer of sensitive data to third parties that are not part of this contract. Transfer becomes possible only with the written permission of the company responsible or with the unequivocal permission of the subject and a contract that requires the third party to provide the same level of data protection. If national laws require the transfer of sensitive data to third parties outside of the SAP group, the company responsible must be informed immediately.

▓ Order control

During order processing, the contract guarantees the principal that personal data will be processed only according to the instructions of the principal and in the context of its original purpose.

▓ Availability control

Appropriate measures must be taken to protect the data against loss or destruction.

Other rights and obligations

▓ Employees and partners who processes sensitive data are obligated to non-disclosure (secrecy) and data protection; they are to be informed about security guidelines (*see* Appendix A). The same holds true for all persons who come into contact with customer information. They must be particularly familiar with the rules for remote services and remote support.

▓ The parties agree that in relation to the subject they will first seek out and make claims against the responsible company for information and rectification.

▓ All subjects must be able to obtain, on demand, information about their personal data, the purpose of any processing, the recipient, and those who can access it. The processing company must respond to the demand of the responsible company without delay.

▓ Incorrect or doubtful data is to be rectified, deleted, or blocked upon the request of the responsible company.

▓ The responsible company obligates itself to support subjects in the exercise of their rights.

Monitoring procedures   The parties to the contract have the right to monitor the orderly execution of the contract at any time. The monitoring officer (and representatives of regulatory agencies) are to be granted unfettered access to all IT systems and documents used for processing the personal data of the contractual partners.

The parties agree to support the monitoring officer and provide any required information.

The responsible company arranges for the investigation and its scheduling.

Responsible contact persons   The parties obligate themselves to nominate a person responsible for security and data protection. That person serves as the contact for all parties and provides support to help fulfill the tasks required by the contract.

The contact person must be kept informed about the processing of sensitive data. The support offered by the contact person includes active cooperation in monitoring activities and the processing requests and complaints.

Appendix   *See* corporate security in SAPNet for German and English versions of the following:

▓ Obligation for non-disclosure and data protection

▓ Security guide

▓ Data protection booklet

▓ Criteria on storing personal data

▓ Privacy policy

▓ Security standard

▓ Security guidelines

▓ Remote service.

6.6.3 "Culture wars"

They that can give up essential liberty to obtain a little temporary safety deserve neither liberty nor safety (Benjamin Franklin).

The US (still) has no general law on data protection because it traditionally prefers a free market. The self-regulation of the market is regarded as sufficient to handle relationships between companies. People simply hope that everyone plays by the same rules of partnership. Government usually intervenes when public health or the environment could be affected. The reports issued by the World Trade Organization (WTO) praises the liberalization (deregulation) of commerce as a basis for recent economic growth. The relaxation of restrictions and the opening of the American economy has led to reduced prices and the increased competitiveness of domestic producers, with more and better-paying jobs.

To follow the conclusion of the WTO a bit further, the improvements in the US must have come at the cost of Europe, which was unable to dismantle governmental limits and restrictions. Europe has not experienced continued economic growth and therefore does not have an opportunity to hold unemployment in check.

Data protection is also a matter of self-regulation in the US. Unlike Europe, damage claims for proven personal harm have an enormous deterrent effect. If a clever lawyer can prove injury to a client's civil rights, the damages involved can often threaten the existence of the company responsible.

And unlike the situation in Germany, citizens in the US demand complete openness from the government. The public has a documented right to view personal data at governmental locations (by virtue of the Freedom of Information Act or other sunshine laws). The court case involving the last census in Germany would have been unnecessary in the US.

6.6.3.1 Safe harbor

The pressure that the EU put on third countries without appropriate levels of security led to the principles of safe harbor in the US regarding data protection that involves Member States of the EU. US companies may exchange data with the EU and private companies only if the companies have freely agreed to undergo monitoring. This principle of economic self-control through self-certification has gained preference among DPOs.

Above all, the Americans must recognize the protection of privacy is seen as a fundamental right in Europe, but that personal data is seen as a normal commercial good in the US.

Superficially, the principles of safe harbor correspond to the principles of data protection as laid down by the EU.

1. **Notice**: information on the purpose and contact persons involved in transfers and indication of the options.

2. **Choice**: option to limit the use of data, especially in transfers to third parties.

3. **Onward transfer** to secure third parties according to principles 1 and 2.

4. **Security** provided by reasonable technical and organizational measures.

5. **Data integrity**: process personal information relevant to the purposes for which it has been gathered and keep data accurate, complete, and current.

6. **Access** of subjects to view and correct or amend their personal data where it is inaccurate.

7. **Enforcement**: implementation of the principles, including the ability of subjects to raise objections and the consequences of non-compliance.

The EU basically regards the model as reasonable and useful, but its main complaint is the failure to include a vehicle to monitor and enforce the principles themselves [WP-27]:

> The pursuance of complaints and the enforcement of rectification are unclear. The principle of enforcement is effective only when it includes the payment of damages for the person harmed and when unresolved issues can be taken to a higher authority for adjudication. In addition, the list does not contain any criteria for lawfulness. It's easy to fear that the self-imposed obligation of the economy can be misused purely as an alibi.

We can easily imagine that the German and French, especially, must see the provision of data protection by self-certification as an oxymoron. Wouldn't the global companies headquartered in Europe be the very first to use the most-favored clause to demand the same relaxation for themselves for competitive reasons?

The discussion on safe harbor – which many already regard as a trade war for data protection – clarifies the different approaches of the EU and the US. The US places the economy's requirements for information exchange in the foreground, and the Europeans proceed strictly according to their guidelines. As pragmatic as Americans are, they accept the principles of data protection, but otherwise do not want anyone looking into the internal matters of a company.

Europeans, however, love and live bureaucracy. They mistrust the free market just like Americans mistrust their own government. They demand that agencies provide a list of regulations, exact export controls, and an extensive monitoring system that cannot be implemented. The protection of privacy gets lost in the middle of a demand for a fundamental right that covers the processing of *all* personal data by *all* companies. The European economy does not have the political voice of the American economy. Are the Americans the only ones to have noticed that, as issued in 1995, the EU regulations no longer correspond to the economy, as clearly seen in practices on the internet or in data warehouses? If you are interested in these topics, please see Chapter 8 on the internet and Chapter 11 on data warehouses.

## CHAPTER 7

Tasks of the data protection officer

Because the German delegation pushed for such a requirement, the EU Directive provides for a data protection officer (DPO). The provisions of national law can set up the position. This position indicates the German preference for a certain amount of self-regulation over general governmental control.

This chapter treats the function and the tasks of a DPO against the background of German experience.

Before we proceed, we must clarify one point. Yes, self-regulation in a company by a DPO is a German invention. But you can find the same or a similar position in other countries as well. We recommend that every company appoint a DPO. The following description of the function and tasks of a DPO and the German experience with this position can help to define the activity areas in which a DPO should operate. At the very least, a company needs someone to convert legal requirements into practice, supplement legal requirements with recommendations and rules, monitor the observance of data protection, and serve as an internal and external contact person to deal with questions of data protection and security.

7.1 LEGAL REQUIREMENTS

According to Article 18 of the EU Directive, the person legally responsible for processing according to national law can appoint a DPO as a subordinate who holds responsibility for the following:

1. for ensuring in an independent manner the internal application of the national provisions taken pursuant to this Directive

2. for keeping the register of processing operations carried out by the controller, containing the items of information referred to in Article 21 (2)

3. thereby ensuring that the rights and freedoms of the data subjects are unlikely to be adversely affected by the processing operations.

International monitoring of data protection moves between belief in the self-regulation offered by the economy (as in the US) without governmental control and wagging fingers and central monitoring by the state.

Germany has previously practiced a mixed form of self-regulation in companies that includes the presence of a DPO along with law at the level of individual federal states and occasional monitoring by regulatory agencies in those states. Several independent auditing agencies at the state and regional level reflect differing requirements and auditing procedures. Accordingly, the practical implementation of data protection must be evaluated differently for each company.

7.2 PERSONS RESPONSIBLE AND TASKS

DPOs in a company must perform specific tasks. This section focuses on the tasks of a DPO, particularly as contained in the new German Federal Data Protection Law:

- monitoring the proper use of programs
- familiarizing employees with the law.

The controller is the internal organizational unit with the sole authority to determine the purposes and means of processing personal data. The controller must provide the DPO with an overview of information as derived from Article 19 of the EU Directive:

- name and address of the controller
- the purpose or purposes of the processing
- a description of the category or categories of data subject and of the data or categories of data relating to them

■ the recipients or categories of recipients

■ validity dates for deletion

■ proposed transfers to third countries

■ a general description of the measures taken to ensure the security of processing

■ persons with authorized access.

Article 19 does not include validity dates for deletion or persons with authorized access. The points are a German addition.

Only the future can tell the arrangement of rights and obligations that this point will bring to the DPO. Here we see an approach to how a DPO can fulfill the duties of that office outside of Germany.

7.2.1 Persons responsible

Section 6.2.7 treated individual areas of responsibility within a company: upper management, system administrators, and application administrators all assist the DPO. In the area of human resources, elected employee representatives such as the works council and the HR department itself are also involved.

The duties of a DPO include raising consciousness of the principles of data protection, training employees, and inspecting programs, authorizations, data frugality, and transfers. The DPO is a contact person for any questions and for complaints. The DPO must be integrated into projects that involve personal data.

Project management should also appoint additional responsible persons (or deputy DPOs) for individual applications and systems. Those responsible for systems also have responsibility for the security of the systems (*see* [SAP-SG]). Those responsible for applications are contact persons for the DPO. They must have the SAP training needed to perform their tasks.

The DPO and employee representatives should be integrated into individual projects that process personal information. The project plan should also include the appropriate basic training.

But the DPO does not need to become an expert. A DPO can depend upon the collegial assistance and specialized knowledge of contact persons, administrators, and SAP consultants.

7.2.2 Information policy

The example of internal SAP information policy can illustrate how to transmit information and internal guidelines to employees within a company.

7.2.2.1 Security and data protection manual

All obligations of and information on data protection and security are kept up to date and published on the SAP intranet. No printed security, employee, or travel cost manuals exist. Employees can call the electronic manuals directly by alias names or bookmarks when needed. They are always kept current and employees can copy or print them as necessary. But what's the value of an obsolete document in a drawer these days?

The corporate security homepage offers an overview of the following areas in both German and English:

- data protection
- development group for security
- IT security
- security service.

Representatives of each group meet regularly to discuss their experience, agree on any measures needed, and create reports for the board of directors.

The information contained in the page is valid throughout the world for the SAP group.

7.2.2.2 Information on data protection and security

The site contains information on the obligations of employees along with additional information for all employees on security and data protection:

- non-disclosure and secrecy obligation
- agreements on recordings of the telephone, internet, and access control systems
- excerpts from various data protection and media laws, copyright laws, and internet links to the complete citations
- criteria for storing personal data
- recommendations for surveys
- recommendations for setting up processing overviews
- security guide
- security guidelines
- security standards.

The security standard contains information on linking partners, desktops, and server networks and dial-up, internet, office, and training connections.

7.2.3 Training

The DPO must employ appropriate means to inform persons involved in the processing of personal data of data protection regulations.

Experience has shown that the number of persons with access to personal data continues to grow. Direct training for all of them is usually not a sensible approach.

Technical

It's a good idea to use modern media, such as an electronic data protection manual on an intranet, to convey the required information. You can target specific groups in this manner. Section 6.4.1 and this section list various pamphlets regarding the obligations of various groups. See the checklist in Table 7.1.

TABLE 7.1	Data protection information and target groups	
Data protection information	**Group of persons**	**Active**
Obligation to observe data protection	All	x
Obligation to observe non-disclosure and secrecy	All	x
Data protection pamphlet	All	x
Recording use of telephone, internet, and so on	All	x
Excerpts of laws	All	
Security guide and guidelines	All	x
Obligations and special pamphlet	Administration	x
Obligations and special pamphlet	Human resources department, project management	x
Criteria for the storage of personal data	Project management	
Suggestions for surveys	Project management	
Recommendation for processing overviews	Responsible application personnel	x

You can send information to the heads of administration, the human resources department, and project management according to delegation and have them redirect the information to the appropriate staff in their departments. Group meetings should include discussions of data protection; if necessary, you can also include those responsible for security and data protection. Delegation offers an advantage: you can transfer responsibility to department heads. You can clarify responsibilities to these personnel who then take responsibility for themselves and their employees. The department heads decide whether or not they will shoulder that responsibility alone or delegate it further within the department.

This approach involves the department heads directly in responsibility for data protection so that they become the first contact person for employees. The security pamphlets should express this reality:

> Should questions of data protection arise, please consult your supervisor or, in special cases, the DPO.

You can maintain any training and register the obligations explained to individual employees directly in the R/3 HR application component: use infotype 0035.

Table T591A stores the info-subtype and maintains the IDs of individual employees. This table can also indicate whether or not a given employee is obligated to data secrecy (*see* Table 7.2).

TABLE 7.2	Table T591A for infotype 0035 for suggestions for training	
Infotype	Sub-type	Text
0035	01	Accident prevention
0035	02	Obligation to observe data protection
0035	03	Training in data protection
0035	04	Information on the storage of general personal data

7.2.4 Inspection

7.2.4.1 Monitoring the proper use of programs

Inspection guidelines issued by the audit group provide accountants and auditors with recommendations on how to perform inspections in the R/3 System. The recommendations are available in English and German. Inspection of the proper use of programs, particularly modifications and enhancement, should be performed by internal auditors upon the basis of audit guidelines and file digests [Guidelines].

The type of inspection depends upon the available time and the scope of the company data to be inspected.

Several variants are possible:

- monitoring data entry
- form and screen templates
- evaluation oriented to transactions
- personnel file (transaction pa10) to display infotypes
- table, field, and program analysis with the ABAP Dictionary.

Additional inspection fields would include:

Modification rules Rules for modifications and in-house development must be created and observed. The DPO must be notified of any planned IT activities in advance. Doing so enables the DPO to ensure that data protection law is being observed.

Authorization concept You can use the SAP authorization concept to protect any objects or functions. The programmer determines where and what is inspected; the user administrator determines who may execute a function or access an object.

Administration of tasks As discussed in section 2.1.2, user administration should separate tasks and work with a division of labor. User administration creates user names and initial passwords. It determines if new users have received instructions on their responsibilities for data protection when processing personal data or if they are obligated to observe data secrecy.

Obligation   We recommend a general obligation to data secrecy for all systems users, even when they do not have access to personal data initially. See section 6.4.1 on obligations.

You can also require other obligations centrally.

- Secrecy of business secrets of the corporate group, customers, and partners.

- Special obligation of administrators and emergency users, who have extensive rights in the SAP systems and the system environment. In particular, you must ensure that no one abuses logons (secure passwords).

- Confidential handling of all information related to accessing the system and working in it: passwords, addresses, data structures, programs, and documentation. This aspect includes knowledge of customer and partner systems.

Use of programs   Report authorizations control the use of programs in SAP R/3. You can use report RSCSAUTH to generate an overview of standard and customer-specific authorizations, and then make any required adjustments. The HR application component of the R/3 System offers a special option to monitor the use of specific programs, including the parameter variants. You can use this feature to find abuse and problems with authorization variables. Labor agreements might require that you inform employees of your intention before turning on this feature.

7.2.4.2 Auditing and the Audit Information System

Auditing a system makes sense only when all the security settings are active in a given environment. Auditing does not make sense for a simple test system for the SAP system as delivered, but for an active production system or one that is being prepared for production.

You must always view the security functions of an SAP system in the context of the corresponding system environment: interfaces, third-party software, customizing settings, modifications, and other environmental factors such as the administrative and departmental staff, the place of a security policy in the company, and the implementation of the security policy.

All security measures are useless if you cannot trust system administration or when the operating or database systems are not completely under control. For just this reason, therefore, the SAP Security Guidelines treat the system environment in more depth than the SAP system itself. You must first find and repair the weaknesses in the environment because they affect all applications.

For the customer, central certification would mean that the customer must insist upon that tested status. Every change moves the customer away from the certified status and might well lead to an increased security risk. That situation would require another audit as an on-site acceptance.

Technical

The Audit Information System (AIS) offers direction in performing an audit based upon the guidelines of the auditing group [Guidelines].

The auditor uses the AIS to determine the security standard in the system – almost at the push of a button. This approach is similar to the ideal formulated by the auditing group. The ideal includes support from a software tool. The tool should not aim at saving time when performing mechanical and automatic tasks during auditing. Rather, it should allow auditors to concentrate on their more important (and lucrative) consulting business.

In AIS, SAP offers a set of tools that matches these requirements. Certain transactions and reports can run with predetermined defaults (SAP variants) for regular audits. The system stores the results as lists. Comparisons with the same parameters provide the required data almost completely automatically upon a repeat inspection.

Checking security is a permanent task, particularly in the SAP environment. The system is almost constantly in flux because of external innovations and customizing modifications to the business processes. The adjustments occur not only in the SAP system, but also in the entire environment, including the operating system, the database, the network, and security products.

It is best to arrange for a data protection audit by a consulting firm that specializes in the processing of personal data, such as outsourcing firms or service and computer centers.

7.2.5 Obligations of employees

All employees who process personal data must be obligated to observe data protection. *See* section 6.4.1 on the obligations of various groups of employees.

7.2.6 Overviews

To create the notifications register required by Article 17 of the EU Directive and maintain oversight of the processing of personal data, it helps to create overviews. A broad overview shows the systems and SAP components that process personal data. Overviews are needed to prove that data is being or has been processed legitimately.

Only the DPO is in a position to define the scope of the overviews. The overviews are intended for the DPO, who must communicate what information is needed for what purpose. Only the DPO can determine if the scope can be processed in the time available. The DPO must interpret and implement the brief formulations of law in a business environment. Whenever an external person offers advice, the DPO should examine the motivation behind that advice (*see* security guideline 12) and ask why and to what end desktop documents are needed.

Of course, the DPO must receive exact regulations, especially from supervisory authorities. But, if these do not exist and several contradictory opinions on overviews do, it's best for the DPO to formulate and implement an internal policy. As we will see, SAP systems live because of their dynamism. A printed overview is obsolete, and therefore worthless, only weeks later. Note that only programming specialists can interpret many overviews properly. The external observer does not see the data field itself, the context in which the program uses it, or the value fields controlled by table fields.

Accordingly, this section illustrates the ways to get to the current data in the system at the desired time. For example, we recommend that the DPO become familiar with the ABAP Dictionary. The DPO's level of knowledge is crucial to determine if hundreds of table overviews with where-used lists in thousands of unfamiliar programs are really helpful.

The inspection measures to be performed determine the scope of the overviews. If only minimal inspections are needed or required, a file register that describes individual fields and their purpose plays a secondary role.

The controller must make the overviews available. To fulfill the requirement for detailed overviews, the department involved must have good knowledge, at least, of table processing, the Repository Information System, the ABAP Dictionary, and the authorization concept. The DPO can get the required basic knowledge from the department responsible.

Since the DPO is to be involved in a project from the very beginning, the officer is also involved in customizing decisions that determine what data is collected and stored. At that point, discussions must consider the following overviews.

7.2.6.1 Categories of data

The R/3 System stores data in relational databases that consist of more than 10,000 individual tables. Database tables can be transparent tables or cluster and pool tables. The latter contain additional tables that are known to the R/3 System but not to the database. Consider the ATAB pool table which has more than 2,000 tables.

Since the EU Directive requires that a file describe all the procedures for dealing with personal data, general comments are usually enough, such as customer management, vendor management, personnel master data, time management, and applicant management.

The victory of databases meant the demise of transparency in many systems because neither the program coding nor a data dictionary was available. That situation makes a program inspection with a file overview or with coding impossible in many systems. SAP systems do not suffer from this limitation. Standard delivery includes coding and dictionary; comprehensive training enables customers and partners to become familiar with programming techniques and specific programming areas. Nonetheless, direct coding changes remain a risk and make upgrades more difficult.

Those responsible for data protection must determine the depth of information they require to perform their tasks. Experience and common sense are essential.

With the appropriate knowledge, you can follow personal data in the R/3 System to an individual field in a table or in a program.

Nevertheless, it's best to create only the file overviews you need to determine their legality. You don't need to print the overviews; display in the R/3 System is sufficient. Comprehensive registers for a filing cabinet quickly become obsolete and superfluous.

The Audit Information System and the ABAP Workbench provide tools that support dynamic analyses in the system. You can perform additional selections or display where-used lists. Icons permit automatic searches for terms. You can use the Data Browser with a table key to determine specific vendors or personnel numbers.

With the ABAP Dictionary, SAP offers various options to create a general or very comprehensive file register. *See* section 7.3 for further information.

A first step creates a broad overview of the applications that use personal data (*see* Table 7.3 for an example). You can then create additional overviews of critical systems as required.

TABLE 7.3   **Broad overview of applications with personal data**

Area	Application	Au	Tr	Bp	LB	Ca	Da	Re
Employee	R/3 HR	A			L	2, 3	3	1
	Advanced HR	B			L	2, 3	3	2
	Self-Service	C			L	2	3	3
	SAP BW	D			A	2	2	4
	Telephone recording	E			C	2	1	1
	List of employees	F	tp		C	1	1	2
	Skills database	G	tc		A	2	3	3
Contractual relationship	Customer master	H			C	2	1	4
	Vendors	I			C	2	1	1
	Partner database	J			C	2	1	2
	Remote access	K			C	3	3	3
	Orders	L			C	2	1	4
External	Applications	M			C	3	3	1
	Internet	N	tc		C, A	2	2	2

Au	Authorized for access: name and department
Bp	Business purpose
Da	Danger level: 1–4
Ca	Category of data: 1–4
LB	Legal basis: **C**ontract, **L**aw, or **A**greement
Re	Risk estimate: 1–4
Tr	Transfer to third parties (tp) or countries (tc)

This overview can also show management the condition of data protection in the company at the end of each quarter.

7.2.6.2 Persons with authorized access

Employees who may access data also have the appropriate authorizations. *See* section 2.3. The reports and transactions of the Audit Information System can inspect authorizations. *See* section 9.6 for an example.

7.3 TOOLS FOR DATA ANALYSIS

The ABAP Dictionary enables central description and administration of all the data definitions in the system. The most important object types in the ABAP Dictionary include tables, views, types (data elements, structures, and table types), domains, search helps, and locked objects. Use of the ABAP Dictionary presumes basic knowledge of the R/3 table structure.

You can use the ABAP Dictionary to obtain information on tables, structures, field names, data elements, and domains in addition to how they are used in programs, screens, and tables.

During an inspection, you can dynamically access information right up to the individual table filed. The ABAP Dictionary provides the following information (transaction se11):

- structure of tables with fields and domains
- where-used lists for tables, fields, and domains in programs, screens, and tables
- online documentation of tables and fields
- value tables for the permitted values of a domain
- table contents
- number of up-to-date entries in the table
- versions of the table definition.

How can a controller provide the DPO with a file overview?

7.3.1 Table overview

Legal requirements demand that an employer store more than 2,000 individual entries on an employee. HR processes the master data in over 300 tables (infotypes) with more than 10,000 fields. Tables PA0000 through PA0999 are reserved for the master data (structure P0000 through P0999).

The menu paths in the following examples may differ among releases of SAP R/3. The examples use Release 4.6C.

Technical

A table overview can create a short description of the infotypes or tables for the DPO.

Menu path:

Tools • ABAP Workbench • Development • ABAP Dictionary (se11)

Once you have entered the ABAP Dictionary, you can display the structure of all tables. Figure 7.1 shows the initial screen of the Dictionary. From this screen you can also display and search for database tables, views, domains, and help (with the F4 key).

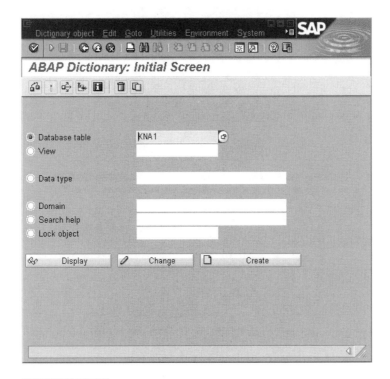

| **FIGURE 7.1** | Transaction se11 for display a table (Copyright © SAP AG) |

| **TABLE 7.4** | **Frequency of tables with personal data** |

Table	Description	Number
PA0*	Personnel master data	459
PA2*	Personnel time data	13
PBO*	Applicant master data	34
PB4*	Applicant data	6
KN*	Customer master	30
LF*	Vendor master data	20
SADR*	Address management	19

The following screen in Figure 7.2 shows the fields of the selected customer master table, KNA1, with field types, data format, field length, available decimal points, check tables, and a short description. You can click on each field for more information in order to see domain or field information.

Table 7.4 illustrates an example from a 4.6C test system: the number of tables with personal data. Here, PA0* means that all tables whose names begin with PA0 have been evaluated.

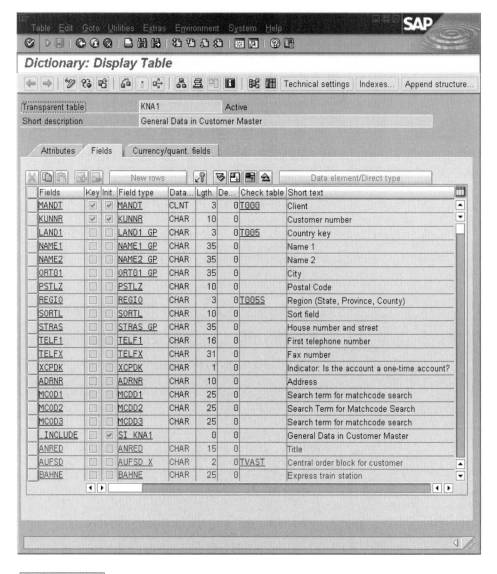

Fields	Key	Init.	Field type	Data.	Lgth.	De...	Check table	Short text
MANDT	✓	✓	MANDT	CLNT	3	0	T000	Client
KUNNR	✓	✓	KUNNR	CHAR	10	0		Customer number
LAND1			LAND1_GP	CHAR	3	0	T005	Country key
NAME1			NAME1_GP	CHAR	35	0		Name 1
NAME2			NAME2_GP	CHAR	35	0		Name 2
ORT01			ORT01_GP	CHAR	35	0		City
PSTLZ			PSTLZ	CHAR	10	0		Postal Code
REGIO			REGIO	CHAR	3	0	T005S	Region (State, Province, County)
SORTL			SORTL	CHAR	10	0		Sort field
STRAS			STRAS_GP	CHAR	35	0		House number and street
TELF1			TELF1	CHAR	16	0		First telephone number
TELFX			TELFX	CHAR	31	0		Fax number
XCPDK			XCPDK	CHAR	1	0		Indicator: Is the account a one-time account?
ADRNR			ADRNR	CHAR	10	0		Address
MCOD1			MCDD1	CHAR	25	0		Search term for matchcode search
MCOD2			MCDD2	CHAR	25	0		Search Term for Matchcode Search
MCOD3			MCDD3	CHAR	25	0		Search term for matchcode search
.INCLUDE		✓	SI_KNA1		0	0		General Data in Customer Master
ANRED			ANRED	CHAR	15	0		Title
AUFSD			AUFSD_X	CHAR	2	0	TVAST	Central order block for customer
BAHNE			BAHNE	CHAR	25	0		Express train station

FIGURE 7.2   Transaction se11 with a display of fields from table KNA1
(Copyright © SAP AG)

7.3.2 Determining tables with personal data

The R/3 System does not label tables with personal data as such, but you can still determine those tables. During customizing, project management decides which infotypes the company will use. Which tables are needed is also checked. If the DPO is involved in the project, the field analysis for individual tables can occur here in the ABAP Dictionary. This approach avoids comprehensive lists of all fields.

The ABAP Dictionary can not only branch to the individual fields of tables, but can also determine the contents of tables and the number of entries. You can also store the lists created by the ABAP Dictionary on a PC for further processing.

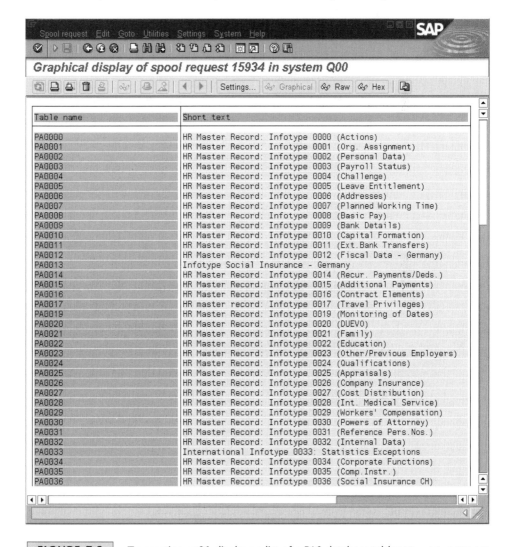

FIGURE 7.3 Transaction sp01 displays a list of a PA0 database tables (Copyright © SAP AG)

Technical

■ Display and print tables with personnel master data

Menu path:

Tools • ABAP Workbench • Development • ABAP Dictionary (se11) • Database Tables PA0 • Display • Print list* (shift F10)

Figure 7.3 shows the beginning of spool output from the Dictionary: a list of all tables that begin with PA0.

■ Display or print tables and fields (also printable as a table manual with report RSS-DOCTB)

Menu path:

Tools • ABAP Workbench • Development • Overview • Information System • ABAP Dictionary • Fields • Structure fields >P000< Print icon* (se84)

■ Where-used list of tables, data elements, and domains

Menu path:

Tools • ABAP Workbench • Development • ABAP Dictionary • Domain >KUNNR< for customer number • Utilities • Where-used list • Indirect application • Tables on Programs (se11)

■ Further processing with Office products

You can store the generated lists on a PC as an Excel, Word, or spreadsheet, HTML, or text file and then use them as a register, providing that downloads are permitted.

Menu path:

System • List • Save • Local file • Unconverted or Spreadsheet, Rich text format or HTML format

7.3.3 Audit Information System

The AIS provides reports and variants that enable you to create a comprehensive file register at the push of a button. You might well need to produce these reports for consulting firms whose customers must comply with the data protection laws.

Technical

Menu path:

Information Systems • Audit Info System • System Audit • Human Resources Audit / Data Protection Audit • File Register for Personnel-Related Data

Figure 7.4 illustrates the initial screen of the Audit Information System.

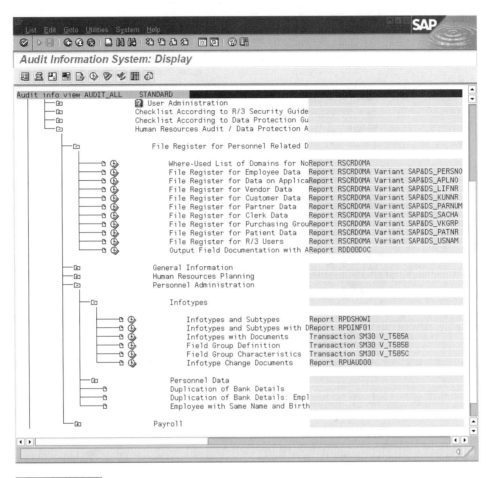

Path to the file register in the AIS (Copyright © SAP AG)

7.3.4 File register with default variants

The AIS path to the file register refers to report RSCRDOMA with the variants given in Table 7.5. The variants are grouped into domains that refer to the tables used in the report evaluation. The variants do not guarantee determination of all tables that can contain personal data. Conversations about the contents between customers and the data protection group have hopefully produced a good approximation of the tables needed for intensive inspection in practice.

To determine the fields and tables in which a clerk's name can appear, variant SAP&DS_SACHA contains the domains illustrated in Figure 7.5. Unlike the individual display offered by the ABAP Dictionary, the report has the advantage of creating only one list with the appropriate references. But the list is alive: from it you can branch to where-used lists in the corresponding reports. This is therefore a current, completely dynamic file register.

TABLE 7.5	Variants for report RSCRDOMA
Variant	Meaning
SAP&DS_APLNO	Applicants
SAP&DS_KUNNR	Customers
SAP&DS_LIFNR	Vendors
SAP&DS_PARNUM	Partners
SAP&DS_PATNR	Patients
SAP&DS_PERSNO	Personnel number
SAP&DS_SACHA	Clerk
SAP&DS_USNAM	User
SAP&DS_VKGRP	Purchasing group
SAP&DS_XUBNAME	User

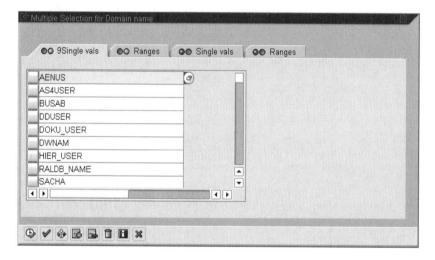

FIGURE 7.5	Variant SAP&DS_SACHA of clerks from report RSCRDOMA
	(Copyright © SAP AG)

When you start report RSCRDOMA, you can select the display of only those tables that are actually populated. With this approach you gain an immediate overview that shows you whether or not any agreements not to use specific tables have been honored. Even those unfamiliar with the SAP R/3 System can easily execute and interpret this report.

7.3.5 Where-used list for populated database tables

With this AIS selection, you enter a domain and/or a data element and receive all the corresponding tables that contain at least one record.

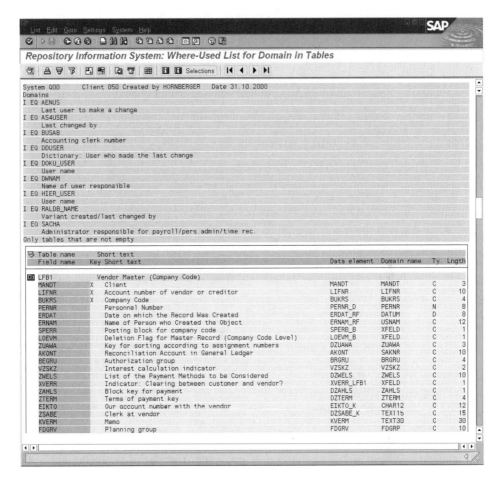

FIGURE 7.6 List output of all tables with variant SAP&DS_SACHA
(Copyright © SAP AG)

Technical

You can select output as a simple list of Data Dictionary tables or as a list of table fields as illustrated in Figure 7.7. You can double-click on the individual fields of each table to drill down to more detailed information.

From the display of the tables used, you can also display special tables and their fields (Figure 7.8).

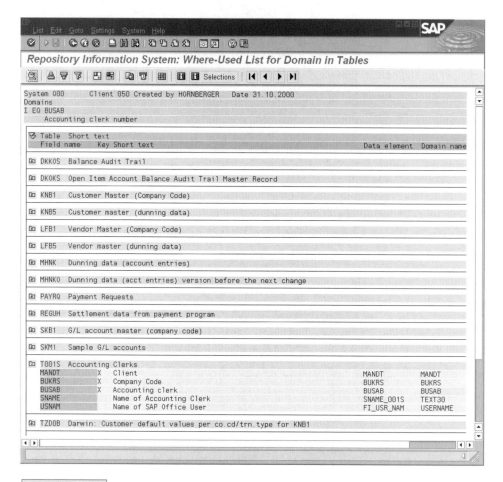

FIGURE 7.7 The use of domain BUSAB in tables and fields (Copyright © SAP AG)

A special challenge for data protection and rectification is the requirement that calls for the ability to display and maintain table contents for special keys (*see* Figure 7.9) from within this simple Dictionary list, assuming that the user has the proper authorizations.

Menu path:

Utilities • Table contents

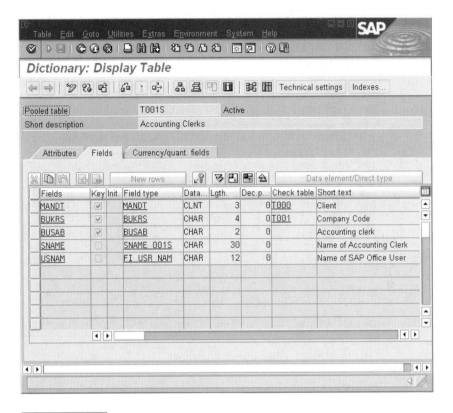

FIGURE 7.8   Field display T001S with field BUSAB (Copyright © SAP AG)

7.3.6 Overview of infotypes in HR

You can start an evaluation of populated infotypes with report RPDINF01. You can generate both a short overview for specific personnel numbers and a general overview that does not require entry of a personnel number. The latter option is particularly interesting to auditors and works councils to help them determine which infotypes are populated in a given client. Once the overview appears, you can drill down and perform a detailed analysis.

Technical

Menu path:

Information Systems • Audit Info System • System Audit • Human Resources Audit / Data Protection Audit • Personnel Administration • Infotypes • Infotypes and Sub-types with Database Statistics

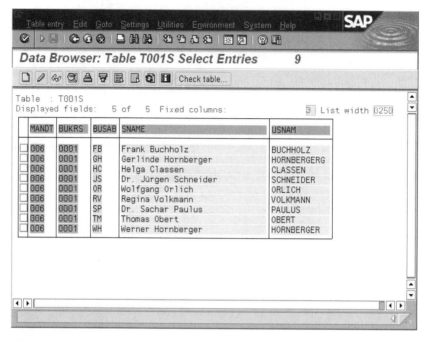

FIGURE 7.9 Table contents of T001S (Copyright © SAP AG)

▨ You can enter one or more personnel numbers and generate an overview of all the populated infotypes for this person or these persons with report RPDINF01. You can limit the overview by personnel number or by infotype (*see* Figure 7.10).

▨ You can enter no personnel number or a group of personnel numbers to generate a list of all populated infotypes. You can also limit the infotypes being examined (*see* Figure 7.11).

7.3.7 Where-used lists

Within the ABAP Dictionary display, you can also generate where-used lists of programs, screen, function modules, domains, tables, and so on.

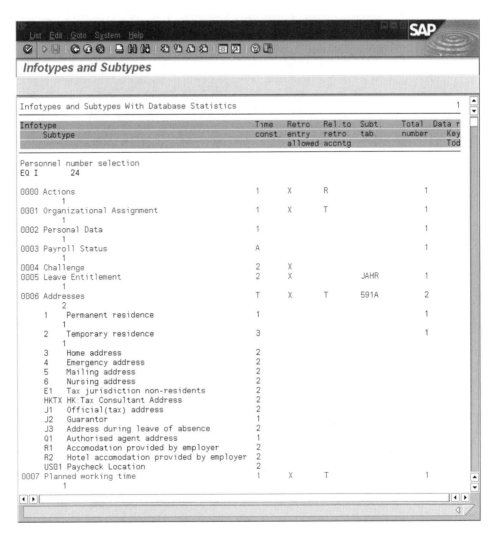

List Edit Goto System Help

Infotypes and Subtypes

Infotypes and Subtypes With Database Statistics						1
Infotype Subtype	Time const.	Retro. entry allowed	Rel.to retro. accntg	Subt. tab.	Total number	Data r Key Tod
Personnel number selection						
EQ I 24						
0000 Actions	1	X	R		1	
1						
0001 Organizational Assignment	1	X	T		1	
1						
0002 Personal Data	1				1	
1						
0003 Payroll Status	A				1	
1						
0004 Challenge	2	X				
0005 Leave Entitlement	2	X		JAHR	1	
1						
0006 Addresses	T	X	T	591A	2	
2						
1 Permanent residence	1				1	
1						
2 Temporary residence	3				1	
1						
3 Home address	2					
4 Emergency address	2					
5 Mailing address	2					
6 Nursing address	2					
E1 Tax jurisdiction non-residents	2					
HKTX HK:Tax Consultant Address	2					
J1 Official(tax) address	2					
J2 Guarantor	1					
J3 Address during leave of absence	2					
Q1 Authorised agent address	1					
R1 Accomodation provided by employer	2					
R2 Hotel accomodation provided by employer	2					
US01 Paycheck Location	2					
0007 Planned working time	1	X	T		1	
1						

FIGURE 7.10   Display of all populated infotypes for a personnel number
(Copyright © SAP AG)

Technical

Menu path:

Tools • ABAP Workbench • Development • ABAP Dictionary • Display <database table> •
Where-used list

Figure 7.12 displays entry to the where-used list for table T001S in programs.

The exact reference for programs is very detailed. For example, a specialist can

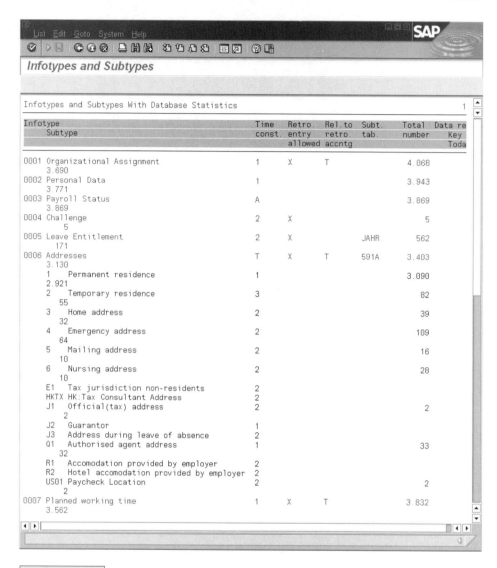

FIGURE 7.11   Display of all populated infotypes without limiting personnel numbers
(Copyright © SAP AG)

determine precisely which programs or screens access which tables. The system is transparent for those authorized, in this case for development in a development system.

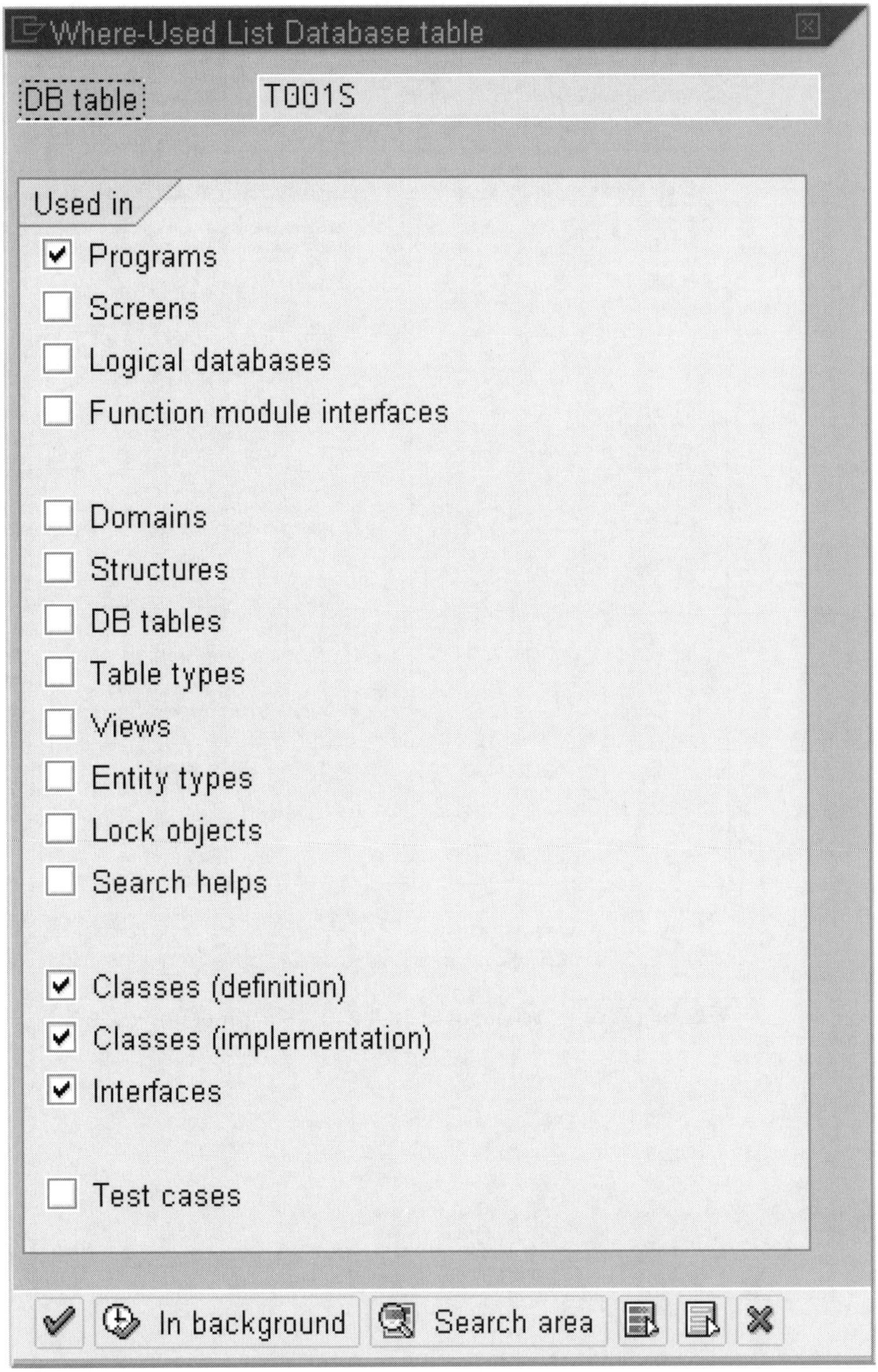

Where-Used List Database table   ⊠

DB table	T001S

Used in

☑ Programs
☐ Screens
☐ Logical databases
☐ Function module interfaces

☐ Domains
☐ Structures
☐ DB tables
☐ Table types
☐ Views
☐ Entity types
☐ Lock objects
☐ Search helps

☑ Classes (definition)
☑ Classes (implementation)
☑ Interfaces

☐ Test cases

✔ ⊕ In background   ▣ Search area   ▤ ▤ ✖

FIGURE 7.12   Call of a where-used list for T001S (Copyright © SAP AG)

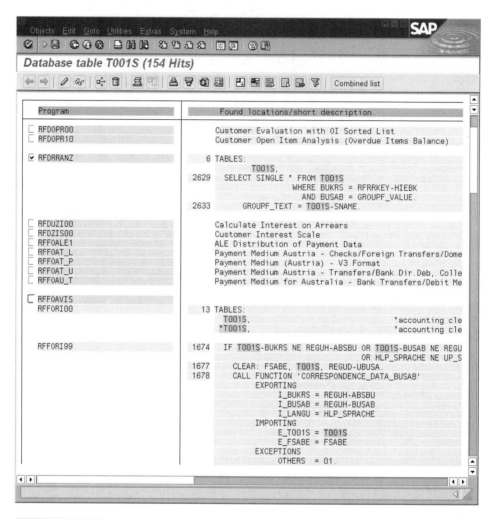

FIGURE 7.13 Where-used list for T001S in programs (Copyright © SAP AG)

## CHAPTER 8

Use of the internet

This chapter enhances the treatment given in Chapter 4 on internet security with mySAP.com by adding a discussion of data protection.

8.1 INTRODUCTION

Let's briefly summarize technical aspects of security discussed previously.

- The internet poses multifaceted dangers. The absolute preconditions for commercial use of the internet include secure connections, secure systems, authentic (non-counterfeit) data, uniquely identifiable subscribers, and the security of law for electronic commerce.

- Secure transactions in the mySAP Marketplace presuppose reliable identification of users and systems. Authentication of users can range from a simple password procedure to the use of PKI and chip cards with secure user ID.

- Digital certificates make the exchange of information secure over SSL connections or with X.509 certificates.

- Digital signatures make electronic transactions provable. The signature need not belong to a single user, but can be used centrally by an entire company.

■ The infrastructure of mySAP.com supports the assignment of authorizations that allow you to determine the services that different users can employ.

■ Encryption of transactions and integrity of transaction processing guarantee the security of transactions. These features ensure that all documents reach their recipients and exclude multiple transmissions. A log belongs to each document.

■ The Message Store in mySAP.com logs transmissions and receipts for all orders and confirmations (business-to-business procurement). In the event of a dispute, this feature can prove that an order was issued and confirmed.

This chapter does not treat security techniques as such, but the self-understanding of a company that is moving toward international e-commerce. Such companies must consider internal norms for etiquette on the internet (netiquette) and ways to treat external visitors fairly and legitimately relative to the storage and use of their personal data. In some cases, companies will need to solicit the agreement of visitors to process and transfer their data.

8.1.1 Stormy development

We have frequently emphasized that we are still at the start of developments on the internet, developments for which we have no overview. Many commentators see these developments as a constitutive element of the service revolution, others speak of a continuation of the industrial revolution. Many claim that in a few years nothing will be as it was.

This stormy development has also affected SAP. The security functions described or intimated here are tested continually. It will be interesting to see where the demands of the economy and of interest groups will lead us. One of the main strengths of SAP is its ability to react to market demands and customer desires in a short time, so we can assume that in a few years parts of what we have described here will become amusing and seen as insufficient or unrealistic.

8.1.2 Political assessment

In a ministerial statement on the topic of opportunities for global information networks [Minister], ministers of the EU, the European Free Trade Zone, Central and Eastern European countries, and Cyprus summarized their expectations at a meeting in Bonn in 1997.

■ The creation of global information networks is an extremely positive development of significance for the future of Europe and an opportunity for everyone: large and small companies, citizens and agencies, commerce, public health, training, and leisure (points 1 and 2).

■ Global information networks allow the right to freedom of expression and the right to information access to become realities. They foster democracy (5).

- European companies have committed comprehensive expertise and finances to position themselves successfully in the global multimedia and information market (10).

- The expansion of global markets must arise from commercial initiatives in the market (14).

- European industry has taken a leading role with the Trans-Atlantic Business Dialogue to opening global communications markets and eliminating obstacles (15).

- Personal data on the users of global information networks should be collected and processed only when the user is aware of the fact and has given express permission, or when the collection and processing is permitted by law. Corresponding security measures in the legal and technical areas must be taken to protect privacy (49).

At the beginning of 2000, the EU heads of state and government met in Lisbon and called for equipping all schools with internet access. And to counter the American role as leading economic power, one EU commissioner also wanted to ban all US software from European classrooms. In her opinion, such as step was necessary to inoculate European youth against American culture.

8.1.3 Rigid legislation

The creation of global information networks has one certainty: global internet offerings will not respect existing, "ancient" laws; the internet clock runs much faster than a normal clock. By the time European laws run through the legislative process, the practices described in the legislation are often already obsolete. At the international level, the laws are ridiculed, ignored, and circumvented, or the market moves to third countries with lower levels of data protection.

The rigid process of legislation can no longer apply. It must become as flexible as developments in the market. The long process in Germany and France for implementing the EU Directive serves as an example of the need to update communications and media laws.

The legislative process must adopt a procedure similar to that of software development, a procedure that focuses on dynamic, continual adjustment rather than long-term planning. The market drives legislation; the global economy will not wait until national governments create national contexts for it.

This is an opportunity to rethink, to redesign. The global availability of the internet will affect other areas. The numerous demands for thinner and uniform communications and data protection laws must be implemented.

The statement issued by European ministers in Bonn provides a glimmer of hope for legislation [Minister].

■ Every legal framework for e-commerce must be clear and reliable; it must strike the correct balance between freedom of thought and the protection of private or public interests (point 21).

■ Given the speed at which new technologies appear, rules must be neutral to technology and unnecessary rules avoided (22).

■ The consideration of fundamental human rights and the interests of society must be guaranteed. Manufacturers and consumers must be protected by fair and transparent service offerings (29).

■ Brokers, network operations, and access providers should not be responsible for content (42).

8.1.4 English as the internet language

The internet will force another trend: English will be the primary language used on the internet. Rapid development will make it impossible for providers to offer various languages. Only global companies, whose language for internal communications will also become English, will be able to translate any or all of their products into other languages. But here, too, the market will decide. If large numbers of customers refuse products in English, companies will be forced to provide a translation at least for their major markets.

A problem of comprehension will arise here for data protection. Both legal requirements (conditions of commerce) and privacy policies will remain unclear to many. Free, unambiguous agreement based upon exact information will remain an illusion.

To avoid this confusion of tongues, we see two options. The same innovation that drives the internet will create automatic translation computers (chips) that can translate understandably and immediately into another language, or users must give in to the trend toward English. Regarding the latter, we see that rather conservative Europe does not feel compelled to achieve economic prosperity at any price, especially one that disregards existing cultural perceptions.

The language of programming and system administration has always been English, and documentation frequently exists in a mixed language. English terms have always characterized program development at SAP and its customers. Basis development has documented every R/2 assembler statement in English since 1979 – even then a feeling of EnjoySAP colored the choice of terms.

8.1.5 Free exchange of information and the consideration of privacy

The objective is the agreement on basic binding principles allowing for the free flow of personal data in worldwide electronic commerce while respecting the individual's right to privacy and thus ensuring trust and confidence in electronic commerce.

This recommendation comes from a group dedicated to the protection of subjects affected by the processing of personal data. The European Council established the group after approval of the EU Directive. The group is to ensure that the rights of users and the protection of their privacy are properly considered within further development of the internet. This approach will increase trust in commercial and private applications. The group also believes that the basics of data protection also apply to the internet. An Internet Task Force is analyzing the technical and legal aspects and will issue its own recommendations [WP-16].

Note the significant expansion. Talk is now of global business – beyond the EU – and the emphasis on proper measures.

8.1.6 Demands of the software and hardware industry

Presently, it is almost impossible to use the internet without being confronted with privacy-invading features which carry out all kinds of processing operations of personal data in a way that is invisible to the data subject. In other words, the internet user is not aware of the fact that his/her personal data has been collected and further processed and might be used for purposes that are unknown to him/her. The data subject does not know about the processing and has no freedom to decide on it. [WP-17].

As described in Chapter 6, this clearly formulated insight is based upon the reality of internet traffic: European legislation either limps behind the reality or a majority of internet users simply ignore the legislation. Almost with resignation, everyone seems to admit that the privacy of internet users is continually abused.

There's no shortage of laws. If you look at the current laws on data protection (§§ 4 and 28) and telecommunications services (§§ 3, 5, and 6 TDDSG) in Germany, you realize that many cases cannot point to a subject's permission or to a legal basis for storing data. Subjects are usually uninformed that their data is being stored, to say nothing about what data is being collected for what purposes and placed into long-term storage.

In its Working Paper 17, the EU group sees no need to create new laws; the EU Directive defines the context of data protection. Instead, the group demands that the software and hardware industry produce secure internet products that enable the following.

▪ Informing subjects of processing

The group is concerned about processing that occurs on the internet without the knowledge of subjects and is therefore invisible to them: supplemental information taken during chats, automatic hyperlinks to third parties, or cookie characteristics.

▪ Information on data processing

Internet users must know what data is being collected, stored, transferred, and for what purpose:

- the browser must provide information on the purpose of connections to a web server

- display of all hyperlinks sent to users

- warnings in comprehensible language on the contents, purpose, and life-expectancy of cookies.

▨ Information on stored data

Internet products should enable users to access data about themselves without any difficulties.

▨ Standard configurations should not support the storage of client data

Browser software should process only the data needed for an internet connection. Cookies should never be stored as a standard feature.

When installing a browser, the user's profile data on the computer must not be evaluated.

▨ Users' free decisions about storage

The design of the software must enable users to decide for themselves about the storage of their personal data with agree/disagree buttons or with configuration options:

- the ability to decide what data may be collected

- the option to refuse cookies altogether

- to collaborate on the contents of cookies.

▨ Removal of client-persistent information

Users need sufficient information to remove client-persistent information themselves or to block its use with reliability.

8.2 DELIMITATION OF THEORY AND PRACTICE

The suggestions given here should help subjects remain masters of their own data at all times. Subjects should be optimally informed and able to agree to the use of their data without coercion and unequivocally.

The market wants the ability to assume agreement from specific behavior because gathering express permission from subjects can be impossible or very expensive in many cases. If subjects do not expressly prohibit processing, the market wants to take their silence as consent (Schleutermann, 1995).

If the existing guidelines and laws are to be observed, any agreement must consider technological innovation. Attitudes must become looser and more relaxed, or every website will force users to read often incomprehensible legalese and give general consent to the use of their data. Who really knows what's in all the agreements you have to sign at the bank, the doctor's office, or the hospital? You really can't talk about free will in a situation where all hospitals function like a cartel and demand the same release. Refusal to agree in one location within the healthcare system can put your life in danger. Do legislatures really want the same situation to apply to the internet just because some commentators place the right of self-determination in the foreground in any discussion about data protection? The needs of the economy are often not addressed, and those needs include not only the desires of upper management, but also the needs of employees and the need for jobs.

As is noted, often, business on the internet is still at the beginning of its development, and this reality is mirrored in legislation. Both subjects and providers of information need unambiguous predictions of legal decisions. Laws are national, but the internet is global. It knows neither temporal nor spatial borders. The EU Directive is a first step toward softening national barriers. It seeks to equalize national laws – at least in the European market.

The example of the internet clarifies that the search for a uniform level of data protection in Europe becomes counterproductive when it ignores the economic power of third countries and the flexibility of the global economy. The US is clearly the leader in the internet market. It sets and will continue to set many standards. If Europe proves unable to find a reasonable approach, hardware and software manufacturers along with service providers will relocate wherever they find the fewest restrictions to economic development. In that case, a brain drain from Europe to the US will become more intense, and sorely needed jobs in the IT sector will go to countries outside the EU. And in conclusion, let's recall the first six preambles to the EU Directive noted in Chapter 5, preambles that refer to a free flow of information and a free market.

We must ask ourselves who sets the priorities for the goals of the EU. If you read legal commentaries on data protection, the law and its prohibitions remain in the center, leaving little room for human collaboration. You would easily get the impression that the leading position is taken by absolute protection of personal rights ahead of all other goals: economic and social goals usually go unmentioned. But real life operates in exactly the opposite direction. Human beings prioritize their goals and regard data protection a luxury until the fulfillment of the high-level goals creates a situation worthy of human dignity.

Isn't current behavior on the internet an expression of subjects who clearly place economic prosperity, peace, freedom, and social stability (see the preambles to the EU Directive) ahead of the security of their personal data? Otherwise, how else could you explain how job applicants who are thoroughly familiar with the weakness of the internet nevertheless use it to transmit the most personal information (resumés, grades, diplomas, and sometimes even police records) to prospective employers and leave the door open to publishing the data publicly? Even the unemployed reveal their situation at the time of need and increasingly use the internet for sensitive data.

We by no means wish to speak of illegal activities here. We believe that the right of self-determination for each individual and existing law must be observed. The recommendation of Working Paper 17 draws only one conclusion from the EU Directive: personal data must be treated fairly and legally; subjects must have the right to determine how their own data is used.

But particularly for the internet, Europe needs some connection to the outside world, particularly to the philosophy of self-regulation in the US. A growing trend sees internet companies issuing privacy policies that avow security and data protection and that provide enough information to subjects. In the US, customers are also informed that the provider assumes no liability for any damages; internet users are responsible for themselves. Courts have repeatedly tested this principle and found it valid; it excludes claims for damages from the outset (think of the rules in a hospital here).

8.3 PRIVACY POLICY

A privacy policy must rest upon the foundation of mutual trust. Providers and suppliers depend upon fair partnership and upon equalized give and take. Fair treatment of the available data, be it confidential or personal, must be seen as self-evident (see data protection guideline 4).

Like the faint-hearted suggestions of EU organs, the SAP privacy policy was developed in light of customer demands and the needs of individual projects. It is not our goal to develop a one-size-fits-all solution for all cases, but to react to the specific needs of each case. For example, a statement of agreement is not always necessary – a purely informative notification may be sufficient.

The current SAP privacy policy is available at the SAP homepage under Privacy Statement. It contains the following points.

▦ Remarks on data protection

Protecting the individual's privacy on the internet is crucial to the future of internet-based business and the move toward a true internet economy. SAP has created this privacy statement to demonstrate its firm commitment to secure and trustworthy internet commerce and the individual's privacy. Read more about our practices for gathering and distributing information on our websites.

▦ Privacy across the SAP network

As a global company, SAP operates a number of websites around the world. Any information that you submit to one of our sites in any one country or language may be sent electronically to a server for one of these sites in another country. As such, the information may be used, stored, or processed outside the country where it was recorded. However, we safeguard your data security interests around the world by ensuring that this SAP site adheres to our international privacy principles described in this policy.

■ What information do we collect?

– IP addresses

We use your IP address to help diagnose problems with our server, to administer our website, or to gather broad demographic information.

– Cookies

We may use cookies to enhance the user experience and deliver personalized content. Cookies help us to deliver information specific to your interests, to save you having to re-enter your password each time you visit our site, or to keep track of your shopping cart. Cookies also allow us to better analyze our site traffic patterns so that we can bolster our web offering.

– User registration

You may choose to fill out a registration form on our website with contact information that we or our business partners may need. This information is used to send you requested information or products, to contact you with other product information, news, or promotions and to learn more about our web visitors.

– E-mail addresses

If you give us your e-mail address, we will communicate with you via e-mail. However, we do not share your e-mail address with others outside the SAP group of companies. You can choose not to receive e-mails at any time.

– Registration for third-party services at mySAP.com

At mySAP.com you can register for third-party services. Those services are available through mySAP.com, but are provided by a third party, which is typically not affiliated with SAP. When you sign up for one of these services, it may be necessary to transfer some of your mySAP.com registration information to this service provider. Also, if the service you chose requires your e-mail address to fulfill this service, we will also give your e-mail address to the service provider.

– Shopping

Our site includes order forms that you fill out to request information, products, and services. These forms collect your financial information, such as your banking details or credit card. We will use any financial information that you submit solely for billing and payment purposes.

– Online surveys

From time to time, we may conduct online surveys. Our surveys may ask you for demographic information, such as zip codes or your industry sector. If the online survey collects contact data, we may use that data to send you further information only if we specifically asked for your permission in the survey. You are free to opt out of receiving future mailings at any time.

– Links to other sites

This site contains links to other sites. SAP is not responsible for the privacy practices or the content of other websites.

▨ Online security

SAP wants your shopping experience to be simple and safe. We support secure online shopping using secure server technology. The secure server technology used on SAP Store encrypts your personal financial information before it is transmitted over the internet. That means information such as your name and credit card number is protected in a secret code until we receive them.

▨ Opting out

Rest assured – you can opt out of receiving communications from us now or at the point on our site where we request information from you. An e-mail is enough to have us remove you from the SAP Web registration database or the SAP e-mail list.

▨ Your consent and our revisions

By using this website, you consent to the collection and use of the information as described here. If we decide to make changes to this privacy policy, we will post the changes on this page so that you always will know what information we collect, how we use it, and when and how we will disclose it.

Critics of American data protection practice will wave their fingers, warn, and ask if this policy can also be used outside of Europe.

We can only reply that this policy originated in the US. That's where the first mySAP Marketplace was created and that's where a statement on data protection was seen as necessary to explain how user data was being used. Readers can judge for themselves how close the SAP privacy policy comes to meeting the requirements of the EU group.

8.4   HOPES AND WISHES

At the end of the section on data protection, we want to summarize the recommendations made in previous chapters as we close this presentation on the internet. After all, the internet is one of the main reasons that federal or national laws can hardly regulate global communications that now threaten to become completely independent.

In general, we have pleaded for a convergence between the philosophy of data protection in private enterprise between the EU and the US:

▨ strengthening self-regulation in private enterprise

▨ simplifying rules based upon international data protection principles.

8.4.1 Self-regulation versus government control

Welcome to the USA: we have George W. Bush, Johnny Cash, Bob Hope, and Stevie Wonder.
Welcome to the European Union: we have Romano Prodi, no cash, no hope, and no wonder.

Does this easily modified T-shirt slogan that once applied to the competition between Canada (Brian Mulroney) and the US (George W. Bush) speak to our present and even more to our future?

After implementation of the EU Directive, Europeans do not live on an island of data protection happiness. The efforts of the EU to create distinct data protection rules with the US indicate that Europe is ready for wide-ranging concessions. The European Commission does not wish to place either international trading relationships or the exchange of personal data in jeopardy.

Will we enter into a two-class economy? Will the EU have meticulous and exact regulations along with varied levels of governmental monitoring and sanctions (*see* sections 6.5.6 on the prosecution of a pizza shop and 6.5.2 on the internet disclosures in Italy)? Will third countries have no regulations or a very generous program of self-certification for companies and a lack of any monitoring?

The demands of an economy that operates globally force a move to global regulations. The European economy will exercise tremendous pressure with the argument of competitive distortion when competing firms in third countries can certify themselves as having an appropriate level of protection but European countries are subject to strict regulations and governmental controls. In particular, global groups of companies will either demand the same rights in Europe that they enjoy elsewhere or simply move the affected applications, such as data warehouse solutions, portals, service computing centers, or service providers in the telecommunications market to a third country. Those who don't play along will lose.

8.4.1.1 Responsibility for data protection in companies

If private enterprise companies in third countries are allowed to certify themselves, European companies should be allowed to do the same. The German approach that calls for a data protection officer in the company is the correct approach. As usual, data protection officers report to upper management and their expertise does not depend upon their commissions. If Member States in the EU want to offer the market a greater sense of self-responsibility, the appointment of data protection officers (DPOs) serves as a precondition for that process. But since legislation in the other EU nations will hardly follow the German example, European companies must appoint their own DPOs.

The following overviews summarize previous insights; references to other sections of this book appear in parentheses.

So far, we've reached the following insights.

- Despite 20 years of data protection laws in Germany, the laws are abused in many cases and the obligation to appoint a DPO and notify subjects is simply ignored. The data protection reports in individual states bear constant witness to this situation.

- Countries that have traditionally implemented data protection measures have been unable to implement the EU Directive on time (5.3). Other countries have implemented the Directive quickly, but have not taken the corresponding measures to implement real data protection (6.5.2).

- The mistrust of citizens for Big Brother in government is thoughtlessly transferred to private enterprise (6.2.2).

- The demand for data protection among subjects is just as small as the publicized occurrence of problems (security guideline 8)

- Even experts can hardly unravel the legal regulations on data protection. DPOs are insecure (6.5.1).

- A flourishing market offers contradictory commentaries and non-practitioners offer seminars for practitioners (6.2.2).

- Legislation cannot keep pace with technological development (8.1).

- Users cannot recognize the recording of user data on the internet (8.1).

- Third countries mistrust governmental control and trust self-regulation by companies and the market (6.6.3).

If we draw conclusions from these insights, we can write our own wish list.

1 Distinguishing between the public and the private sectors

- Complete openness must exist in the relationship of government to citizens (6.6.3). The fundamental right to self-determination of data (derived in Germany from legal challenges to the last census) must enjoy particularly high regard when subjects are forced to provide private data (6.2.2). All citizens must be informed about the processing and transfer of their data, and must be able to delete stored data at any time. In particular, transfers to other governmental agencies must be strongly prohibited and monitored closely by supervisory authorities.

- Self-responsibility and the regulation of the market should be trusted in the private sector (6.1.1). This should hold especially true when personal data is managed because of contractual relationships and legal requirements. Companies have a strong self-interest in protecting employee and customer data as a valuable economic good (6.1.2). Market participants can decide if they want to surrender their private data without any guarantee of security. Security will become competitive in many segments of the market according to security guideline 3: functionality often comes ahead of security.

The role of the DPO in companies must become stronger.

Companies with legal notification obligations, especially those that transfer data without a contractual relationship, must remain under governmental control (6.1.1).

- Supervisory authorities must still monitor the reasons behind processing and regularly inspect both public companies and those with notification obligations.

2 New self-awareness for DPOs

- The rights and obligations of the DPO must be expanded. The DPO determines the data protection measures required by a company, based upon international data protection principles and the particular needs of the company. A DPO must not depend upon a commission: internally or externally.

- A security concept lists the security measures and is made available internally (employees) and externally (contractual partners) as a means of building trust.

- Auditing and certification based upon the security concept can publicize the security standards of a corporate group. Especially in business on the internet, companies can gain a competitive advantage by marketing their security standards globally and guaranteeing their implementation credibly.

- The demand for security and data protection is actually an artificial creation of various interest groups. The market will make its own decisions in the long term. On the internet, it will be interesting to see the level of interest in companies that provide neither a security guarantee nor a privacy policy. In the private sector, internet customers decide if security comes before functionality; in the public sector, official agencies make the rules.

- The DPO must be able to delegate tasks and responsibilities independently. Upper management and the IT staff must accept this approach as the precondition for self-regulation. A security instance must provide monitoring (security guideline 5).

- The DPO uses the principle of proportionality to decide on the proper technical and organizational measures needed in the company. The DPO monitors progress toward the goals and regularly reports to those responsible and to management. They, in turn, support the DPO in implementing the measures.

3 Persons responsible for security (security guideline 6)

You must first define the responsibilities for security in the company. Only a few people are involved in a small company; different departments are involved in a large company.

- Upper management appoints a security coordinator (CSO).

- The security coordinator develops security management.

- The security coordinator creates a security instance (security council).

- The security instance is responsible for the creation of a security concept.

- The security instance makes the required decisions and prepares reports for the board of directors on a regular basis.

4 Contents of the security concept (1.3 and 6.4.2)

Those responsible create a security concept that aims at establishing a uniform level of security and data protection in the corporate group.

- Security analyses: determining risks, probabilities, and potential damages.

- Definition of security steps and the goals of protection.

- Management signs off on the security concept and makes the means to implement it available.

- Distribution of tasks and the determination of those responsible and of contact persons.

- Implementation and global rollout.

- Information, awareness-building, and training of subjects.

- Monitoring compliance.

- Auditing the security processes.

5 Contribution of the DPO to the security concept (Chapters 6–8)

Based upon the requirements and needs of the company, the DPO determines the appropriate data protection measures and has the security authority approve them. Because the DPO enjoys a great deal of leeway, the approval of this body plays an important role in securing and monitoring the situation (see security guideline 6).

Only someone inside the company is in a position to determine the appropriate measures in light of the organization, the system landscape, the corporate culture, the categories of data, the partners, the level of IT, and the agreed-upon goals. Someone outside the company can use these factors to monitor the situation.

The situation requires constant inspection and review, especially for modifications, upgrades, release changes, new systems, and new system components. You can expect constant adjustment of the security measures in a dynamically changing system landscape. Management makes its decisions based upon the risks and costs formulated in the security concept.

The following contributions of the DPO to the security concept illustrate both the responsibilities and leeway that exist within a company:

- co-determination of definitions for the protection zones of critical systems (1.3)
- determination of the system landscape (test, qualification, and production: 3.6.1)
- distribution of administrative roles (9.6.2), especially user management (2.1.2)
- collaboration in setting rules for password protection (2.2.1)
- agreement with employee representatives on the type of logging (2.5)
- determination of what is to be encrypted (2.6)
- decision on the limits for uploading and downloading (3.4)
- determination of data categories (6.2.4)
- determination of the appropriate technical and organizational measures (6.4.2)
- Agreement with employee representatives on recording and evaluations to detect abuse (6.5.4)
- context for the scope of auditing (7.2.4)
- decision on data exchange with selected companies in third countries (6.6).

6 Additional tasks of the DPO

For the sake of completeness, we list additional duties of a DPO as they apply to the person who organizes a company's approach to data protection. We see a great opportunity here for consultants and consulting firms to instruct and assist the DPO.

Such aids, however, must remember that they can only express recommendations on specific, theoretical constellations. The DPO must take the responsibility of translating them in accordance with the needs of the company.

- Determination of persons responsible for systems and applications (6.2.7 and 7.2).
- Obligating those responsible, administrators, and human resources staff (6.4.1).
- Releasing new projects that involve personal data (6.2.7 and 7.2).
- Weighing the interests of the company and subjects (6.2.2).
- Contributing a section on data protection for the electronic security manual (6.4.1 and 7.2.2).
- Supporting a process to obtain information in the creation of processes (6.3.2).
- Drafting statements of obligations, determination of those who will take on the obligations and those responsible for performance (6.4.1).
- Conversations with employee representatives (6.3.4).
- Checking the need for contracts when transfers to third countries are involved (6.6.2).

- Determination of training needs (7.2.3).
- Templates for overviews (7.2.6).
- Contributing to the privacy policy on the internet (8.3).

8.4.2 Uniform regulations

The following points summarize our wishes.

1 Self-responsibility before legal leashing

Let's take the example set by the US, swear off bureaucracy, and trust companies and a functioning economy (6.6.3). Let's prefer practical recommendations to obsolete regulations.

2 Uniform, simple legislation

The goals of the law must be clearly indicated as an introduction: protection of fundamental human rights from the power of the state and companies, along with regulations for free, secure, and global exchange of information to secure economic and social progress and the well-being of humanity (5.3).

The center here contains the principles of data protection as outlined in Article 6 of the EU Directive, which has been ratified by several states since 1981 as Convention 108 of the European Council (6.2.5).

Technical regulations require too much change: they are to be removed and published when needed as guidelines on data protection.

3 Consideration of market demands

Globalization of the economy demands as free a flow of data between companies as possible, and especially within a corporate group. European economic associations have demanded an exception (privilege) for corporate groups since 1992 (6.1.2).

The addition of "on the free movement of such [personal] data" in the title of the EU Directive must be respected (6.1.1). The private sector has a fundamental right to process data, which should be anchored in law. Data protection regulations should be liberalized; laws should govern gross abuse (6.5.1 and 6.5.4). Data protection concerns must not limit detailed logging to track abuse.

Data protection laws should be liberalized in the private sector but strengthened to protect citizens in the public sector. The public sector, especially, must respect demands for the right of informational self-determination of the individual. Relationships between contractual partners are to be liberalized according to the principles of the market (6.2.2).

4 Practical guidelines for implementation

Those responsible for the security of data protection need practical directions on how to implement data protection in a company. The law can only define the context: guidelines can deal with new needs that arise from technological innovation and undergo regular updating.

The market, data subjects, and associations of interested parties should demand these guidelines and supplement them with constructive suggestions. Governmental authorities should approve them and then legal experts should formulate them. And everything should occur in that order.

We also see a market for private and public consulting. Public agencies should use this opportunity to learn from consultants and to evaluate private recommendations.

The DPO needs guidelines with an official character for the following points. We believe we have made a contribution here.

- Not all personal data is the same: the DPO needs support in defining data categories and protective zones (6.2.4).

- Subjects have various demands of data protection. It often helps to classify matters according to their relationship to the subjects (6.1.1): contract (voluntary transfer), law (forced transfer, employee data, or employer as government agent), address broker, *and* information brokers (of unknown origin and raising questions of authorization).

- The EU Directive does not require written agreement. Certain cases should allow for electronic agreement or legally conclusive agreement. This should apply especially when subjects consciously entrust their data to others after having carefully selected partners and had the opportunity to gather sufficient information (8.2).

- Which data can be transmitted to companies in third countries? Which data can be transferred within an international corporate group? What may occur within group networks to monitor abuse (6.5.4 and 6.6)?

- When do internal services for a group of companies turn the group into a service provider, and what does that mean for recording, transfer, and monitoring abuse (6.2.3 und 6.5.4)?

- Details on technical and organizational measures and agreement with the security concept (6.4.2).

Part 3

Special Topics

## CHAPTER 9

The special role of the administrator

To accomplish their tasks, administrators possess all rights and authorizations. They can grant rights to other users. As the highest authority, administrators know everything, see everything, and can do everything.

9.1 INTRODUCTION

Even many responsible experts are truly shocked when system, database, or network administrators display their cornucopias of access options and demonstrate how they can display salary or private information without the knowledge of the applications involved.

Data protection officers and security staff note that projects, contracts, and explanations do not mention administrators as such. Insiders know that any mention is unnecessary because the presence and activity of administrators is self-evident.

At the end of this chapter, it will be clear that trust and self-responsibility, two terms that do not appear in the laws and guidelines, are an absolute precondition for efficient implementation of security and data protection in a company.

At this point, it's good to recall some security guidelines from Chapter 1 (section 1.2.2):

■ it's certain that nothing is certain (1)

- functionality must not compromise security (3)
- the employee is the greatest risk to security (4)
- respect employees' sense of responsibility (5)
- coordinate the security staff (6)
- improperly implemented transparent security regulations can be misused (10).

Once again, we emphasize that we look at security and data protection from the viewpoint of development. We don't want to demand additional legislation to prevent administrators from working or to place them under total control. We do hope, however, that this chapter helps illuminate the almost infinite options available to administrators. You can take the appropriate countermeasures, even if they merely increase the level of trust, to an internal threat in the company only when you know what the potential dangers are.

9.1.1 Terms

The following uses the terms typical of each operating system. Microsoft operating systems use the user manager, administrator account, and user accounts. Siemens uses the same terminology for Siemens Nixdorf and Fujitsu-Siemens Corporation: system administrator, user ID, and account number. We hope that the use of these familiar terms will make specialized readers feel at home.

9.2 SOME EXPERIENCE WITH SECURE OPERATING SYSTEMS

To deal with the issue of administration, we need to look back at our personal experience with system administration. You can correctly judge the responsibilities and options of administrative activities only if you have enjoyed those privileges in practice and have been able to plumb their nuances over the course of several years.

We believe that those responsible for data protection and security must have this background knowledge before they can correctly determine where the risks lie and if the countermeasures they take are efficient. People with those responsibilities see security measures from the viewpoint of an abuse of power or of a burglar. Just like modern criminologists, they and their assistants must keep pace with potential perpetrators in the use of technology. Their experience has taught them that a too-rapid implementation of technology does not create advantages, but security risks, especially when time constraints or a lack of knowledge means that even publicly available security measures are not implemented. Internal employees who read security instructions can easily give in to the temptation to check if system administrators have done their homework (*see* guideline 10 on transparency). Curiosity can quickly lead to a breach of data protection law and possible penalties. Too much transparency can be harmful here.

9.2.1 Rights of system administrators

First, let's look at the options available to a system administrator of a mainframe system considered secure.

From the very beginning, SAP has not only developed system-independent applications, but also prepared interfaces to system software. That approach was necessary to deal intensively with operating systems, databases, and transaction monitors and to operate and maintain the systems themselves.

For about 20 years, SAP R/2 has supported the DOS/VSE and MVS from IBM and the BS2000 operating system from Siemens. In this period we have maintained a BS2000 system technically and have enjoyed an active exchange of experiences with the development department at Siemens. After the name was changed to Open Server Dimension (OSD), we worked together to examine the possibility of connecting the R/3 System to BS2000/OSD. With the R/3 database server DS2000, Fujitsu Siemens Computers now offers a database server of mainframe quality: BS2000/OSD functions for hardware availability, maintenance, data backup, job control, and printing are integrated. The R/3 database itself runs under a UNIX system.

To design an optimal development environment and simultaneously create an efficient and high-performance interface to SAP systems, we still need the rights held by system administrators. The following treats these rights in more detail not only because of our practical experience, but also because mainframe operating systems are generally considered more secure than UNIX and Windows platforms.

BS2000/OSD guarantees user IDs and the files available to those IDs a high level of security. Only those with access to a user ID via user name, account number, and password can access the files located there. Users with one set of IDs have no idea of the existence of foreign files. Passwords protect individual files from read or write attempts and are generally available only to one's own user ID. But you can also share these files. A productive SAP system runs under a specific user ID and you can limit access to this user ID to the SAP system administrator and operations scheduling. Normal users cannot display the contents of files or list files. In addition, the address entries are completely sealed off from each other: users cannot end up in the address area of another program. Although address areas can be shared, you can also limit sharing to a user ID and protect it with a password.

The system administrator works with a special user ID, TSOS, which you should protect with frequently changed passwords.

This system of file and memory management based upon strict assignment to users was developed as early as 1968 by RCA. The Americans had already developed user-oriented security measures in earlier systems, the TSOS (Time Sharing Operating System) and VMOS (Virtual Memory Operating System). The discussions on data protection in the 1970s could highlight the beauty of these measures as they appeared in BS2000. At customer seminars, we too sang the praises of the security available in the system, both as system consultants and in light of the first German data protection law.

The system area is completely sealed off from the normal user. Only the system administrator can work in this area and make portions of it, such as system programs, available for general use.

You can store both customer and log data in individual files in the application and keep them relatively transparent within the SAP user ID. The system handles sealing areas off from each other. But woe to anyone who enables file sharing or has an untrustworthy system administrator. The administrator can and may do everything, including displaying or hiding the files and address areas of other users. Abuse or simple errors in administration can nullify the security in the system.

Can system administrators really do anything and everything? Yes, they can!

If someone gets into the password-protected TSOS user ID, all catalog limitations are rescinded and the following permitted:

- changes to all file and program libraries, including deletion
- replacing current files with older ones
- sharing privileged programs with all users
- finding the passwords for files
- access to the virtual address area of all running programs, including the operating system
- changing the coding of the operating system
- starting programs, even the SAP system, in interactive mode, with the ability to set stopping points at any point, display and manipulate the contents of memory, and trace operations instruction by instruction
- starting programs that work in privileged operating system mode – only these programs have the privilege of working in the physical IOCS, which means they can read and change every address in main memory or on disk.

9.2.2 Rights of those responsible for applications

Users with access to the user ID for productive systems have a high level of rights within the ID. Such users can manipulate files, share them, restart an online application on the screen, and read or manipulate data at paused points. They cannot, however, discover passwords.

We obviously use these functions in Basis development in the SAP development system. During courses on debugging, we inform our customers of the privileges given to administrators and demonstrate how to read from main memory and, if authorized to do so, manipulate (change) it.

Particularly in the R/2 System, the SAP administrator can use the display and replace function in the productive system. Of course, you must protect this function with authorization, and, according to well-known principles, never release it in the productive system.

Since the majority of SAP R/2 programs are written in assembler language so that the computer code can be interpreted directly in main memory, it's easy for those with privileges to interpret the contents of memory. They know where the buffers are, what the buffers contain, and can even use debugging to become familiar with the secrets of buffer management. And since SAP makes no mystery out of its programs and delivers the source code to its customers, the customers can also understand programs line by line and read statements in main memory. In fact, they must do so during testing or when trying to discover the source of an error.

We should note that at one time, those with privileges in the R/2 System could use direct manipulation of memory to turn off authorization checks. At the very beginning, they could even change clients and disguise themselves as another user with another set of authorizations. All changes are, of course, logged, but a clever user with administrator rights can also turn off logging.

All this shows us that the operating systems and the SAP systems are normally very secure for normal users. However, even required administration can introduce a significant level of insecurity.

9.3 ADMINISTRATORS AND WINDOWS NT

Let's move from old technology to modern, such as the Windows NT operating system from Microsoft.

An understanding of the security concept in the Windows NT operating system depends upon a good comprehension of the principles of users and user groups. Users and groups are represented internally with SIDs, security identifiers. The system automatically generates SIDs, which guarantees that a SID is assigned only once in the entire lifecycle of a system. Whenever a user is assigned rights in the system, it stores the user's SID.

Users are either predefined or created with the help of the user manager. In either case, a user account stores system rights. The creation of non-predefined users occurs best with an assignment to a predefined or self-defined user group.

One of the predefined user accounts is that of the administrator, which belongs to the administrators group. The administrator is a privileged user who normally has the right to execute all privileged operations in the system. Accordingly, the administrator can create, delete, and change user accounts, install and configure system software, change security settings, and release directories. The administrator is the most powerful person in the NT environment.

An important principle in computing systems states that you should always work with the lowest possible rights. An administrator, therefore, should use the administrator account only when the privileges stored there are truly required. In other cases, the administrator should use the normal user account used for logon. For specific activities that administrators also perform, Windows NT offers a specific user group with customized authorizations. *See* table 9.1.

TABLE 9.1	Administration groups
Group name	**Activity**
Server Operators	Administration of domain servers
Account Operators	Administration of domain accounts and user groups
Print Operators	Administration of domain printers (print requests)
Backup Operators	Performing backups
Replicators	Synchronization of files in a domain

Members of this group possess exactly the rights they need to perform their tasks. They cannot, however, create new rights for themselves or others. For example, a backup operator may save directories and files, but not OK them for restoration.

The administrator account cannot be deleted or blocked. This is one reason why hacker attacks often prefer this account. The name is already known, and attackers can repeatedly try out different passwords in a brute force attack. Of course, you can rename the account, but it's still rather easy to determine which accounts belong to administrators. It's much safer to create a new account for an administrator and then assign it to the administrator group. You can also block this account after a specific number of invalid logon attempts. The predefined administrator account is protected by a strong password and cannot be accessed over the network.

You can block some files from administrators, but they can circumvent the block by taking ownership of the files. Nonetheless, this action is logged and the intended user of the file loses access to it, which offers the user indirect information on the administrator's takeover.

9.4 THE SUSCEPTIBLE PERSONAL COMPUTER

For their working devices, their PCs, users also serve as administrators, albeit with no or poor training. Have technological advances contributed more to security? If you think of your own experiences, you'll probably answer "no." Who isn't familiar with destroyed boot sectors, unexplained system crashes, and virus infections in a system for which the user is supposed to be the only master of the data involved?

System administrators from the mainframe sector react with disgust when they see the system directory mixed in with program files during installation of a simple application. Although the display of file storage locations and the path provides some openness, it's far more likely to confuse normal users. And users don't even wonder any more when the installation of new software makes it impossible to run programs or utilities that worked fine previously, and that actually have nothing to do with the new software.

The person with the responsibility here also has all available privileges, including those of destruction. System and application programs are mixed and it's no problem that simple games can read and change every area of memory and the disk. Doing so depends upon the programmer's knowledge, and how much criminal energy the programmer has to use that knowledge openly or secretly.

The destruction of personal property in the PC environment has become a sport. The goal seems to be causing the most damage possible to the largest number of users and to eliminate all traces of the offender. To circumvent discovery, virus producers must know exactly what's going on in the system and what opportunities exist for logging. They can then work around or deactivate transparent logging.

Experience shows that one weak leak in the security chain is enough to damage overall security. Once you've lost control over a PC or a server, it can become a permanent source of danger. Foreign users, manipulated data, viruses, and Trojan horses can all be sneaked into other systems. Since a PC user is normally responsible for the PC, and the user has administration rights, the computer itself demands protection. The identity of the person responsible for it must be unique and available at any time.

We'd like to present an example here of how open networked PCs can be. We know of a case in which ftp service was normally available on a Windows NT network. Under NT 3.5, this configuration made it possible to access all C drives with ftp and thus display or copy the contents of directories and files. The ftp user had rights similar to those of an administrator. An industrious employee who used every means available to access his company PC from home discovered the weakness. The worst part of this story is that company experts and administrators had long since had information about the weakness, but took comfort in the knowledge that few people knew about it. They chose not to fix the problem and make access more secure because, as they indicated, doing so would have required an upgrade to NT 4.0.

An unprotected PC practically invites users to infect open registry files on 32-bit systems, or win.ini, system.ini, autoexec.bat, and config.sys files in older operating systems, with viruses to investigate their effects. The protective measures offered by operating systems are usually the only reactions to virus attacks. They not only limp behind developments by attackers, but also are complicated to implement. In any case, attackers understand them. But it's encouraging that you can also prohibit registry changes from the outside. All transactions in the registry should be logged, but be sure to consider some points that avoid system lockups in the event of bottlenecks.

9.5   MULTI-USER PCS

It is against this background that you must view the demand made on SAP development by data protection authorities to create a special lock for a PC used by several users. Particularly in hospitals, several nurses typically use one computer. Each nurse logs on to an SAP R/3 System with a unique user name. Should a nurse leave the application, a function key, or hot key, should block the connection so that the next user cannot work with the nurse's application. The connection can be restored with entry of a password. The option of blocking the PC in general does not exist in this case.

During direct conversations with those affected, we see the inept attempt against the background of an all-powerful administration to open a security gap and then blame the follow-up systems for the problem. When several persons share a "personal" computer, appropriate security measures must be taken at the desktop level. For example, rules must define who has administration rights for the PC and is therefore responsible for its security. A PC has a complex operating system with millions of lines of code and numerous service programs.

Settings on the PC can establish automatic recording, which trustworthy users often fail to notice. Especially noteworthy for data protection are the temporary internet files. Without the awareness of most users, the PC records and stores the internet activities of users (the URL addresses of all sites visited, the data and time of the visit, and the amount of data transferred). This is a rich fount of information for employees working together. They can not only determine how much time another employee spends surfing the internet, but also see the content of the pages visited by their colleagues. Links to other log files enable someone to identify what persons visited what URL addresses. Earlier versions of NT reserved 3 percent of disk capacity for these files. The *recycle bin* file was even more wasteful, reserving 10 percent of the disk for deleted files.

Several arguments speak for user groups with specific profiles as a precondition for several users using one computer under Windows NT. Besides the role of the administrator, the question here involves the desktop as a whole. The desktop not only stores open connections to SAP systems, but also provides access to office services such as spreadsheet programs, text processing programs, databases, and archiving systems. Users can also start these programs from within SAP systems. Much like the situation with additional open SAP modes, the original program cannot control these programs any longer; they often become independent with no option for reverse coupling.

If you want to create an additional level of security with single sign-on, you soon reach a limit with multi-user PCs. The user ID and password are available only uniquely: all users log on to the application under the same name.

There's only one answer for SAP: if several users share a PC, appropriate security measures must be implemented at the PC level. Specific users may see and use only their own desktop, the workplace administration of their own files (including temporary internet files and files in the recycle bin), their own archive, and only the SAP applications they have opened in any mode. These tasks can be performed by the Windows Terminal Server or by a solution from Citrix ICA Technology. All users have their own windows that display all the applications they have opened. Users have access to their personal desktop only with their own user ID and password. Single sign-on carries a unique user ID with the corresponding PSE in each desktop session. Users identify themselves once and are linked to the desired application under their own names. The system logs users off automatically after a period of inactivity: users must re-enter their password to resume work with the application.

Here, too, you need a trustworthy administrator with rights for all desktops.

Administrative rights must be taken away from individual users or uniquely assigned to a user from the group.

9.6 RECOMMENDATIONS

We recommend that those responsible for data protection and security directly examine the abilities of administrators. When doing so, note that good administrators can do almost everything, including the inconceivable. If you find administrators who can't do anything, they either have not earned the title, have too little training, or are in over their heads.

As soon as you have an idea of the capabilities of individual administrators, you can choose between two extremes. You either trust them completely, or rigorously limit their power.

Limiting their abilities can lead to paralysis; blind trust can lead to abuse. Both have unforeseeable results. Try to steer a middle course. Without some trust, you can't operate a company. Regard administrators as assistants in creating a secure system. They need cooperation. But trust should also be accompanied by monitoring activities.

But before you get involved, take our guidelines on security and data protection to heart. You know that there's no such thing as 100 percent security, that you can improve security and data protection only in cooperation with specialists, and that you must build upon the self-responsibility of administrators.

We encourage security and data protection experts to work out clear rules in companies, to make the rules transparent, and to implement them among the persons responsible by consensus. Since PC users are not experts in data protection or security, you must translate legal requirements into the language of users. Refer to the literature for detailed rules on PCs, but consider the following highlights:

- documentation of PC components
- responsibilities, administration, and obligations
- internal and external communications (periphery, network, and internet)
- logging and access control
- storing personal data
- private use: private devices and private data storage
- procurement of new components
- cyclical deletion of data (data minimization)
- security features (access to rooms, screen savers with passwords, automatic logouts after a period of inactivity, and the encryption of data on disks and on the network)
- secure passwords (check passwords with crack programs, minimum length, and validity periods)

- central and local security (backup) copies
- storage of disks and storage media
- security software and up-to-date virus programs
- maintenance, remote support, and repair.

Technical

The SAP system includes opportunities for logging, monitoring, and task distribution. User management falls under the purview of a high level of responsibility.

This list clarifies that an out-of-the-box system, taken as is, does not meet the requirements of security and data protection without any further action. The system can only offer specific tools for security that you must use to the full within the available environment. The environment itself demands additional security measures: strengths and weaknesses appear in different system variants, in employee knowledge, in the security policy, and in the corporate culture.

9.6.1 Distribution of roles

9.6.1.1 Distribution of rights

An important principle in the security of computer systems states that you should assign only those rights required to perform a specific task.

Following the principle usually poses no difficulty in practice. The real danger lies in piling up roles. Over a long period, administrators take on various roles. They retain the rights they received earlier, even if only to support their successors from time to time. But even when the successors are secure in their positions, the original administrators often retain all their rights.

You should therefore use all the means available in the SAP system for user management

9.6.1.2 Controls

You can use the Audit Information System (AIS) and its reports to filter an overview of current administrators and their rights.

An excerpt from the AIS is shown in Table 9.2.

You can place time limits on the assigned user profiles and activity groups. Once roles have changed, you should impose the limitations immediately, whether they take effect that day or after a maximum transition period.

You can also assign access to specific users for specific periods. You should grant emergency users only short and very limited access rights, and require logging.

TABLE 9.2	Reports for user control		
Menu branch		**Report**	**Variant**
Users by name		RSUSR002	SAP&_BENU
Users by authorizations		RSUSR002	SAP&_AUTH
Users according to transactional authorization		RSUSR002	SAP&_TRANSAKT
Users according to critical combinations		RSUSR008	
Users with incorrect logons		RSUSR006	
Users with critical authorizations		RSUSR009	
Authorizations according to the last change		RSUSR030	SAP&_ÄNDERUNG
Activity groups according to user assignment		RSUSR070	SAP&_BENU
Executable transactions for users		RSUSR010	SAP&_BENUTZER
Change documents for users		RSUSR100	
Change documents for profiles		RSUSR101	
Change documents for authorizations		RSUSR102	

9.6.1.3 Distribution of roles during user and authorization maintenance

As noted in section 2.1 on user management, SAP recommends a distribution of roles and separation of functions when maintaining users and authorizations.

- The authorization administrator creates authorization profiles but cannot activate any authorization.
- The authorization activator has authority to activate authorization profiles.
- The user administrator creates user master records and assigns users to authorization profiles.

9.6.1.4 Distribution of systems

SAP recommends dividing the system landscape into three parts. This approach allows organization of administrative responsibilities and monitoring over a few systems. You should have a production system with its own valuable data that needs protection, a development system, and a quality assurance system. Only the production system may contain real data that needs protection: allowable administration must be read out manually. Other systems may contain only test data. Because of audits, development work should not occur in the production system: the privileges of developers allow them to take on authorizations illegally, to turn off checks, and to manipulate programs and data.

9.6.1.5 Organizational measures

The power of a system administrator can also be limited by the forced distribution of functions. For example, you might give several administrators only a partial password so that they can dial in to the system only when working together. You can also obligate them to perform any emergency work in the system together.

In an extreme case, you can distribute the password to an R/3 System to nine administrators, each of them dependent upon the others. Assuming a password length of eight characters, each administrator knows one character and the ninth knows only the correct sequence. This distribution is clearly impractical: experience shows that security is the last consideration in an emergency situation. Emergency situations usually occur when superiors want a newly written evaluation or when you can avoid restarting the system after a minimal correction to a program.

9.6.2 Logging and controls

Section 2.5 treats the options available for logging and how to evaluate logs.

At this point we want to remind you of the use of the security audit logs. Although designed as an instrument for system administrators to use in observing and recording security-relevant events in the system, you can also use it to record the activities of system administrators.

We recommend that you create emergency users in the system as a precaution. Organizationally, these users are released only in an emergency, either by unblocking or by issuing a password. When unlocked, their validity period should be limited. The security audit log can be set to record all actions performed by an emergency user. A special account number for this user enables you to monitor settlement if you have agreed to do so. Once the action has been performed, you should block the user (again) or reset the password. Our discussions with data protection officers have proven that this option is much more transparent and offers more advantages than assigning emergency authorizations to an active user dynamically.

To control and monitor the situation, you can review the temporary authorizations with the log. The advantage here is the ability to discover problems immediately and to demonstrate clearly that the appropriate security measures exist in the system. Obviously, a potential user is to be informed of the recording from the very beginning and obligated to confidentiality.

Additional options for logging exist at the system level. Here, too, you must ensure that this function cannot be temporarily turned off or manipulated. Under Windows NT you can monitor the following events:

- logging on and off
- file and object access
- use of user rights
- user and group administration
- changes to security guidelines
- restarting or shutting down the system
- tracing processes.

## CHAPTER 10

Remote support

With its Remote Service, SAP offers special services for customers, partners, and interested parties with a remote connection. The offerings include implementation services and a worldwide network of services for productive operation. The services include consulting, training, testing, problem resolution by local, regional, and development support, software maintenance, and other services.

Whenever a remote entity dials in to a customer system, the question always arises of how much adequate security and data protection can be guaranteed. Remote access to productive HR systems poses particular challenges to human resources staff and data protection officers. Can they still trace individual processing steps, or still perform their task of providing data protection in the company?

The resulting insecurity can be countered only when all those involved have the greatest amount of information possible on the technical connections and access options. Accordingly, we first describe the individual services and treat them in light of security and data protection.

However, we must begin by saying that effective protection becomes possible only when both parties to a remote connection work together and when individual tasks are executed according to definitions. Defense against unauthorized access is possible only when the customer's side consistently implements measures and guidelines for security. Only the information available at a given time can be taken from an external system. It's the customer's responsibility to keep the connection and user ID open at a given time and provide support personnel with exactly the authorizations needed to perform their tasks. Support personnel do not always require authorization to access a productive system. It's often possible to detect problems in a test system.

Consider the results of a study on data protection in a physician's practice [Hamburg].

Although doctor–patient confidentiality should provide additional protection to patient data and professional standards require special protection for physicians' electronic notes, the data in many physicians' practices does not enjoy sufficient protection. Remote Services provide only insufficient IT knowledge for smaller tasks. The system administrator IDs and passwords are usually unknown. In many cases, maintenance technicians use super-user rights with comprehensive access rights. Remote service is regarded as particularly risky. The staff at the practice should initiate access to data – exclusively. Maintenance activities must be logged and traced, on site, on the screen. Test data should be available for maintenance, as recommended by the German association of physicians.

Additional problems include trivial group passwords, screen savers without mandatory passwords, a lack of logging, and no encryption. Common administration of patients in most practices violates doctor–patient confidentiality.

10.1   SAP SUPPORT SERVICES

SAP Support Services are described in various publications such as SAPNet, the SAP Magazine, and in SAP Info.

SAP Magazine has published an article on remote services by SAP. SAPNet offers the list of publications shown in Table 10.1. You can order individual publications in printed form.

Customers who take advantage of Remote Services should order the appropriate literature and make it available to all those involved.

At this point we wish to offer a brief description of the most important services, based upon SAP literature, and then discuss the security measures that must be implemented on the SAP side and the customer side.

Remote Services are available to all customers throughout the world. The task of Remote Services is not limited to helping customers with emergency situations and problems. They also seek to free customers from maintenance and conversion efforts that do not belong to day-to-day IT work. Remote Services can also perform preventive system checks to guarantee the uninterrupted operation of SAP systems in the future.

Taking advantage of SAP Remote Services can make the visits of consultants to perform the same services at a company superfluous. Customers will find the costs of Remote Services significantly lower than the travel costs for on-site work and that they can react more quickly to critical problems. If needed, they have access to SAP specialists from around the world.

TABLE 10.1	Overview of publications on Support Services

Support Services publications	Order number
Support Services	50023845
SAP EarlyWatch Service	50007166
SAP EarlyWatch Alert	
SAP GoingLive Check	50018796
GoingLive Functional Upgrade Check	
Remote Upgrade Service	50023201
Conversion Services	50030677
R/3 Remote Services	
Remote Connections to SAPNet	50017380
Remote Consulting	50012462
Security for Customer Connections	50028244
SAP Security Review Services	50030902
Technical System Security	50026500
Secure Network Communication	50014335
R/3 Security Mechanisms	

It's important to remember that customers themselves control and monitor security and data protection for a remote connection. They establish the connection and allocate authorizations to SAP employees. Customers can provide the responsible SAP employees with router and user passwords securely – over the telephone is the best method. That information should never be documented in a problem notification. Along with the network provider, SAP makes every effort to provide a high level of security for access to customer systems.

10.1.1 Remote Support

Some customer problems can be analyzed and corrected only in the system that contains the problem. In these cases, SAP specialists dial in to the customer system directly, which is not limited to the customer's SAP system. The specialists might have to examine the entire system environment, so they might also need authorizations for the operating system, the database, or the network.

A direct dialup connection guarantees quick and effective resolution of the problem.

10.1.2 Remote Consulting

If a company experiences special problems with its SAP systems – problems with no immediate solution – the company can engage the services of SAP Remote Consulting. SAP consultants help solve the problem over the phone or via a videoconference. If those approaches do not work, consultants can set up a remote connection to the customer's system and examine it themselves. If required, they agree on changed settings with the customer and perform some light programming.

10.1.3 EarlyWatch

EarlyWatch offers customers the opportunity to have SAP experts analyze their systems at regular intervals. The service aims at keeping the performance and availability of the customer's system at the highest possible level. EarlyWatch examines R/3 applications along with the technical environment such as configuration, database, operating system, and network. The Computer Center Management System (CCMS) provides the basis for the examination. It monitors the system and contains information on the current status of the system and the expected consumption of resources. The customer receives a monitoring report and a list of recommendations for optimizing the system after every inspection.

EarlyWatch sessions occur with a user ID provided by the customer and in a dedicated client (066). The session does not offer access to company data.

10.1.4 GoingLive Check

When a company implements an SAP system, the system should be prepared for production as well as possible. Experience teaches that many performance problems can be solved even before the start of production. As a Remote Service, SAP offers a GoingLive Check, which examines the performance and availability of SAP systems in detailed system tests. The GoingLive Check consists of three inspections, each separated by one month. The first two occur before production begins, the third about one month after going into production.

10.1.5 Remote Upgrade

Customers can access new functions at periodic intervals. A small upgrade project performs the required maintenance activities, during which the customer and SAP work closely together.

Here, too, only the customer establishes the data connection between the service center and the customer system. The customer also grants all the authorizations involved.

10.1.6 Technical Security Check

The Security Consulting Group performs security analyses of customers' systems. Three to ten-day investigations include risk analysis, development and implementation of a security concept, study of the authorization concept, implementation of security guidelines, and individual consulting on the security environment.

The goal is the highest possible level of security within the context of laws and regulations. The analysis not only examines the internal security of the SAP system, but also studies the weaknesses of components associated with the system: database, operating system, network, and front ends.

10.1.7 SAPNet

The database of SAP notes is available on SAPNet around the clock for employees, customers, and partners. In it, you can search for similar problems among solutions already provided. If your research does not discover a satisfactory answer, you can create a problem message or a query. Employees at Remote Services will process the notifications and offer customers the appropriate feedback.

SAPNet also provides customers with access to Hot Packages – corrections to the R/3 System – for download into customer systems. It also offers Hot News – information of interest to all customers.

10.2	**SAP SECURITY MEASURES**

To guarantee the security of networks, various security systems at network gateways are kept at the latest level of technology.

10.2.1 Network security

SAP offers customers Remote Services over a wide area network (WAN). Customers need a connection between the company network and the nearest SAP support server. Working with network providers, SAP attempts to guarantee the highest possible level of security for access to customers' systems. But reaching that level becomes possible only when all security measures and guidelines have been implemented.

10.2.2 WAN protocols

The WAN protocols can serve as the first level of protection for access.

- Service providers should set up an X.25 connection so that the customer can establish only outgoing connections. This approach ensures that the customer alone controls the establishment of connections.

- The virtual private network (VPN) area includes exclusive TCP/IP networks for SAP and its customers; only they can access these groups. The routing tables are maintained only for a connection between SAP and an individual customer, not for customer-to-customer relationships.

- With frame relay networks, a service provider offers a permanent, virtual connection between a customer and SAP. The disadvantage of this constant connection can be countered with a strongly limited list of persons with authorized access or a firewall on the router.

- With ISDN, the connection is created only when needed and only the two parties to the connection know the telephone numbers. A list of those authorized or a firewall can be set up to allow access only to authorized ISDN numbers.

10.2.3 Hardware router

SAP recommends that you use and configure a hardware router that supports various WAN protocols. Hardware routers are easy to configure and offer additional security to the WAN with their integrated access-protection mechanisms. During configuration of its hardware router, SAP has made sure that routing between customers is impossible.

■ Routing protocols such as RIP, IGRP, and OSPF are deactivated, and only static routes to customers' networks are implemented. This means that routing data is never accessible over the WAN.

■ Lists of persons with authorized access control lists limit access on the SAP network to customers.

■ Only specific service ports, those used for R/3 services, such as SAP EarlyWatch, SAPNet, Remote Consulting, and anonymous FTP, are activated.

■ SAP enables complete TCP/IP access from the SAP support server (sapserv(x)) to the customer network.

Customers are responsible for setting up firewalls to secure their networks. Specific service ports are important for SAP Remote Services and should be considered when setting up lists of persons with authorized access or firewalls.

10.2.4 SAProuter

Besides the recommended hardware router, customers also need the SAProuter software that functions as part of the firewall system and regulates access to the network. SAProuter controls and monitors communications between a company and the SAP support server. SAProuter is installed on only one of the customer's computers; it directs information on all linked systems to SAP and external requests to the correct computer in the company network. The appropriate authorizations must be set up in advance. SAProuter also handles network security and the stability of the connection.

SAP customers configure the SAProuter, provide SAP with the data needed to set up a TCP/IP connection, then access SAPNet. SAP employees in the Service Support Center can connect with customers only when they notify SAP of the connection and establish it actively. Customers also need the SAProuter password, which they must maintain in the router permission table.

See section 3.1.2 for more information on SAProuter.

10.2.5 Encryption

SAProuters can use an SNC interface to set up external security procedures and thereby create secure communications tunnels through insecure networks. Secure Network Communications (SNC) creates the opportunity for providing security at the application level or end-to-end security, a single sign-on procedure, or authentication with smart cards.

External security products use a public key method for server authentication and can also be used for encrypting connections between SAProuters. To implement this approach, you need a personal security environment, and can obtain the software for it from SAP.

10.2.6 Connections with customers

SAP employees can use a remote connection to log on to an SAP installation directly from the customer service system. An authorization protects this function. The customer must give the SAP employee the password for the SAProuter before this connection can be established.

Customer connections are presented in different categories, depending upon the type of service activated by the customer. SAP employees can access customers' installations only with the types of services for which they have authorization. For example, employees in First Level Customer Support cannot use EarlyWatch connections.

The following lists the types of Remote Services there are:

- First Level Customer Support
- EarlyWatch
- Remote Consulting
- Telnet Connection.

10.2.7 Transmitting passwords

To enable remote access, you must transmit passwords in addition to system and user IDs. Customers must release users and must block them or change their passwords as soon as users have completed their activities. The password rules noted above apply particularly to access to sensitive production systems.

Special security measures are required to transmit the initial password. The customer must transmit the password to the correct employee and SAP must transmit it internally when solving the problem.

Neither the author nor the recipient may include the written password in a problem notification for a sensitive system. The first disclosure of the password to SAP should occur over the telephone.

The distribution of tasks involved in problem resolution by local, regional, and development support sometimes makes it necessary to redirect passwords that have been given to SAP to solve the problem quickly. In these special cases, you can assign the required access information, including the password, to a specially protected table. Only the staff member currently working on the problem has access to this table. A popup informs the employee that the password may be stored only when it is absolutely required for further work on the problem by another staff member. The action log in the problem notification logs all accesses (including reads) of this information. The system notifies all users of the logging at each access.

The access data is deleted when the problem notification is closed. In addition, all passwords are deleted after three days, even for open problem notifications.

Along with the option to provide passwords over the telephone, customers can give staff members passwords in this protected table. These options allow customers to eliminate fraud completely (especially by their own employees) or at least to control abuse by monitoring.

The entire procedure conforms to password rules: the initial password is stored and transmitted securely. Abuse can be controlled at any time.

10.2.8 Monitoring connections

SAP has various options to monitor connections. For example, SAP can perform the following tasks:

▦ define the access list on the hardware router

▦ define the route permission table for SAProuter

▦ provide an autonomous system for remote connections (CSN) to ensure that remote connections can be created only from this system

▦ offer CSN logging functions to monitor the remote connection

▦ split types of service into categories

▦ limit the access authorizations of CSN users.

The checks performed by the logging functions can help the administrator of the CSN system to monitor remote connections to SAP and determine who has registered for what type of service and when in the customer system.

Access occurs exclusively via SAP means (SAPgui and SAPtelnet), so that complete control of functions for the SAProuter lies on the customer's side.

10.2.9 Logging

The activation of a user ID can trigger user-specific recording, such as that performed by the Security Audit Log. The logging options in the production system (change documents and changes to customizing tables) should be activated automatically. *See* section 2.5 for more detailed information on logging.

Up to R/3 Release 3.1, you could use echo mode to display the screen image of a second user on another monitor, but this feature is no longer available as of Release 4.0 for technical reasons. An even better substitute is provided by pcANYWHERE. Establishment of a service connection requires that you satisfy the security mechanisms built into pcANYWHERE (such as password protection for creating a connection), and other, SAP-specific hurdles.

As is true of every service connection established by a customer, access over pcANYWHERE must be released explicitly. Establishment of a pcANYWHERE connection consists of two steps:

1 release of connection type pcANYWHERE in SAPNet
2 maintenance of the SAProuter configuration files to allow pcANYWHERE connections explicitly.

You can use a log file on the customer computer to trace the work of the SAP employee at a later time. The log file contains all mouse movements, entries, and so on, so that you can see the same screen contents that the SAP employee had while working on the case.

Customers with special security requirements can use pcANYWHERE to log all activities on their systems, including work with the SAPgui or Telnet.

10.2.10 Obligations of employees

SAP employees and contractual partners are obligated to observe data protection throughout the world. They sign a non-disclosure agreement that binds them to secrecy about all confidential matters, including information on trade secrets of SAP customers and partners. The current confidentiality agreement is found in SAP note 35493 and is reprinted as Appendix A.

SAP employees who leave the company lose their access rights to all SAP systems the day that they depart.

10.3 CUSTOMER SECURITY MEASURES

Customers direct and monitor data security and data protection because their own companies establish connections and grant authorizations to SAP employees. They should create specific user IDs for remote access and block the IDs as soon as a session ends.

Router configuration can enable connections only to specific partner systems, such as the SAP Support Server. The opportunity also exists to limit access to specific support services.

In addition, responsible parties in the company can follow the actions of SAP specialists on their screens and intervene if necessary. As a side effect, observation of the SAP specialist also works as a teaching tool.

As we will see later, an on-site visit to a customer is not necessarily any more secure than a remote connection. You have to decide if an on-site visit might not create new problems: costs, access to buildings and facilities, access to documents on desks, the ability to view screens, and the chance of overhearing telephone and other conversations.

10.3.1 Monitoring the connections

Customers have various options to monitor connections. We strongly recommend the following measures to strengthen access protection at customer installations.

- Configure the network connection only for outgoing connections.
- Define access control lists on hardware routers.
- Set up a route permission table for SAProuter.
- Integrate the SAProuter into a firewall system.
- Supply a password in the SAProuter so that the SAP consultant can use it to establish a connection.
- Use non-trivial passwords and change them frequently.
- Analyze the SAProuter logs to trace current and past connections to the SAProuter.
- Define the user profiles in the SAP system that depend upon the type of service.
- Monitor the current user with transaction sm04.
- Monitor users with echo mode (up to Release 3.1) or with pcANYWHERE.
- Lock user or change passwords immediately after an activity ends.
- Activate or deactivate remote connections with the service connection button in SAPNet.
- Set a time limit for the connection with the service connection button.

10.3.2 The necessity and advantages of remote service

To begin, we want to indicate how, in certain cases, a remote dialup to the customer system can offer advantages to both sides, particularly if a trusting partnership already exists. The vast majority of cases do not require access to authentic, personal data, so that the authorization concept can prevent access to it. SAP has a great deal of experience with remote support, dating from the development of the R/2 System. SAP knows the problems associated with security and has dedicated highly qualified personnel and significant resources to Remote Service.

In many cases, customers can solve the problem directly from the notes database. The effort SAP has contributed to this database is hardly selfless. Practice has shown that several customers often experience a similar or identical problem that they can (and must) solve quickly with the application of a note rather than waiting for the installation of a Hot Package or a new release.

However, it is unsafe to assume that a specific programming error will affect all customers. Were this the case, the problem would have been discovered and corrected during the comprehensive, internal tests under standard customizing conditions at SAP. SAP customers have the option of finding a solution for an initially unknown problem.

Nonetheless, some cases require adjustments directly at the customer site. After all, only the customer has the exact customizing or modification data combined with specific hardware, operating system, and database version. It is not always possible to re-create this constellation externally, even in a similar, on-site test system. Experience has shown, however, that inexplicable errors often appear only in a production system and not in a supposedly identical test environment. Especially in development, we have learned that many errors occur only in a specific, not-yet-tested constellation that cannot be reconstructed at SAP or on-site in the customer's test system. These cases demand tedious work directly in the production system, work that analyzes the system environment, the customizing settings, and the level of modification step by step. And it's not unusual for these efforts to uncover errors that have slumbered unobserved for years in a system without being discovered or causing any actual damage to operations.

When deciding between local and remote maintenance, you must observe the principle of proportionality, as is true of data protection. Remote Support is significantly less expensive and faster. It can also dedicate more experts to a complex problem. Local support can involve long waiting times. In both cases, network connections with a user name and password are used to dial in to a system. Both parties work to minimize the risks involved in a WAN dialup, as described in this chapter. With an on-site visit, the parties can get to know each other personally. Frequently changing partners means that familiarity is often limited to a name, which then has no more value than a user name. During Remote Service, SAP keeps a record of which users were connected to systems at any given time. Local service has the advantage of direct observation. One side offers recording and logging, the other side offers observation, which, however, cannot be constant. The potential risks increase if logging is neglected, assuming unreliable partners on both sides.

If a customer problem demands an immediate solution that requires a dialup connection to a production system, the customer may well feel that an exceptional situation exists – particularly when the person responsible at the customer site is also responsible for a quick solution. Of course, some cases will exist in which the right amount of effort might have re-created the problem in a test system even without actual data, but no one took this approach. It's far more comfortable to take the approach authenticated by experience: direct support from a reliable partner is the optimal way to avoid service interruptions. After all, you can measure the costs of downtime exactly, but not the costs of a theoretical danger.

Those responsible for personnel and data protection might appear to be in a weak position here. But trusting collaboration among all parties can minimize security risks even here, as long as everyone recognizes them. We recommend that you analyze the frequency of remote dialups to various systems and that you evaluate the risks with those responsible. Most companies can use the data from such an analysis to recommend or agree to remote maintenance.

RECOMMENDATIONS FROM SUPERVISORY AUTHORITIES FOR DATA PROTECTION

In their annual reports, German data protection authorities at the state level have taken a position on remote maintenance.

10.4.1 Required security measures

As you might expect in a federal system, the data protection officers in each German state list their own recommendations, each of which consists of 6–20 individual points.

This section groups and evaluates these recommendations.

The data protection authorities recommended the following general security measures:

10.4.1.1 Technical and organizational measures for customers

▨ Remote software maintenance is to be excluded completely or limited to specific, exceptional cases.

When customers develop problems, they should decide for themselves what kind of support they require. They remain masters of their own data. If they must grant a third party access to their personnel system, they must view the situation as an exception. SAP uses all its resources to create the same high level of security during remote support that exists during an on-site visit.

Optimal customer support presupposes quick reaction times and communication paths.

▨ Access to personal data should be excluded, along with remote maintenance that occurs in parallel to productive operations.

As noted, some special situations will arise that demand immediate solutions in the production system. The authorization concept can limit an SAP employee's access to personal data. But the required analysis often targets Customizing and tax tables, and sometimes even the personnel data on a specific employee with an unusual combination of data. Here it's reasonable to consider making the problem anonymous to allow further research.

▨ Direct access to personal data should occur only in conjunction with anonymous data.

This approach is recommended when it can be executed without excessive effort.

But the theory can prove counterproductive if making the data in a personnel system anonymous leads to inaccuracies that make the data unusable.

▨ Only the customer can establish a connection.

This is always the case.

▓ Strict access checks for the maintenance technicians, who may act only within the context of their maintenance privileges.

SAP customers must set up a user ID and password in the appropriate client. Customers also assign authorizations to users.

▓ The maintenance technician must use an agreed-upon password to authorize each maintenance step.

A password secures every user ID. The password must be changed at the first logon as regulated by the company norms.

▓ To prohibit uncontrolled access to files, all executable programs must be protected.

When it assigns authorizations, customer administration decides which activities can be performed. The program level is usually hidden in a real-time system, so that users call functions via transactions that stand before other programs, screens, and function modules. Only a specialist can see the program level, especially during batch input or during a CATT procedure, for example.

In the R/3 System, customers themselves decide upon the permitted transactions and which reports, if any, can be called.

▓ If access to user data is required, you must first check to see if you need to remove sensitive, personal data before access may occur.

Authorizations determine the types of records (infotypes in the HR area) that can be accessed. You might need to block table groups and some individual tables. The customer must decide which personal data to consider sensitive and therefore to remove. This data differs from the sensitive data defined in Article 8 of the EU Directive as racial and ethnic origin, religious and political opinions, and health-related behavior.

▓ No direct changes to the software are allowed: changes may occur only on site.

On-site changes are not necessarily any more secure; the local connection is not necessarily any more secure than a remote connection. However, it is important that any changes will be implemented, tested, and documented in the test system and then transported officially through the QA system and into production. SAP recommends this three-tiered division of systems; not all customers adhere to it.

Remember that changes to tables can affect program controls.

▓ Maintenance data in the log files must be inspected and kept for one year.

This approach requires an organizational solution.

▓ Users determine the depth of involvement, not the maintenance company.

Users determine access authorizations.

▓ Those responsible for systems must receive enough training on the options for remote maintenance and must regularly check the security measures in force.

The appropriate SAP documentation must be kept up to date. In particular, system administrators must be familiar with the literature noted at the beginning of this chapter and the White Paper on security for customer connections, particularly for system administrators.

10.4.1.2 Customer measures supported by the maintenance company

- An employee of the company who is also a user must observe all maintenance activities and have the authority to intervene at any time.

  This approach requires an organizational solution.

- Logging and display of all transmitted data, tracing screen displays, and after-the-fact monitoring of the transmitted data.

  The activation of a user ID can trigger user-specific recording, such as that in the Security Audit Log. The production system should automatically activate the available logging options (change documents and changes to Customizing tables). *See* section 2.5 for more information on logging.

  pcANYWHERE can handle detailed monitoring and logging. The ability to store the recorded data in its own log file enables customers to check the work of an SAP employee at a later date.

  Since customers establish communications, they can also disconnect at any time.

- A maintenance contract must specify the type and scope of maintenance, competencies, and obligations.

  See section 10.4.3 on maintenance contracts.

- The maintenance staff must be obligated to confidentiality, even with appropriate non-disclosure agreements if appropriate.

  All SAP employees and partners are obligated to observe data protection and secrecy.

- A contract must prohibit transfer of user data to third parties. Once the maintenance has ended, the data must be returned or deleted.

  During Remote Support, personal data is displayed on the screen but not transmitted in table form for later processing. Remote Support includes the possibility of SAP subsidiaries or partners connecting to customer systems. As noted above, these parties, too, are obligated to observe data protection and secrecy.

10.4.3 Maintenance contracts

The data protection authority for the German state of Baden-Württemberg offers the following positions on maintenance contracts for remote maintenance (see the commissioner's 18th report, dated 1997).

A contract that sets the rights and obligations of both parties is the basic precondition for minimizing risk. The remote maintenance company must be engaged in writing. The contract must clearly regulate the data protection considerations that must be observed. General references to the level of data protection to be observed are insufficient. The contract must include the following.

1 The IT company describes the exact work to be done.

2 Access to personal data is to be refused. In exceptional cases, data may be used only for maintenance purposes. Further transfers to third parties are forbidden.

3 Subcontractors must be regulated.

4 The required technical and organizational measures must be spelled out.

5 Maintenance personnel must be obligated to secrecy.

SAP customers already enjoy a contractual relationship and contractual regulations. In its general terms and conditions, SAP agrees to observe data protection. The security of the network is documented extensively, as are the obligations of SAP employees and partners to observe data protection and secrecy. Regulations exist within the SAP group of companies to establish a uniformly high level of security and data protection throughout the world. The EU Directive on data protection and German data protection requirements determine the level for which SAP strives.

10.5 CLOSING REMARKS

We stand at the beginning of a development that seeks to link systems to each other. The internet is a gigantic network of networks that no one can really comprehend any more. Data warehouse systems that function as collection points for group-wide data are gaining wider acceptance and will concentrate information from legally independent companies within the group. Standard business software such as SAP solutions will be used in international corporate groups to avoid redundancy and to provide a basis for real-time decision making.

These systems must be economical over the long term.

The demand of many data protection officials to prohibit the transfer of personal data has proven very negative to corporate DPOs. They faced the danger of being ignored in the rush to progress and not being incorporated into future projects.

As noted at length, the dangers of transferring data in the course of SAP Remote Service are relatively small given the context.

## CHAPTER 11

Data warehouses and data protection – a contradiction?

Today's corporate decision makers urgently need precise information from production, sales, marketing, finances, and human resources along with a complete and current view of their corporate group and its environment. But this information is distributed across various platforms and in a huge number of applications throughout the IT structures of the group and beyond. Getting to the correct facts and numbers can prove a complicated and time-consuming endeavor.

The technical conception that meets these challenges is called data warehousing. A data warehouse is an independent application environment with its own database that takes data from various sources and enables both queries and analyses. Although data warehousing was on everyone's lips in the 1990s, it was often unable to fulfill the demands made upon it. It frequently led to high costs and delivered results of little use.

Data warehousing means more than the availability of a relational database, which, like an R/3 System, links tables and data elements into new relationships to achieve new insights. The database of a data warehouse should collect (in a compressed format) all the information available on the corporate group from all databases of the most varied systems. If needed, even the smallest units of information can be decrypted. Especially for mixed groups that offer a wide palette of goods and services, it's interesting to treat the customer master of individual areas as corporate stock. For example, an automotive group often includes insurance, savings banks, and commercial banks.

These members of the group would gladly use the master data on customers who have bought cars to create their own customers.

Customers become:

> . . . predictable and transparent in their buying patterns. An invaluable jump on the competition that commercial managers know how to use…. Globalization floods companies with ever more information, and high-performance storage media make it possible to store more and more of this data somewhere…. Knowledge is power [Manager].

11.1   MASTERING THE FLOOD OF INFORMATION

The forms of information on offer today make it impossible to get an overview. The internet features free, home delivery of electronic information that can easily be processed further. Economic advantages in the future will increasingly go to companies that place value on individuals, those that truly differentiate significant from insignificant data, and those that can filter significant data from the mass of data available to them.

Such filtering can occur automatically with search engines that support searches with free text, at least for data stored electronically. The future might bring a "scanning engineer," whose tasks involve evaluating important information throughout the world, summarizing it, and formatting it for decision makers. Professional experience for such occupations already exists among secret services or authorized wiretaps on telecommunications services. In these cases, the goal is to recognize the essential in a mass of data. The German Federal Intelligence Service already uses an "electronic vacuum cleaner" to search all international wireless telecommunications for specific terms. The Service finds 20 hits in 15,000 overheard conversations every day [SZ-BND].

11.2   THE SAP BUSINESS INFORMATION WAREHOUSE

The example of a data warehouse clearly illustrates the data protection problems that affect internationally active corporate groups. The precondition here is a thorough description of the individual components in a data warehouse. Only such descriptions can offer those responsible for data protection an overview of the field that lies between the problems and the solutions. Let's take a brief look at the production information on the SAP Business Information Warehouse (SAP BW).

An invitation to a SAP BW congress spoke of the advantages to be gained:

The dynamics of today's business world demand efficient decision-making processes in all areas and at all hierarchical levels of a competitive company. But companies can make the right decisions at the right time only when they have access to the required information in a timely manner, without gaps, and in degree of summarization that is optimal for the decision-makers. . . . Unlike traditional data warehouse systems, SAP BW enables a completely new look at enterprise data because it's based directly upon company processes.

Preconfigured business models keep implementation efforts at a reasonable level and thus avoid any compromises between customization and analysis functions. SAP now offers quick and simple access to the required information. The SAP Business Information Warehouse was designed especially for R/3 environments, but can also be used with other systems.

SAP BW can answer the following typical questions.

- What products are the most profitable this quarter?
- Who's buying them?
- Who are our best customers?
- What do those customers have in common?
- Which suppliers are the most unreliable?
- What alternatives are there?
- What are our decisive success factors?
- Who are our competitors?
- Where are our competitive advantages?

Information is data with a purpose. According to the classic definition, this orientation toward a goal makes information out of data. The information that a data warehouse provides its users must therefore be oriented on the requirements that arise from questions posed by the business.

The SAP BW was designed with the same consistent business orientation that characterizes SAP R/3 software. From the very beginning, the SAP BW not only extracts data from R/3 applications, but also considers the company's business processes. The goal is to make data available to decision makers almost in real time. Lengthy and expensive programming efforts to extract data and create metadata models are no longer necessary, because these functions are already available.

11.2.1 The components of the SAP BW

The main components of the SAP Business Information Warehouse support customers in the rapid creation and evaluation of information for business decisions.

11.2.1.1 Business Explorer

The report and analysis interface, Business Explorer, can be easily, graphically, and practically tailored to the needs of users. It includes clusters of defined, standard reports, and freely definable favorites that users can select with drag and drop.

11.2.1.2 Administrator Workbench

The Administrator Workbench is the control mechanism to assign data from the source systems to the SAP Business Information Warehouse. The Administrator Workbench provides a hierarchical overview of source systems, InfoSources, InfoCubes, and the relevant InfoObjects. All source systems access data from one database, data from either SAP or non-SAP systems.

11.2.1.3 InfoSources

From a business perspective, InfoSources are collections of logically related data needed by a source system. This data can include customer number, delivery data, product, quantity, amount, and plant. InfoSources are created with the Administrator Workbench, but can also be found, for technical reasons, in release-independent source R/3 Systems.

11.2.1.4 InfoCubes

The reporting functions in the SAP BW provide information for the analysis of all factors that influence a company's business activities. The data of the SAP Business Information Warehouse is distributed across various data areas called InfoCubes. The viewpoint of individual companies is vital here. An InfoCube consists of InfoObjects: characteristics and key figures. Characteristics are organizational terms such as company code, product, customer groups, fiscal year, period, or region.

11.2.2 New features in Release 2.0

With the option of accessing SAP BW with mobile devices, business information becomes available at any time and from any location. The information is always correct, current, and can be presented in a clear form that speaks to customers.

The new version also offers additional user roles that employees can use to obtain strategically important information more easily than ever before. The combination of Business Intelligence and mySAP.com provides a uniform information structure that enables an integrated view of economic viability. The scope of services includes about 75 of the user roles integrated into the mySAP Workplace and about 500 preformulated queries that enable users to perform their tasks quickly and efficiently.

THE PROBLEMS OF DATA PROTECTION

Decision makers in global corporate groups must be able to include data stored in all locations throughout the group in their decisions. They want to redeem the promises made by the IT staff when they requested large budgets for a modern IT infrastructure and pleaded for standardization. Management doesn't regard it as a feat of magic to combine data in almost infinite forms throughout the corporate group, summarize it, and present it to decision makers in an appropriate form.

Problems with the security of data transmission are still accepted (protecting ownership of customer data), but the requirements of data protection are seen as a burdensome evil. They are seen as a brake to the flow of information within the group. Data protection officers are seen as hindrances to innovation or are simply ignored during project development.

11.3.1 Application of the principles of data protection

Article 7 of the EU Directive forbids processing of personal information stored in files and its transmission to third parties unless:

1 subjects unambiguously give their consent

2 processing is necessary to fulfill a contractual relationship with the subject

3 processing is necessary for the purposes of the legitimate interests of the company, except where such interests are overridden by the interests for fundamental rights and freedoms of the data subject.

Regarding the first point, written permission can involve a great deal of effort. Many have problems with the legally binding character of permission that appears in the fine print of a contract.

Regarding the second point, the customer or labor contract is usually written with significant advantages for the company. It cannot justify company-wide transfers of employee data, for example. Legally independent subsidiaries are regarded as third parties.

Regarding the third point, the interests of subjects can be injured when private data is transmitted insecurely or stored at a subsidiary outside the EU. The dangers include eavesdropping on the data during transmission or having the end-user send the data to a third party.

In an annual report for 1997 on mining in banks and warehouses, the Data Protection Commissioner in Berlin treated the problems of data mining [Berlin].

The process of data summarization enables BW users to create new connections by applying statistical methods to large quantities of data. What remains veiled from the viewpoint of one company in the group can result in a new insight at the group level.

With a computer search for clients, users can understand the buying patterns of customers and the behavior of competitors exactly. The goal, of course, is to predict and thus influence that behavior.

In particular, the Data Protection Commissioner in Berlin does not see a sufficient legal basis to combine data because the purpose of such combinations is not always clear. The report also states that the interests of subjects for protection in a data warehouse system must be given more weight than they receive in a company's individual system, for which a contractual relationship might exist:

> The considerable legal basis for the processing of personal data in the Federal Data Protection Act permits the processing of personal data when legitimate interests of the processor are present and have resulted in a judgment that the rights of the subject are not being unduly harmed. These categories assume a specific usage context or a specific goal. Although the data in data warehouses was originally collected and stored for specific usage contexts, when it is combined and used to analyze new, previously unknown connections, it is separated from its original purpose and used to gain any kind of new knowledge about persons. This procedure means that it is no longer possible to assume that the interests of the subjects (for protection) take second place to the legitimate interests of the processor. For the processing of personal data, whether the persons involved be customers, employees, or citizens, data warehouses represent a special risk to informational self-determination.

At the end of 1999, thousands of SAP BW installations were in operation, some 200 of them in Germany. Several other commentaries repeatedly claim that the data warehouse cannot stand up to the demands of the data protection law; practice has shown that SAP has received hardly any enquires on the topic of data protection. The following might serve as reasons.

In many cases, access to personal data is not even required; the SAP BW is used exclusively to optimize the business process chain. In other cases, a reference to the authorization concept, borrowed from SAP R/3, is sufficient. Those responsible for the project seem independently to have made the adjustments required by data protection, obligated the appropriate parties, obtained the required permissions, or made the data anonymous with specific authorizations. In Germany, the works council will keep a sharp eye on the combination and summarization of employee data.

Effective data warehousing requires its global use throughout the corporate group. Secure transmission of data that adheres to the requirements of data protection is an absolute precondition. Although the data must be relatively current and secure (timely and without gaps), it does not need the same depth as traditional data (an optimal level of summarization). Data protection has an opportunity here to achieve minimization of data and data frugality.

11.3.2 Corporate self-interest

One of these chances arises because the corporate group can have no interest in allowing customer or personal data to end up outside the company. The corporation's own self-interest dictates that the data enjoy the highest possible level of security.

> The entire discussion of data protection among users misses the company's own interests. Ultimately it's not only about observing lofty legal principles. Companies have their own significant interest in protecting their customers. None of the surveyed data warehouse experts know of a top manager who would transfer data to a third party [CWfocus].

Management increasingly is becoming the end-user in data warehouse scenarios. The security of the overall system is tested at the very highest level. The self-interest of executive management and the gentle support of data protection and security experts should foster an awareness of security at the highest levels of a company. Those responsible for security and data protection should use this opportunity to introduce their conceptions of company-wide data protection and to gain support. Perhaps the board of directors should ask those responsible if everything really is secure.

11.3.3 Reference to persons

Predefined rules in a project extract originally very sensitive data for the data warehouse and format it for evaluation. In most cases, the evaluation does not require any reference to concrete persons.

Global personnel planning might well require group-wide information on the number of employees, personnel movements, and employee structures that include age, operating unit, gender, hours worked, nationality, working conditions, training, personnel, continuing education, and sick days.

The evaluation is broken down to the level of company, area, and cost center. End-users should not be able to drill down to individual persons.

The person responsible for data protection must be involved in project planning. Making the data anonymous takes the most explosive data protection issue out of the data warehouse discussion. Individual cases can decide if evaluation really requires references to natural persons.

If no drilldown to a natural person is required, other questions would arise. What personal data must be transported to the BW system at all to create InfoCubes and how long must that data be stored? InfoSources, in particular, can contain data that the end-user will never display, but that is needed to create the information units. But administration has access to this data and can be compromised if the SAP BW does not possess as high a security level as the human resources system or the customer database.

Those involved in a project determine the personal data, its level of detail, and those authorized to access it. If third parties have access to the data, its level of detail should be reduced. Remember that personal data on employees can be used only when it is connected to a business purpose. Examples include organizational unit, personnel area, position, cost center, annual salary, and employment status. Private data should be taboo.

11.3.4 Administration

As is the case in all systems, special attention must be given to BW administration, which can have comprehensive rights. The view of the end-user may be limited, but the administrator works directly in SAP BW and usually has privileged, almost complete rights. If the system does not permit aggregation of data in the data warehouse database to person-neutral units, the administrators have the same options for examining data that they enjoy in the original systems.

System administrators must also guarantee the security of the overall SAP BW system. As is true of R/3 Systems, security depends upon the following components: operating system, database, network infrastructure, authorization concept, user authentication, the communication methods in use, logging, and inspections.

To limit the risk of abuse, you should distribute administrative tasks to different persons. This approach applies to both system and BW administrators.

Because various groups with tailored access authorizations work in both the delivering applications and the receiving SAP BW systems, you can easily distribute tasks. The tasks include the BW development administrator, the BW modeler, the BW operator, the BW report developer, and the BW report user.

11.3.5 Access authorization

Only authorized end-users may access reports with sensitive data. As does an R/3 System, the SAP BW offers comprehensive access control at various levels. Access rights can be assigned for complete areas, specific key figures (such as salary in a personnel InfoCube), and even for specific maximum values (such as for a specific cost center). You change access authorizations in the Administrator Workbench.

11.4 RECOMMENDATIONS

To satisfy the requirements of data protection, the following measures must be taken in SAP BW. Most of the recommendations deal with organizational issues.

11.4.1 Obligating all users in a project

All project members and administrators should be advised of their obligations and responsibilities regarding data protection. During the normal course of a project, it's normal for participants to have occasional access to data beyond that permitted by their normal access. From the very beginning, everyone should be clear that project management and those responsible for data protection know the opportunities that additional privileges give project members.

11.4.2 Security contracts with third parties

If personal data within a corporate group is transferred to subsidiary companies located in countries with an inappropriate level of security, we recommend that a contract regulate a uniform level of security (*see* section 6.6.2). Contracts must include: regulations on data security procedures, access authorizations, limitations on transfers, right to information, damages, penalties, and regular audits.

11.4.3 Limiting data storage to the absolutely necessary scope

Only the data that the SAP BW actually needs should be taken from OLTP (online transaction processing) systems: the unnecessary infotypes and tables should be deleted immediately after transfer. The data must be kept correct and up to date; obsolete data must be deleted immediately, especially if a person is leaving the company. Access rights are to be tailored to end-users whenever roles change.

11.4.4 Purpose

The collection and processing of personal data may occur only for specific and legal purposes. Any further processing that is not aligned with the original purpose must be forbidden. The data must correspond to the purpose for which it was collected and not exceed those limits.

11.5   DATA PROTECTION CHECKLIST FOR SAP BW

The checklist given in Table 11.1 uses a sample SAP BW to represent the tasks to be performed by the persons responsible in an SAP BW project. Those responsible for data protection and security and employee representatives are to be integrated into the project. Their tasks are listed under project management. This checklist also contains tasks that go beyond those required by the SAP BW. It can also be used and enhanced for other projects.

TABLE 11.1	Data protection checklist for SAP BW	
Person responsible	**Tasks**	**Date**
Project Management	Inclusion of DPO and employee representatives in the BW project	
	Fixing the scope of training for all project members and end-users	
	Distribution of different administrative rights to several persons	
	Obligating all administrators to secrecy, maintenance of data protection, and secrecy of access authorization	
	Giving information to all subjects on the processing, access to, and transfer of personal data	
	Setting the level of anonymity	
	Setting rules for deletion	
	Setting end-user access to personal data	
	Setting end-user access by third parties to personal data	
	Monitoring the data to be provided in the OLTP system, such as the HR system	
	Maintaining a file overview for the DPO to ensure that only the data required is stored and revealed	
	What personal data is available?	
	Who has access to the data?	
	Is data being transmitted to third parties within and without the corporate group?	
	Supporting requests for information from subjects	
	What evaluation programs are available?	
	What are the storage locations of data?	
	Regular audits of guidelines regarding or limitations of:	
	authorization concept and access control	
	implementation of security guidelines	
	minimizing data, deletions, and making data anonymous	
	obligations and file overview	
Administration	Implementation of SAP security guidelines	
	Setting up authorizations	
	Implementation of efforts to make data anonymous	
	Implementation of deletion guidelines	
	Hindering unauthorized storage (download blocks, for example)	
	Supporting registration for the data protection officer: how, where, and when data is being used and to whom it is being transmitted	

Obligation to secrecy

A.1   NON-DISCLOSURE STATEMENT

The undersigned undertakes to maintain secrecy regarding all confidential matters about which he/she obtains knowledge during the course of his/her activities for SAP, including any information about trade and business secrets of SAP customers and partners. This obligation shall remain in force after termination of the undersigned's assignment on behalf of SAP.

The undersigned undertakes to keep secret from third parties any knowledge about trade and business secrets of SAP customers and partners that he/she obtains during the course of his/her activities for SAP. He/she shall be permitted to discuss such confidential information with other persons only as and when the fulfillment of his/her duties requires him/her to do so. SAP emphasizes categorically that it has no interest whatsoever in business or trade secrets of other companies that are not in the public domain. In particular, the undersigned shall be prohibited from disclosing documents containing business or trade secrets of partners or customers to third parties or from enabling third parties to obtain access to documents of this nature.

| A.2 | **TRADE SECRETS AND COPYRIGHTS OF OTHER COMPANIES** |

The undersigned undertakes to respect the copyrights, particularly software copyrights, held by third parties. Unless the copyright holder has issued authorization to do so, non-SAP software in particular shall neither be used nor modified, either independently or in conjunction with SAP software.

The undersigned undertakes not to disclose knowledge about business and trade secrets or information protected by copyrights of other companies to any employees in the SAP Group, nor shall he/she store documents of this nature on the premises of the SAP Group.

| A.3 | **OBLIGATION TO OBSERVE DATA SECRECY** |

Mr/Ms . . . . has been informed about his/her obligation to observe data secrecy according to Article 5 of the Federal German Privacy Act and the penal consequences facing him/her in case of violation.

You are prohibited to process, publish, disclose, or otherwise use protected personal data without authorization for any purpose other than in the course of your lawful business.

Your obligation to observe data secrecy shall remain in force after termination of your assignment. This commitment expressly includes any protected personal data that is in the possession of business partners. Violation can lead to a fine or imprisonment in accordance with Article 43 of the Federal German Privacy Act and other applicable legal provisions.

Article 5: Data secrecy

Persons engaged in the processing of data are prohibited from processing or using personal data without authorization (data secrecy). Such persons, inasmuch as they are employed in the private sector, shall undertake to maintain data secrecy when taking up an assignment. The obligation to maintain data secrecy shall remain in force after termination of their assignment.

Article 43: Penal provisions

1 Anyone who:

1. stores, changes or transmits

2. makes available using automated procedures

3. calls up or procures from files for himself/herself or another party personal data that is protected by this law and has not been publicly disclosed will be punished by a prison sentence of up to one year or a fine.

2 Penalties will also be imposed on anyone who:

1. makes false statements to surreptitiously acquire data that is protected by this law and has not been publicly disclosed

2 uses the transmitted data for ulterior purposes, by forwarding it to a third party or third parties, contrary to Article 16, Section 4, Subsection 1, Article 28, Section 4, Subsection 1, also in conjunction with Article 29, Section 3, Article 39, Section 1, Subsection 1 or Article 40, Section 1 or

3. combines the attributes referred to in Article 30, Section 1, Subsection 1 with personal details, contrary to Article 30, Section 1, Subsection 2, or combines the attributes referred to in Article 40, Section 3, Subsection 3.

3 Should the offender act in return for payment or with the intent to enrich himself/herself or another party or to harm another party, he/she shall be liable to a prison sentence of up to two years or a fine.

4 The offender will be prosecuted upon complaint only.

Glossary

SAP online help contains a glossary that includes additional entries.

ABAP (Advanced Business Application Programming)   A programming language developed by SAP for writing application programs.

ABAP Dictionary   Directory that contains the following information:

- description of all application data for an enterprise
- relationships between the application data
- use of the application data in programs and screen templates.

The descriptive data for the ABAP Dictionary is also known as metadata since it represents data about data.

AcceleratedSAP (ASAP)   A standard methodology for the efficient implementation and continuous optimization of SAP software. ASAP supports implementation of the R/3 System and mySAP.com. It can also be used for upgrades and release changes.

Activity group   Collection of activities that cover a specific work area. For example, the activity group "accounts payable accounting" contains all the transactions and reports that accountants need to perform their daily tasks.

You can create a user menu for an activity group. You assign transactions, reports, and internet/intranet links to the user menu. This menu is displayed when users assigned the activity group log on to the system. Authorizations are automatically granted for the activities included in the activity group. These authorizations can be changed.

Application Link Enabling (ALE)   Technology for the setup and operation of distributed applications. The basic concept of Application Link Enabling is to guarantee a distributed, but integrated, R/3 installation. This includes a controlled exchange of business messages during consistent data storage on loosely coupled SAP application systems. The applications are integrated via synchronous and asynchronous communication rather than via a central database.

Audit Information System (AIS)   Auditing tool aimed at improving the quality of audits. The AIS consists of an audit reporting tree and is a structured, preconfigured collection of SAP standard programs.

Business Application Programming Interface (BAPI)   Open, stable, and object-oriented interfaces that help you integrate business applications, even over the internet. BAPIs enable you to couple systems based upon different technologies.

Business Framework   Open architecture for converting the functions of the R/3 System to an integrated package of modularized components. Components can be mixed together with each other and with compatible components from other manufacturers.

Building upon BAPIs, the SAP Business Framework represents a component-based, open, and integrated solution. The Open BAPI Network is a free network for BAPI developers at www.sap.com/bapi.

Business Object Repository (BOR)   Directory of all object types in a hierarchy format. The object types are each assigned to a development class (and therefore indirectly to an application component as well).

Cluster table   Table type in the ABAP Dictionary. The data of several cluster tables is stored together in a table cluster in the database. A cluster table is thus known only in the ABAP Dictionary, but not in the database.

Computing Center Management System (CCMS)   An integrated suite of tools for monitoring, managing, and configuring R/3 and independent SAP business components, for automating operations such as resource distribution, and managing SAP databases. The CCMS supports 24-hour system management from an R/3 System. You can analyze and distribute the system load and monitor the resource consumption of various system components.

Consulting Services   Support for all questions on the R/3 System. Consulting Services include customer-specific on-site or remote consulting on customizing questions, project tasks, QA review of an implementation project (SAP Review Program), technical system checks (SAP GoingLive Check and SAP EarlyWatch), remote execution of system upgrades and data archiving (remote upgrade and remote archiving), conversion of business data (conversion services), and support for conversion to the euro as the internal currency (Euro Services).

Cookie   An information entry that is placed by a web server in a user's computer so that the server can identify the user at a subsequent visit and offer additional information to the user. An SSO cookie is information stored in the user's web browser that is used to identify the user in the mySAP Workplace.

Customizing   The configuration of a system by the system administrator during implementation. In customizing you can introduce SAP functions into an enterprise quickly, securely, and economically, tailor the enterprise-neutral functions delivered by SAP to the specific needs of the enterprise, and use a simple tool to document and administer the phases of the implementation and the adjustments. Customizing is mandatory before the system goes into production; it is performed in R/3 System via the Implementation Guide (IMG).

Data element   Object that describes the data type and semantic meaning of a table or structure field. Fields with the same purpose should have the same underlying data element.

Domain   Object that describes the technical attributes of a field such as its data type and length. A domain defines a value range containing the valid values for fields that refer to that domain. You can group fields that have similar technical or business purposes together under a single domain. All fields based on a domain are automatically updated when you change the domain. This guarantees the consistency of the fields.

Dynpro (Dynamic Program)   A dynpro consists of a screen image and the underlying flow logic.

Employee Self-Service (ESS)   Easy-to-use internet applications that enable employees to view and update their own personal data.

EnjoySAP   A uniform design for the development of individual user interfaces characterized by a visual design that identifies functions at the first glance and uses interactive elements to let users accelerate their daily tasks. With EnjoySAP (R/3 4.6), SAP focuses upon user concerns. Users should experience as much support as possible.

ERP Enterprise resource planning stands for a package of standard software, such as financials, human resources, production planning and control, and logistics: the data for all applications is stored in one database.

Field name Name of a field in a table (transparent table, pool table, cluster table, table pool, table cluster). Each field references one data element, and therefore one domain, to accept their characteristics.

HTML (Hypertext Markup Language) Graphical, document-description language to create HTML pages for the internet. They are transmitted by web servers to web browsers, which then implement and display them.

HTTP (Hypertext Transfer Protocol) Application protocol for the world wide web. HTTP controls communications between web browsers (HTTP clients) and web servers (HTTP servers).

Implementation Guide (IMG) Tool for configuring the SAP System to meet customer requirements. The Implementation Guide (IMG) explains all the steps in the implementation process, tells you the SAP standard (factory) customizing settings and describes the system configuration activities.

Infotype (information type) The data fields for personnel master data, time management, and applicant data are combined into logical views, called information types, or infotypes for short. Typical infotypes include "family/person referenced," "organizational assignment," or basic reference. The following naming conventions apply for infotypes:

- infotypes 0000–0999 for personnel master data and possible-applicant data
- infotypes 1000–1999 for organizational management
- infotypes 2000–2999 for time data
- infotypes 4000–4999 for applicant data
- infotypes 9000–9999 reserved for customer use.

Internet Business Framework The Internet Business Framework is oriented toward a new model for business software that enables simple modifications, simple access, and simplified business collaboration and interoperability. With a view toward new technological possibilities for use of the internet, the model describes the dynamic cooperation between users, business partners, and customers within individual communities of interest and markets. The Internet Business Framework essentially includes three factors: the new mySAP Workplace, data transfer over the internet, and WebFlow based upon XML.

mySAP.com   The mySAP.com e-business platform is a family of solutions and services that empower employees, customers, and business partners to collaborate successfully – anywhere, anytime. It allows optimal integration of all relevant business processes over the internet. mySAP.com offers seamless, comprehensive integration between SAP solutions and non-SAP systems for all business processes. It provides a complete business environment for electronic commerce.

mySAP Marketplace   As a part of mySAP.com, the mySAP Marketplace provides one location on the www for communities to exchange goods and services electronically. SAP makes marketplaces available at www.mysap.com.

mySAP Workplace   As a part of mySAP.com, the Workplace represents a role-based and personalized web browser portal for the SAP System. The screen is tailored to the specific role of the user in his or her company or at his or her place of work. Single Sign-On gives the user access to all functions, services, and information that he or she needs for his or her work.

All in all, the mySAP Workplace provides access to all web-based systems, functions, and services.

Note   A solution to a customer problem known to SAP. Notes are stored in the notes database and can be accessed over the SAPNet Web Frontend or the SAPNet R/3 Frontend.

Online Transaction Processing System (OLTP)   A system that processes transactions. The OLTP system can be an R/3 System or a different ERP system.

Personalization   mySAP.com offers users an individually customizable user interface that offers users the most important functions, services, and information they need to perform their jobs.

Pooled table   Table type in the ABAP Dictionary. The data of several pooled tables are stored together as a table pool in the database. Therefore, a pooled table is known in the ABAP Dictionary, but not in the database.

Profile Generator   Tool for generating authorization profiles in role maintenance. You use the Profile Generator to generate authorization profiles based on the activities in a role.

Remote Function Call (RFC)   RFC is an SAP interface protocol. Based on CPI-C, it considerably simplifies the programming of communication processes between systems. RFCs enable you to call and execute predefined functions in a remote system – or even in the same system. RFCs manage the communication process, parameter transfer, and error handling.

SAPNet   The SAP information and communications medium on the internet. The SAPNet Web Frontend is accessible to customers and partners over a remote connection and provides them with a view to SAPNet over a web browser. The SAPNet R/3 Frontend offers access to SAPNet via the Online Service System and a remote connection.

SAProuter   SAP program that acts as part of a firewall system. The SAProuter simplifies network security and the routing of traffic to and from the R/3 System. It also establishes an indirect connection between the R/3 network and external networks. You can define which connections are allowed, which are not allowed, and which are protected by password access.

Secure Network Communication (SNC)   Interface that allows R/3 to communicate with an external security product to protect the communications links between the components of an R/3 System. The features of the security product can be implemented in addition to the standard functions provided by R/3.

Secure Store and Forward (SSF)   Interface for secure data storage and transmission that allows the R/3 System to communicate with an external security product. In this way, digital signatures and digital envelopes can be used to protect data and documents as independent units as they are saved on data carriers or when transmitted over communication paths.

Security Audit Log   Log containing security-related system information such as configuration changes or unsuccessful logon attempts. This information is useful for monitoring changes to the R/3 System or for tracking a series of events.

Single Sign-On (SSO)   Mechanism that eliminates the need for users to enter passwords for every system that they log on to. The Single Sign-On allows users to authenticate themselves once, and then log on to all of those systems that operate in the Single Sign-On environment without further intervention.

Structures   Defined and activated like tables, but no databases are generated from structures. Data can be permanently stored in transparent tables, but data in structures exist only when the program is running.

Subtype   A subgroup of infotypes. The subtypes of an infotype can have different temporal connections and create their own history.

Tables   You can define tables in the ABAP Dictionary that are dependent upon a database. To do so, you define the table fields with the database-dependent data types and lengths. In addition to the table definition already created in the ABAP Dictionary, the activation of a table creates a physical table definition in the database. This process translates the table definition in the ABAP Dictionary into a definition in the database.

WebFlow Functions that enable SAP Business Workflows to be executed over the internet. WebFlow enables:

- XML documents to be sent to other systems from a Business Workflow
- a Business Workflow to be started in another SAP System from your SAP System
- response to be made to the results of a Business Workflow executed in another system
- a Business Workflow to be started when an appropriate XML document is received.

XML Enhancements in data transfer over the internet based upon the XML formatting protocol enables the Internet-Business Framework to simplify access to business information. With the SAP Business Connector, the Internet Business Framework also supports the exchange of messages based upon XML and thus offers a standard process for transferring data to and from business software applications.

References

As SAP is a German company much of the relevant material is only available in German. We have included details here for interested parties. References beginning with square brackets are marked that way in the book (indicating Online Media or that the piece was authored by an institute, rather than an individual); all other titles follow the author–date system.

C.1 PRINTED MATTER

Bergmann, L., Möhrle, R. and Herb, A., *Datenschutzrecht: Ergänzbarer Kommentar*, Stuttgart, Richard Boorberg Verlag, 1998.

Bizer, F. and Brisch, K. M., *Digitale Signatur*, Heidelberg, Springer, 1999.

Bornstein, N. and Freed, N., "Multipurpose Mail Extensions (MIME) Part One. Format of Internet Message Bodies." In: *IETF Request for Comment*, No. 2045, November 1996.

[Comer, D.E., *Internetworking with TCP/IP*. Vol. I, 2nd Ed., New Jersey, Prentice Hall, 1991.

[CWfocus] *Mehr Sensibität in Puncto Datenschutz*. In: Computerwoche Focus, 2nd Ed., 1992, p. 42.

Däubler, W., *Gläserne Gesellschaften?* 3rd Ed., Cologne, Bund-Verlag, 1993.

Däubler, W., "Grenzüberschreitender Datenschutz – Handlungsmöglichkeiten des Betriebsrats." In: *RDV*, 3: 1998, pp. 96–101.

Dammann, U. and Simitis, S., *EG-Datenschutzrichtlinie*. 1st Ed., Baden-Baden, Nomos-Verlagsgesellschaft, 1997.

Dierks, T., and Allen, C., "The TLS Protocol Version 1.0." In: *IETF Request for Comment*, No. 2246, January 1999.

Diffie, W., Hellman, M. E., Whitfield and Martin, E., "New Directions in Cryptography." In: *IEEE Transactions On Information Theory*, 22: 1976, pp. 644–54.

[DSA] National Institute of Standards and Technology. NIST FIPS PUB 186: *Digital Signature Standard*. U.S. Department of Commerce, May 1994.

Ehmann, H., "Prinzipien des deutschen Datenschutzrechts – unter Berücksichtigung der Datenschutz-Richtlinie der EG vom 24.10.1995." In: *RDV*, 6: 1998, pp. 235–243 and *RDV*, 1: 1999, pp. 12–23.

Ellison, C. and Schneider, B., "Ten Risks of PKI. What You're Not Being Told About Public Key Infrastructure." In: *Computer Security Journal*, 16: 2000, No. 1.

Esslinger, B. and Müller, M., "Secure Sockets Layer (SSL) Protokoll." In: *Datenschutz und Datensicherheit*, 21: 1997, No. 12, pp. 691–697.

Eul, H., "Übermittlung personenbezogener Daten ins Ausland nach Ablauf der Umsetzungsfrist der EG-Datenschutzrichtlinie." In: *RDV*, 5: 1998, pp. 185–94.

Fielding, R. et al., "Hypertext Transfer Protocol – HTTP/1.1. In: *IETF Request for Comment*, No. 2616, June 1999.

Fiedler, H., "Zerreißprobe für den Datenschutz." In: *CR*, 1989, pp. 131–139.

[GDD-1994] *GDD Arbeitshilfe: Datenschutz im Unternehmen. Arbeitshilfe für betriebliche Praxis*. 4th Edition. Gesellschaft für Datenschutz und Datensicherung e.V.: Bonn, 1994.

Heckner, M., "The SAP ITS Architecture: The SAP Internet Programming Model, Part 1." In: *SAP Technical Journal*. Vol. 1: 1999, No. 1, pp. 7–16.

[IT-Sicherheit] *IT-Sicherheit. Praxis der Daten- und Netzsicherheit.*, Cologne, Datakontext-Fachverlag.

[ITU] *International Telecommunications Union Standard X.509: The Directory – Authentication Framework*. ITU: 1993.

Kaufman, C. et al., *Network Security – Private Communications in a Public World,* New Jersey, Prentice Hall, 1995.

Kristol, D. and Montulli, L., "HTTP State Management Mechanism." In: *IETF Internet Draft* (obsolete RFC 2109), August 1999.

Linn, J., "Generic Security Service Application Program Interface Version 2." In: *IETF Request for Comment*, No. 2078, January 1997.

[Manager] "Manager: Daten an die Macht". In: *Manager-Magazin*, August 1998.

Menezes, A. J. et al., *Handbook of Applied Cryptography*, New York, CRC Press, 1996.

Rawolle, J., et al., "Wege zur Absicherung eines Intranets." In: *Informatik-Spektrum*, 22: 1999, pp. 181–91.

Rivest, R., Shamir, A. and Adelman, L. M., "A Method for Obtaining Digital Signatures and Public Key Cryptosystems." In: *Journal of the ACM*. 21: 1978, No. 2, pp. 120–26.

[SAP-ALE] *SAP Basis Modeling (Bluebook): Application Link Enabling*. Material number 50017938, Walldorf, SAP, 1996.

[SAP-BC] *SAP In Focus: SAP Business Connector*. Material number 50033842. SAP: Walldorf, 1999.

[SAP-CTS] *SAP Basis Modeling (Bluebook): Change Management and Transport System*. Material number 50017931. SAP: Walldorf, 1994.

[SAP-DBA] *SAP In Focus: SAP Tools to Manage the Oracle Database for the SAP R/3 System*. Material number 50016522. SAP: Walldorf, 1999.

[SAP-Enqueue] *SAP Basis Modeling (Bluebook): Enqueue Server and Update Task*. Material number 50017934. SAP: Walldorf, 1994.

[SAP-MP] *SAP White Paper: mySAP.com – Der mySAP.com Marketplace.* Material number 50037182. SAP: Walldorf, 2000.

[SAP RFC] *SAP Basis Modeling (Bluebook): Remote Function Call.* Material number 50017930. SAP: Walldorf, 1999.

Schleutermann, M., "Datenverarbeitung im Konzern." In: *CR* (1995), pp. 577–85.

Schneier, B. *Applied Cryptography: Protocols, Algorithms, and Source Code in C,* Chichester, John Wiley & Sons, 1995.

Seidel, B., "Peoplesoft beißt sich an Siemens die Zähne aus." In: *Computerwoche,* September 25, 1998, p. 2.

[SZ-BND] SZ BND: "BND darf alle Telefonate ins Ausland abhören." In: *Süddeutsche Zeitung* July 15, 1999, p. 1.

[TBS] *TBS: Einführung von SAP-Programmen. Technologieberatungsstelle beim DGB Landesbezirk NRW e.V,* 1997.

Wahl, M., Howes, T. and Kille, S., "Lightweight Directory Access Protocol (v3)." In: *IETF Request for Comment,* No. 2251, December 1997.

Weise, K., "Datenschutz-Management im Betrieb – Erfahrungen und Ziele." In: *20 Jahre DAFTA.* Datakontext-Fachverlag: Cologne, 1997, pp.225–32.

Wildemann, H., "Das Wissen im Netz der Spezialisten." In: *Süddeutsche Zeitung* July 20, 1999, p. 26.

C.2 ONLINE MEDIA

Please note that both the address and the contents can change for online media. The entries below were accurate at the time of publication.

[BC-SNC]	SAP: Complementary Software Partner Program. Secure Network Communications. In: http://www.sap.com/csp/scenarios. Business Technology.
[BC-SSF]	SAP: Complementary Software Partner Program. Secure Store and Forward. In: http://www.sap.com/csp/scenarios. Business Technology.
[Berlin]	Excerpt from the annual report of the data protection official in Berlin, 1997. In: http://www.datenschutz–berlin.de/jahresbe/97/teil2.htm
[CW-Online]	In: http://www.computerwoche.de/info–point/top–news/
[D-Krypto]	Federal (German) Ministry of the Interior: Cornerstones of German Policy on Cryptograhpy. In: http://www.bmwi.de/presse/1999/0602prm1.html

[ECHOLON]	Interception Capabilities 2000. In: http://www.iptvreports.mcmail.com/ic2kreport.htm#Summary
[EU-DigSig]	EU Commission: European Guidelines for Electronic Signatures. In: http://europa.eu.int/comm/dg15/de/media/infso/sign.htm
[EU Crypto]	EU Commission: European Regulations for Dual-Use Goods. In: http://www.bundesausfuhramt.de/vorschri/eg–dual/eg_vo.html
[Europarat]	European Council: Agreement on the Protection of Persons During Automatic Processing of Personal Data (Convention. 108). In: http://www.datenschutz–berlin.de/recht/eu/eurat/dskon_de.htm
[Hamburg]	In: http://www.hamburg.de/Behoerden/HmbDSB/tb16/
[Heise]	In: http://www.heise.de/newsticker/
[IDG]	In: http://www.idg.net/idgns
[Guidelines]	In: http://www.sap.com/germany/discsap/revis/index.htm
[Minister]	Ministerial statement of July 1997 in Bonn. In: http://www2.echo.lu/bonn/finalde.html
[MS-Bulletins]	Microsoft: Security Bulletins. In: http://www.microsoft.com/security
[MS-WTS]	Microsoft: Windows NT Terminal Server. In: http://www.microsoft.com/office/enterprise/deployment/termserv.htm
[Mühlen]	10 Commandments on Security. In: http://www.siline.com/200_ratgeber/211_gebote.html
[PKCS7]	RSA Laboratories: PKCS #7: Cryptographic Message Syntax Standard. In : http://www.rsa.com
[PKCS10]	RSA Laboratories: PKCS#10: Certification Request Syntax Standard. In : http://www.rsa.com
[Riehm]	Riehm, Ulrich: Reflections on Aspects of New Media. In: http://www.itas.fzk.de.deu.itaslit./rieh98a.htm

[SAP BFA]	SAP: Business Framework Architecture (on SAPNet for SAP customers and partners). In: http://sapnet.sap.com/bf
[SAP-CSP]	SAP: Complementary Software Partner Program. In: http://www.sap.com/csp
[SAP LIB]	SAP: Online Documentation System R/3 (SAP Graphical User Interface Help Menus, on SAPNet for SAP customers and partners). In: http://sapnet.sap.com/r3docu
[SAP Notes]	SAP: Notes. In: http://sapnet.sap.com/notes
[SAP-Router]	SAP: Note No. 30289. SAProuter Documentation. See [SAP-Notes]
[SAP-Scan]	SAP: Note No. 189727. Virus Scanning During Uploads and Downloads.See [SAP-Notes]
[SAP-SG]	SAP: Security Guidelines (on SAPNet for SAP customers and partners). In: http://sapnet.sap.com/securityguide
[SAP-SNC]	SAP: Secure Network Communications – Users Guide (on SAPNet for SAP customers and partners). In: http://sapnet.sap.com/systemmanagement.
	Security. Media Center. Literature
[SAP-Up/Down]	SAP: Note No. 28777. PC Download: Logging and Authorization Checks. See [SAP-Notes]
[SAP-X509]	SAP: X.509 Certificate Logon over the Internet Transaction Server (on SAPNet for SAP customers and partners). See [SAP-SNC]
[SafeHarbor]	International Safe Harbor Privacy Principles. In: http://www.ita.doc.gov/ecom/shprin.html
[Sig]	In: http://www.sicherheit–im–internet.de
[SSL3.0]	Netscape: Secure Sockets Layer 3.0 Specification. In: http://home.netscape.com/eng/ssl3/index.html
[USA Crypto]	Electronic Privacy Information Center: Revised U.S. Encryption Export Control Regulations. In: http://www.epic.org/crypto/export_controls/regs_1_00.html

[W3C-XML]	W3Consortium: eXtensible Markup Language. In: http://www.w3.org/TR/REC–xml
[Wired]	A European's Net View of US. In: http://www.wired.com/news/politics/story/21476.html, 20.8.1999
[WP-12]	Working papers: Transfers of personal data to third-countries: Application of articles 25 and 26 of the EU Data Protection Directive. In: http://www.europa.eu.int/comm/dg15/de/media/dataprot/wpdocs/
[WP-16]	Working papers: Processing personal data on the Internet: See [WP-12].
[WP-17]	Recommendation 1/99 on the invisible and automatic processing of personal data on the Internet by software and hardware. See [WP-12].
[WP-26]	Recommendation 4/99 on the acceptance of basic laws on data protection in the European catalog of basic laws. See [WP-12].
[WP-27]	Statement 7/99 on the basics of safe harbor. See [WP-12].
[Yahoo]	In: http://www.yahoo.de/schlagzeilen/
[ZDF]	In: http://www.zdf.msnbc.de/news

Index